THE STOPETTE DRIVE-IN

HOME OF THE SLAW DOG

J.Q.D. SALT-WORKS

FRONTIER CULTURE MUSEUM

APPALACHIAN SOUTH FOLKLIFE CENTER

MARY DRAPER INGLES COMES HOME

SALTVILLE, VA

Virginia

"*Victuals* is so much more than just another cookbook. It's a marvelous travelogue and history of an underappreciated and often misrepresented part of America, its people and culture, written lovingly by my friend Ronni Lundy. Still, as I finished the last pages, with their stunning illustrations, I couldn't wait to get in the kitchen and try my hand at the delicious recipes she has gathered for all of us who just plain love good food."
—EMMYLOU HARRIS

"Flipping through these pages makes me want to hug my mom and plant some greasy beans. I've been waiting a long time for Ronni to write the definitive story of Appalachian cooking, because she is the only one capable of doing so. Sit back and prepare yourself to discover the wonders of the Appalachian Mountains. The wisdom and flavors within these pages deserve your full attention."
—SEAN BROCK

"Ronni Lundy is the consummate guide to the dynamic food movement that's developed in the mountain South, a native daughter of eastern Kentucky and a graceful raconteur with the sensitivity to let the people she encounters tell their own engaging stories."
—MATT LEE AND TED LEE

"Ronni Lundy's *Victuals* captures the hope inherent in food born of the love of each other, the land, and what the land bears. I wish it came with a string attached so I could wear it around my neck as a constant and mouthwatering reminder of the best of what Appalachia has been and will be."
—ROBERT GIPE

"Ronni Lundy's passionately written tribute to the people and food she loves paints a picture of great beauty that is infectious— where sublimely simple dishes and cultural diversity are hallmarks of a region we have been conditioned not to see. Through the people we meet, the recipes she cooks, and the spectacular photographs, we learn to love Appalachia, too."
—TONI TIPTON-MARTIN

"I am fortunate to hold this book in my hands. On a trip to Japan, I read it on the flight over and again on the way back—it nourishes me all the more with every reading."
—EDWARD LEE

"There's a lot of talk these days about 'real food.' In these pages, Ronni has exuberantly chronicled the realest food I know. Our food is deeply connected to the seasons, our people, and our history."
—JOHN FLEER

"Long-shunned as a region of hillbillies mired in poverty and distress, Appalachia has remained 'hidden in the holler' as a land of smoky mountain mystery amidst the recent celebration of American regional cuisine. Well, no more. The luminous photography, well-crafted words, and mouthwatering recipes of *Victuals* will ensure that Appalachian food and culture belong at the forefront of what we consider American food."
—VIRGINIA WILLIS

"Mmmmm."
—ROY BLOUNT JR.

Victuals

PHOTOGRAPHS BY JOHNNY AUTRY

Clarkson Potter/Publishers
New York

Victuals

AN APPALACHIAN JOURNEY, WITH RECIPES

RONNI LUNDY

Library of Congress Cataloging-in-Publication Data
Names: Lundy, Ronni.
Title: Victuals : an Appalachian journey, with recipes / Ronni Lundy ;
    photographs by Johnny Autry.
Description: New York : Clarkson Potter/Publishers, 2016.
Identifiers: LCCN 2016013454 (print) | LCCN 2016017691 (ebook) |
    ISBN 9780804186742 (hardback) | ISBN 9780804186759 (Ebook)
Subjects: LCSH: Cooking, American. | Cooking--Appalachian Region,
    Southern. | Appalachian Region, Southern--Social life and customs. |
    BISAC: COOKING / Regional & Ethnic / American / Southern States.
    | COOKING / Regional & Ethnic / American / Middle Western
    States. | COOKING / History. | LCGFT: Cookbooks.
Classification: LCC TX715 .L9424 2016 (print) | LCC TX715 (ebook) |
    DDC 641.5974--dc23
LC record available at https://lccn.loc.gov/2016013454

ISBN 978-0-804-18674-2
eBook ISBN 978-0-804-18675-9

Printed in China

Book and cover design by Stephanie Huntwork
Cover photographs by Johnny Autry
Endpaper map illustrations by Ash Swain at Great Southern Tattoo Co.
Food styling by Charlotte Autry

10 9 8 7 6 5 4 3 2 1

First Edition

This book is for John Egerton, who invited me to take my place at the table, and for Finn, who sits today at the same oak table where I took my supper at his age. May we continue to look for truth and meaning in our stories.

CONTENTS

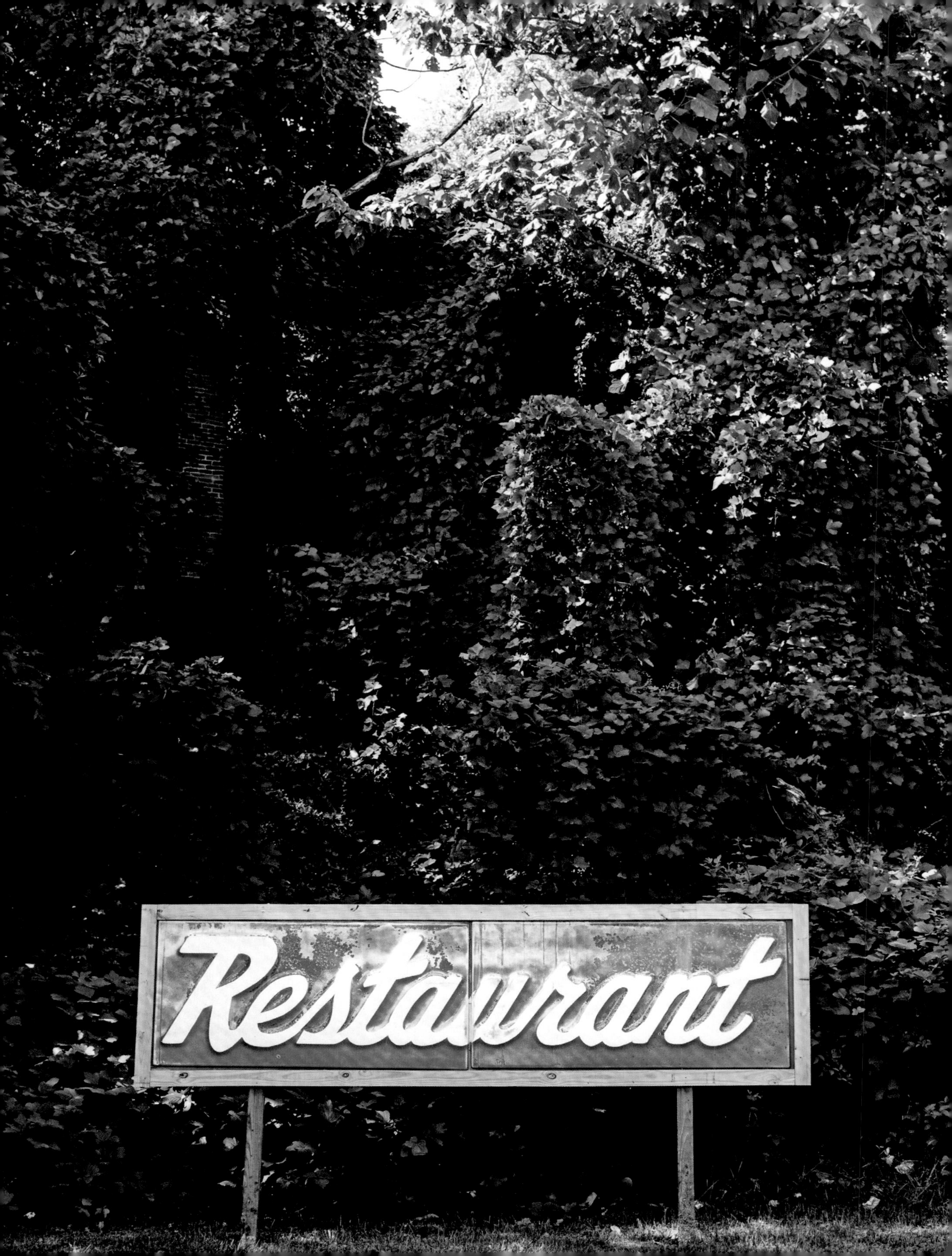
Restaurant

INTRODUCTION

VICTUALS.

Say it the way my people have for centuries: *vidls*.

Maybe you've seen it spelled "vittles" in a cartoon balloon coming from the mouth of Mammy Yokum. Or heard it as the punch line delivered before Granny Clampett clogs off to "roast up a mess of possum." Maybe you thought saying it that way was wrong.

But look that word up in your dictionary. It turns out my people, the people of the southern Appalachian Mountains, have been right about victuals all along. About the way you say them, the way you raise them, the way you cook them, keep them, and share them. About saving seeds, and working the land, and simmering pole beans, and making real cornbread. About the connections between earth and the table, and between the table and the people seated around it.

Victuals. This is a book that tells about those connections. This is a book about present-day people and places across the southern Appalachian Mountains and the ways their stories link to the past. It's about the foods they make and eat, the gardens they grow, the lives they create. It's a book full of recipes and a book full of voices.

To gather them, I drove over four thousand miles—zigzag on switchbacks, straight along ridgelines, weaving and loping through valleys, dark and light—to meet and learn from home cooks and chefs, farmers and shop owners, curers and savers and preservers of both food and traditions. I explored Kentucky, West Virginia, southern Ohio, northern Georgia, Tennessee, Virginia, and North Carolina. I searched back through history and joined others in imagining the future. I ate and cooked up a remarkable amount of really good food. This book will take you back on that journey with me.

But maybe before you call shotgun for a ride in my reliable but rough-countenanced Chevy Astro van, you might want to know a little about who I am and how I came to write this. Halfway through the previous century, I was born in Corbin, a railroad town in eastern Kentucky. My parents and sister were born there, too. Through my grandparents, great-grandparents, and beyond, I have roots that wind through these mountains to Rose Hill and Washington County, Virginia; Buncombe County, North Carolina; East Tennessee; Kanawha, West Virginia; and on. Those roots connected

me to the mountains of my birth even as, when I was a toddler, we moved to the city, Louisville, so my father could find work. Like most who migrated in the many hillbilly diasporas brought on by the regional economic crashes of the 20th century, my parents continued to call Corbin "up home" and to take me there whenever they had a chance. My great-aunts fostered those connections, too, riding up to Louisville on the L&N Railroad in the morning to take me back to spend a few days with them. We rode back in the evening, the train rolling through a velvet darkness that deepened as the landscape edged closer in around the tracks, rose higher to the sky. When we got to the house where my great-aunts lived, where my mother had grown up, I could see a multitude of stars pouring down from the hilltops. The very sound of the night was different— deeper, full of cricket and frog peeps, not car engines and the all-night factory clang outside our apartment in Louisville. When the sound of the train passing by across the creek broke through the deep velvet, it was not a rude interruption, but a reminder that I was surrounded by love. "That's your uncle Clifton a'driving," my great-aunt Johnnie might say, or she'd name one of my other uncles or cousins who worked for the railroad.

Food was magical, too, in the mountains. Corbin had foods I didn't get in the city! Chili buns carried out from the Dixie Pool Room wrapped snugly in red grease–slicked waxed paper were my favorite, along with a bottle of ice-cold Brownie grape soda. This was where I first tasted a Moon Pie, created by a Chattanooga bakery to fill the lunch pails of coal miners. Here a tin of Vi-eeny sausages or a package of Cheese Nabs was available any time a pang of hunger hit. People in Corbin made their own ice cream! Honey came with a comb that my cousins and I would chew like gum. Watermelons were so lush, so sweet and fragrant, that my parents didn't even bother to buy the ones offered in the city.

Food was magical also because I got to be part of the making. I had a little rocking chair out on the porch where I joined the women on summer afternoons as they taught me how to properly string a bean while they told stories. I sat next to Johnnie in the swing as she sliced sourish June apples for drying—my mouth watering as I dreamed of the crisp fried dried apple pies my aunt Minnie would make come fall. I got a handful of warm, sweet, tangy tommy-toes all my own any time anyone went to the summer garden, and I was urged to eat my fill at the tables teeming with summer squash, sliced cucumbers, simmered beans of many kinds, corn cut straight from the cob only moments before it landed in a bacon-scented skillet. When chicken was fried I was always given the pulley-bone, and when I'd eaten all the juicy meat, I was urged to close my eyes, pull the bone, and make a wish with a grown-up who made sure I got the longer, wish-granting end. I often wished that my visit would never end.

So while I didn't grow up *in* them, I grew up *of* the mountains, and all my life I have held that these connections are a beautiful and remarkable gift.

But I also grew up in the 1950s, '60s, and '70s, and I discovered quickly that my understanding of the mountains and the people I knew and loved was not much like the one presented on television, in movies, or in *Life* magazine. And as I left home, moved around, and made friends from other parts of the country, I discovered that when I told stories from my childhood, my new friends didn't hear them as I'd experienced them. Instead they translated them through images from *The Beverly Hillbillies*, the War on Poverty, *Deliverance*.

It became deeply important to me to understand the roots of my experience, and to learn how to tell my stories in a way that people might hear. When I became a newspaper and magazine writer at the age of thirty, music offered that platform. The vibrant progressive bluegrass movement allowed me to hear and say that it wasn't just barn dances, but swing, and jazz, and honky-tonks that fueled those fiddles and banjos in the past as well as the present. (My father and a friend had a nightclub in Corbin for a short time before I was born, a place where bands, stopping overnight on the rail ride from the cities of the north to Florida, would play. His favorite, he told me, was Cab Calloway.)

Writing about food was another way—one that allowed me to talk about the wisdom of mountain foodways, the cleverness of cooks who could make glory out of meager stores, the profound generosity of the people who had raised me. These two threads came together in my first cookbook, published in 1990, based on country and bluegrass musicians' recollections of foods they loved. *Shuck Beans, Stack Cakes, and Honest Fried Chicken* wasn't conceived as an Appalachian cookbook, but because so many of the performers I knew well had mountain roots, and because I was encouraged to include many of my own family stories and recipes, that became—as the title implies—its dominant theme.

When it was published, I began to hear from people with mountain connections and affections of their own. Older people, yes, but also folks, like me at that time, in midlife and even younger. They were happy to see the foods they made, the life they lived, celebrated. They wrote to me in the present tense. But I noticed that often when someone from elsewhere wrote about my book, they congratulated me for recording a dying culture, a people from and fading into the past. I saw the same thing happen when Joe

Dabney's marvelous *Smokehouse Ham, Spoon Bread & Scuppernong Wine* came out in 1998, and when Fred Sauceman's wonderful food travelogues and other Appalachian cookbooks appeared. I read comments about vanishing foodways and a dying culture when John Fleer began to feature Allan Benton's ham, Cruze buttermilk, and Muddy Pond sorghum on his upscale Appalachian menus at Blackberry Farm in the Smokies. Saving a slice of history was a compliment often paid to the Southern Foodways Alliance's (SFA) *Cornbread Nation 3: Foods of the Mountain South*, which I edited in 2005, even though that book featured contemporary stories of the mountains by writers much younger than me: Sheri Castle, Matt and Ted Lee, Tony Earley, and Kelly Norman Ellis among them.

By the time a group of us assembled at former SFA president Elizabeth Sims's request at the Biltmore Estate in 2008 for an eleven-day celebration and seminar on southern Appalachian foodways, I knew we weren't talking about a dying anything. The panels featured several Asheville-area farmers and producers in their twenties and early thirties, many the latest in a line of generations of growers in the region. And when a twenty-something Sean Brock—then the fastest-rising star on the Southern culinary scene, making his name with modernist pucks of solidified black-eyed-pea puree with liquid pepper jelly centers—told me that my simple recipe for cornbread was the same as his grandmother's, and that when he had a restaurant of his own someday, it would always be on the menu, I was deeply gratified but not actually surprised.

It was one of the great unsung pioneers of the contemporary mountain food scene, John Stehling, who zeroed in on what was happening. John and his wife, Julie, opened the Early Girl Eatery in Asheville in 2002 and John, who grew up in the Piedmont, immediately began driving the back roads and up the hollers of the western North Carolina and eastern Tennessee mountains not just to find the best locally raised food, but to talk to the people who made it. "People who come to and from these mountains want to know where they are when they eat," he said as he and his brother, Robert, the acclaimed chef/owner at Hominy Grill in Charleston, South Carolina, answered questions on a panel. Robert might have the James Beard Award, John noted with a grin, "But outside of seafood, I've got truly great local food sourcing way easier than Robert. Restaurants in other places have to start the process a lot of the time. They have to prime the pump by getting small growers to start growing, or encourage large growers to put in some specialties. But here, in the southern Appalachians, it's *always* been small farm world. And the farmers here never stopped growing these things. They *bring* you things you won't see anywhere else, like this squash, this Candy Roaster. It's got a flavor that's deeper, with layers, and you'll start thinking of something new to do with it, just based on that taste. This place and its food has never died off, and it inspires me."

And John's gut-take was empirically validated in 2011, when a study headed by ethnobotanist Gary Nabhan and environmental anthropologist Jim Veteto declared southern and central Appalachia the most diverse foodshed in North America.

"Let's just go ahead and say it," Jim wrote. "People across southern and central Appalachia are crazy about plants and animals. In my lifetime of interacting with Appalachian farmers, gardeners and wildcrafting enthusiasts, I have never ceased to be amazed by their knowledge and love for all things green and growing. Whether they save seeds, graft fruit trees, dig roots and bulbs, can foods, harvest wild plants, hunt game or raise heritage livestock breeds, it is a truism that older people and a smattering of younger people across the region have immense wildcrafting and agricultural skills."

By the spring of 2014, Appalachian foods had become the focus of inventive chefs both in and out of the region. Some were rooted in a genuine understanding of place and history, such as Shelley Cooper then at TerraMáe Appalachian Bistro in Chattanooga. Many were taking adventurous riffs on rooted themes. Sean Brock's first book, *Heritage*, out that October, talked as expected about the Low Country cooking he'd made famous at McCrady's and Husk, but he gave time as well to the foods of his southwestern Virginia upbringing, foods to which he's since rededicated himself.

And so, with a full tank of gas, I lit out on the highways and byways to discover what else was happening. "So much" was the answer, and I knew pretty quickly that I'd not be able to tell everything. But I took as my model the books that had fired up my own imagination and passion when I first encountered them, the Time-Life *Foods of the World* series. Like the authors of my favorites of those marvelous tomes—one part travelogue, one part history, one part recipe—I chose to limn certain places, to tell the stories of certain people, and to weave from them a rich quilt of story.

So, hop in. Let's get going. We'll be stopping for food soon, but if you get hungry on the way, I'm sure there's a pack of Cheese Nabs somewhere in the glove box.

Roots and Seeds

During the Civil War, Staunton, Virginia, somehow escaped the wholesale burning and razing that decimated most significant towns elsewhere in the South. A century or so later, it also survived the concrete pave-over of the late 1970s, and local citizens preserved a downtown that looks as if it might have welcomed Dickens, right in the heart of the Shenandoah Valley.

On Saturdays and Wednesdays, the parking lot in the historic Wharf district is filled with vendors offering fresh fruit, vegetables, sustainably raised meats, bread and buttermilk, soap and flowers, wine and cider at a bustling farmers market. Joel Salatin's Polyface Farm, made famous in Michael Pollan's *Omnivore's Dilemma*, is eight miles southwest of town. For restaurants, there is velvety pecan pie at The Beverley, salt-rising toast and mushroom gravy at Nu-Beginning Farm's The Store. And in 2014, chef Ian Boden's The Shack landed on a number of "best new restaurants" lists, from *Esquire* to *Southern Living*.

But much as I am in love with all this eating in the present, it's the past that has brought me to Staunton. I've come here to look for the seeds of the South's mountain foodways.

Staunton sits at the juncture of two well-traveled interstates, I-81 and I-64. The I-81 corridor follows the ancient contours of the Warrior's Path, the name Europeans gave to the route used by numerous Native American peoples to travel for trade and hunting, as well as for battle. Extending from upper New York State far down into Alabama, this route through the Appalachian Valley (and its many extensions such as the Carolina Road and the Wilderness Road into Kentucky) became the primary passage for the European settlement of the region that began in earnest in the early 1700s. Staunton was a destination for some, but also a taking-off point for those who chose to venture farther into the wilderness.

Driving in and out of the valley on roads that traverse the Blue Ridge and the Alleghenies, my sturdy Chevy Astro strains and sighs as it makes the steep inclines. I try to imagine what this journey was like on foot, as native people made it, and as many of the early settlers did, possessions stripped to not much more than tools for survival and seeds for planting. Switchbacks flanked by walls of rock and furiously rushing creeks

are gorgeous, but equally perilous. And the deep, varied green of the forest that is so pleasing to the eye from inside my car would have offered ominous shelter to unseen enemies. But just when "intrepid" starts to seem a flaccid word to describe the stark will that carried people on this journey, the road will suddenly curve and swoop to enter a sweet meadow, a wide enough stretch of bottom land or the Great Valley itself, stretching open and full of promise. I realize that while this was a passage of risk and hardship, it was also one of great possibility.

The Frontier Culture Museum in Staunton is a living history museum that tells the story of that initial frontier migration. There are three reconstructed working homesteads on the property that represent typical Appalachian farms in 1740, 1820, and 1850. But there is also a homestead from England, typical of the 1600s, and farmsteads from Ireland, Germany, and West Africa, as they would have appeared in the 1700s. These were the dominant cultures from which people came to the southern Appalachians when the territory was opened for settlement.

Spending a day walking through the re-created European and African farms, I see the foreign seeds of what was to become the culture of the southern mountains. There is also an exhibit called Ganatastwi, however, and beginning with it, I see the roots that were already here. Representing a small settlement typical of how natives of this region would have lived around 1730—as European encroachment began in earnest—the exhibit is not attributed to a specific Indian tribe or culture. The museum literature explains that the archaeological and historical records don't definitively tell us which specific groups of native people were here then. But we do know a great deal about how those people lived, and how they ate.

The sun is not yet high but it is already sticky-hot in the clearing dotted with dome-shaped bark and reed huts when I walk into Ganatastwi one early summer morning. Speaking to a group of schoolchildren, a docent tells them that the natives' diet was more varied than that of their European counterparts, ranging from bison and deer to rabbits, turtles, possums, raccoons, birds, and squirrels—all of which became a part of the frontiersman's diet as well. The women gathered wild greens for both eating and medicinal purposes, and grew many types of squash, beans, and corn.

Beans, corn, berries, and meats were dried for sustenance in the winter, we are told. In the spring, women would plant a communal garden at the tribe's settlement, but would also journey far afield to the hunting grounds and plant a garden there. "That way food would be there, waiting for them when they came to hunt in the fall."

Cooking generally consisted of "a lot of soups and stews so everything can go in one clay pot," the guide said. "Another way to make a stew was to take the stomach of a large mammal, open it, and use it to line a pit. You'd put the ingredients in it along with hot stones, cover it over, and let it cook all day while you worked, then open it and eat." I want to call this the first American Crock-Pot. She adds, "When iron and copper pots came in with the Europeans, they were an instant hit."

And there are metal pots aplenty to covet over at the English homestead. This substantial farmhouse would have been that of a prosperous 18th-century English yeoman, someone who owned his own land and so likely would not have emigrated to North America. His brothers or younger sons might well have opted for the adventure, though, as only the eldest sons inherited family land, and America offered an alternative means for becoming landed. A younger son who emigrated to the American colonies was given fifty acres for himself and fifty additional for anyone he brought with him, both family and servants. A small percentage of such gentry continued on inland from the coastal colonies, some braving the Appalachian frontier themselves, becoming the landholding elite. Claiming the lush valleys and the most arable spaces, they made money largely on tobacco, or rye and wheat, with slaves to work the fields.

The vast majority of English-born settlers coming to the southern Appalachians, however, came essentially as slaves themselves: indentured servants, both men and women. Indentured men who survived their sea journey and period of servitude (only about 40 percent did) were promised land and tools if they would head deeper into the frontier.

One of the persistent myths about Appalachia is that these indentured were hardened criminals, but if anything, many were convicted in England of the petty crimes of poverty, such as sustenance hunting on property that landowners had annexed from formerly public land. It became a kind of tidy, but brutal, system: Shipping the convicted to the Americas for five to seven years of indentured hard labor guaranteed workers for the colonies. Offering them land in the wilderness after servitude provided a force to push and ultimately decimate the native peoples and "tame" the land—often for future development by richer settlers and speculators. These previously indentured pioneers were often understandably wary of government and scornful of property laws.

The Ulster Irish who began immigrating around 1718—and ultimately made up the majority of the mountain population—were no keener friends of the government and the manners of England. Perpetually harassed by England's Anglican Church for their

Protestantism, they were actively recruited by colonial landowners and entrepreneurs to come to the New World, to serve as a vanguard against the native tribes in the battle for the frontier. By and large, the Scots-Irish, as they were called, were not given property to own but were tenants who were often told to move farther west to suit the landowners once a section of the frontier was "tamed." (Their skill with a rifle and ferocious fighting spirit were lauded when they won the Battle of King's Mountain during the American Revolution. But later, when industrialists and developers wanted the land they lived on, these same traits were characterized as uncivilized violence and presented as proof that these people, like the natives they'd vanquished before them, weren't worthy stewards of their land.)

At the Irish farmstead, I discover that one of my favorite of the domestic crafts of the Appalachians—the cane-bottomed "setting" chair—has Irish roots. The Irish *sugan*, like its mountain descendant, is armless and sits lower to the ground than a conventional chair; the design allows someone to sit near the hearth to cook below the level of the smoke. My experience is that it's the perfect height for stringing beans, prepping apples, knitting, and whittling—things that require using both lap and floor as work spaces. (These chairs also tip back securely for opining.)

The interpreter at the Irish farmstead, showing me a notebook filled with information on foods and medicinal herbs in northern Ireland, notes that meat was on the table only a few times a week. That echoes how I grew up and is still common among Appalachian families, particularly in garden season. Pigs raised in Ireland were intended for the landowner or the market. The tenant who did the raising got "the pig's feet, tail, and ears, maybe a side or two of bacon. It was a good year if you could afford to buy some of your own pig back." It must have seemed a gift, then, to come to these far mountains and find you could slaughter your own hog, cure the ham and bacon, and eat off it for the whole of a year.

"A lot of Scots called their garden a Kale Garden," the docent tells me, noting that kale and dandelion were brought over and used as eating greens, but the dandelion was also useful for treating urinary tract infections. "The herb gardens were quite extensive, and used primarily for medicine," he says, and I think about my great-grandmother, who had been a "hyarb woman." When my mother was a little girl, Ma Grinstead took her walking in the woods outside of Corbin, showing her the herbs and plants that she knew so well, teaching her their meanings and healing powers. But my mother had no use for them then and soon forgot, except for her longing each spring for a "dose" of poke or creases.

If the English landholder's house was too large, and the Irish tenant's one room too small, the modest German homestead with its compact kitchen, tiny bedroom, and main room feels just right. The first time I visited this place, in 1995, I walked admiringly into the neat but small kitchen area, nodded appreciatively at the rings of apples drying along one wall, then gasped when I turned to find beans, threaded by string, hanging by the chimney.

"You know the leather britches?" Rosa, a sweet woman with a German accent, asked me. I told her, yes, that I knew these dried green beans, that my family called them "shuck beans," and up until that moment I (and many others) had assumed they were a Cherokee tradition.

But, in fact, Rosa had grown up in Germany eating such beans, soaked overnight and simmered long and slow with a piece of pork for seasoning, just as my family cooked them. Rosa told me then that her understanding was that there was a "recipe" that placed the beans in Germany in the 14th century. I have never been able to confirm that recipe, but if you Google their German name, *getrocknete Bohnen* (literally "dried beans"), amid the photos of an array of dried legumes from kidney to crowder peas, you will find several pictures of long sturdy threads strung with green beans in their "shucks," drying, just as people in the Appalachians still prepare them (see page 151).

The Germans who came to the Appalachians tended to stay in the valleys, in towns like Staunton, or to move farther on to the Piedmont. But some traveled up into the backcountry as well. Their foods became some of the most distinctive in Appalachian cooking: stack cakes, pickle beans and sauerkraut, and their Americanized kin, sour corn. And leather britches, or shuck beans.

European threads are visible elsewhere in the mountain culture. The sound of Irish traditional music can be heard in the reels and jigs that became the soundtrack for barn raisings, corn shuckings, sorghum squeezings, and play parties. The ancient ballads of English folk music informed the canon as well, sometimes preserved over centuries in a family. At the German cottage, an interpreter strums a lovely stringed lap instrument called a *scheitholt*. Mountain luthiers adapted it by raising the fingerboard for faster action and the mountain dulcimer came to the dance.

And then, there is the plaintive ache of the blues, as well.

I'd intended my last stop at the museum to be the re-created West African farm, but on the day I am there, it is still in the process of construction. A young man in a dashiki and jeans tells me it's his first day and he doesn't know much about foodways yet, except that Africans taught us frying techniques and introduced peanuts and "yams," by which he means the sweet potatoes so beloved in the Appalachian diet. The story, as I understand it, is much more complicated.

Except for some large tobacco holdings in the valleys of Virginia and the region abutting the Bluegrass in Kentucky, or the cotton fields in northern Alabama, the steep and hollowed terrain of the Appalachians was largely not conducive to the crops or practices of southern plantation farming. Planters with large slave-holdings were scarce, but yeoman farmers often had a smaller number of slaves to work in the fields and in the house. Largely, though, slavery in the mountains took on a different form than private ownership. Instead there was "leasing" of slaves to work in the region's extractive and building economies. Slaves and indentured servants were miners of salt, then of coal and other minerals. They were livestock drovers, railroad builders, and loggers. Slaves were also hired from their owners to work in the frontier inns as cooks, servers, and housekeepers; then in the tourist economy that quickly developed as the region was settled and recuperative spas at medicinal springs were established. (The Gentleman's Pool House at Warm Springs, about fifty miles southwest of Staunton, was established in 1760. Thomas Jefferson bathed there.) Free blacks also lived in the mountains.

Malinda Russell was one such free black Appalachian, born and raised in Washington and Green counties, in the mountains of East Tennessee, probably in the mid-1820s. At the age of nineteen she intended to emigrate to Liberia, but her money was stolen in Lynchburg, Virginia, and she hired out there as a cook, traveling companion, and nurse. She married, had a son born with a damaged arm, was widowed. She kept a wash house in Abingdon for a time, but she largely earned her living and built her reputation as a cook. Before the Civil War, she returned to East Tennessee and established a boardinghouse at Cold Springs, near Greenville, and then a pastry shop, until she moved to Michigan after she was robbed and threatened by war marauders.

Malinda Russell's story is not a part of the narrative at the Frontier Culture Museum. I know this much of it because she wrote about it in *A Domestic Cook Book: Containing a Careful Selection of Useful Receipts for the Kitchen,* the first published cookbook by an African American. It may also be the first published cookbook about the Appalachian South, at least in part. Although it was written and published in 1866, while she lived in

Michigan, the recipes are the ones that she used at her boardinghouse and pastry shop and when cooking for "the first families of Tennessee (my native place,) Virginia, North Carolina and Kentucky."

She begins with a recipe for salt-rising bread and includes a number of other dishes that, while not exclusively, are strongly associated with the mountain South, including boiled custard, chowchow, green tomato preserves, green cornbread, and a fricassee for catfish. Her recipe for molasses custard sounds like the description I've heard from older folks of a fondly remembered Appalachian dish made with sorghum syrup, called egg butter.

Exactly how much of the book specifically represents recipes that would have been common in the region is a question we may not resolve, but Russell's book and her presence as a professional cook and baker broaden our perception of 19th-century Appalachian foodways. So do the arrival of Swiss, Italian, Hungarian, and other Eastern European immigrants to the region, so that spaghetti and goulash become staples of many Appalachian home cooks by the 20th century, and pepperoni rolls a veritable edible icon of West Virginia.

And then there are the cooks arriving today.

———

Like many before him, Ian Boden has come to the mountains to create a life on his own terms. Sitting on the new deck of The Shack with his wife, Leslie, he talks about his journey to get here. He grew up in northern Virginia outside of D.C. and started working in restaurants as soon as he could. Wiry, with a high forehead, red hair, and beard, Ian has a quick, wide smile, but while he talks, he seems to hold himself in anticipation, like a runner wound up and waiting for the sound of the gun.

"My parents are from New York originally and I thought that was my scene. I worked there just shy of ten years and had some good successes, but toward the end of that time, I started to feel like we chefs were losing track of why we were doing what we were doing. The business had become focused on media, on getting attention rather than what brought us here: feeding people."

Ian's parents, Lou and Ellen, were relocating to Staunton and suggested that Ian check out the town. "I went to Staunton for three hours and I knew I wanted to be here.

"So I opened the Staunton Grocery and I wanted to distinguish it from anything else that was here. It was a very artful place downtown, and the food showed everything I'd learned. But I was twenty-six years old and I ended up excluding more people than I included. We were at a high school basketball game and one of Leslie's longtime friends said, 'I looked at some of the photos and it looked a little fancy.' I didn't want that. It felt like I'd just created what I'd wanted to leave in New York.

"I knew that what I wanted was a place where everyone was welcome." So for his next turn in Staunton, Ian and Leslie picked a tiny brick building just outside the hip downtown district and filled it with half a dozen utilitarian tables, mismatched chairs, and photos of Leslie's late grandmother, Tissie, and her house, which she actually called "the shack."

The nightly menu initially offered four different burgers. "We wanted the food to feel familiar, but maybe stretch just a little," Ian explained. But on Friday and Saturday nights, he cut loose with a multicourse small-plate tasting menu, and soon the folks who formed lines for a seat in the sixteen-chair dining room were clamoring for more.

The menu has evolved into a distinct expression of the influences and interests of the chef. It speaks often with a clear southern accent, but is sometimes flavored with French. It flashes occasionally with the lights of New York City, or slides on the schmaltz of a good deli, and the insanely tiny kitchen has both iron skillets and two immersion circulators.

There are also dishes on the menu that are riffs on the region: morel gravy, sausage in sorghum sauce, buttermilk pie with vinegared strawberries, tiny crisp radishes kissed with pork fat and salt. One night Ian served banana pudding with a crackerlike crust that was unlike any I have eaten and yet an eerie throwback to my childhood and how my cousins and I loved that blend of sweet and salty.

"Do you call The Shack an Appalachian restaurant?" I ask him, and he thinks for a minute before answering.

"When you're a part of the community, that comes through when you cook. I try to pay homage, but to do it my way. My pot likker is based on tradition, but it's not traditional. I put fish sauce and soy sauce in mine. So, no, I wouldn't say it is an Appalachian restaurant based on the food. But, yes, it *is* in the fact that everything we do here we do to honor Tissie, and the life she led."

Fannie Grogg Kellison Campbell, known as Tissie, died in 1996 and Ian never met her. "But she had such an impact on Leslie's life. The more Leslie told me about who she was, the more I saw the things I value in Leslie: the strength, directness, but an openness, too. There's no superficiality, no judgment."

Leslie picks up the thread here. A dark-haired, dark-eyed beauty with a heart-shaped face, she was born seven and a half miles up toward the mountains in Churchville. Her parents moved the family into Staunton for work soon after. "I grew up in both the town and mountain. My parents both worked so our grandmother, Tissie, watched me and my siblings and I learned more from her . . ."

"Life." Ian interjects. "She taught a lot of life lessons."

"Tissie was from Swoope," Leslie continues. "Ten miles into the mountains, but lifetimes away. She lived in a house with no running water except a spring-fed faucet that was hooked up to a hose. She did have electric, but we would heat up water for baths on her woodstove. If that hose would freeze in the winter, then your little ass was going to go get jugs of water filled from the spring. Basically we were little worker bees.

"She was very hard, stubborn as a rattlesnake; and if we were bad, we got switched. Had to go out and pick your own switch. But she showed us love in other ways. She would play dress-ups with us, do makeup and wigs, and she'd play right with us. She walked with us, took us to the woods, taught us where we were. And she cooked for us.

"I miss that light bread. She made bread, it was a full-day job, so she'd just ask everybody, 'Y'all want to come over today? I'm making light rolls today.' And she made it for the neighborhood."

Ian nods and then says, "I hired a dishwasher here from Churchville and his first day, he's walking around the dining room, looking at the pictures. So I told him, 'That's my wife's grandmother.' When Leslie came in he went right up to her and said, 'Your grandma used to watch me. She half-raised me.' He was so happy to see her here. He was so happy to be here."

We all sit for a moment, savoring the story. Then Ian leans in and says, "That's Appalachian, isn't it? That seating everyone at the table? That sense that everyone can share?"

Karl Worley's Roasted Chicken & Dumplings SERVES 6

Yard birds cackle and strut around the various homesteads at the Frontier Culture Museum as they still do at farmsteads all across the Appalachian region. Chicken and dumplings is a dish that crosses cultures, demonstrating the ability to make glory out of meager means. The chicken that found its way to the stew pot was most often a stringy extra rooster or old hen, one with spare meat but plenty of sinew to flavor the broth during long, slow simmering. The dumplings of flour, fat, and salt soaked up that goodness.

The free-range chickens most of us get today are a different bird altogether. Plump, juicy, and packing plenty of meat, they perform much better in a roasting pan. Conscious of that and looking for the redolent flavor that reflected the best of what he remembered growing up in Bristol, Tennessee, Karl Worley, who with his wife, Sarah, owns and cooks at Biscuit Love in Nashville, created this magnificent version. Karl discards the skin to make a lighter stock full with the fresh flavor of vegetables and herbs. He then ups the unctuous level in the sauce by adding both butter and cream. This is the sort of "Spread the tablecloth! The preacher's coming!" Sunday dish you'd have been served at a prosperous mountain farm.

Note that you will need two large pots, such as Dutch ovens or stew pots, with wide surface areas—at least 10 inches—for the sauce and the dumplings.

ROASTED CHICKEN

1 whole chicken (about 3 pounds)
Salt and freshly ground black pepper
6 tablespoons unsalted butter, at room temperature
1 lemon, halved and juiced; halves reserved
¼ cup chopped assorted fresh herbs—such as thyme, parsley, and rosemary
1 small yellow onion, halved
4 garlic cloves, smashed
4 sprigs fresh parsley
4 sprigs fresh thyme
4 sprigs fresh rosemary

Preheat the oven to 375°F.

Remove the neck and giblets from the cavity of the chicken and discard them. Pat the chicken thoroughly dry with paper towels. Season the body and cavity of the chicken generously with salt and pepper.

In a small bowl, mash together the butter, lemon juice, and chopped herbs. Rub the herbed butter all over the chicken and under the skin. Put the lemon halves, onion halves, garlic cloves, and herb sprigs inside the chicken cavity. Tie the legs together with kitchen twine. Place the chicken, breast side up, in a roasting pan fitted with a rack. Roast for 1 hour.

Remove the chicken from the oven, and when it is cool enough to handle, remove the skin and shred the meat. Let the meat cool; then set it aside in the refrigerator. Discard the skin and the items from the cavity. Reserve the bones for the chicken stock.

CHICKEN STOCK

2 tablespoons olive oil
2 carrots, cut in large chunks
2 celery stalks, cut in large chunks
1 yellow onion, halved
1 whole garlic bulb, halved
Reserved chicken bones from roasted chicken
4 sprigs fresh parsley
4 sprigs fresh thyme
2 bay leaves

Coat the bottom of a stockpot with the olive oil and place it over medium heat. Add the carrots, celery, onion, and garlic and cook for 3 minutes or until aromatic. Add the reserved chicken bones, 3 quarts of water, and the herbs. Bring to a boil over high heat, and then reduce the heat so the stock simmers. Let it simmer for 1½ hours or until it is reduced to 6 cups. Strain the stock to remove the solids. Discard the solids and set the stock aside.

SAUCE

2 tablespoons butter
1 tablespoon vegetable oil
1 large carrot, small diced
1 large celery stalk, small diced
3 garlic cloves, minced
2 bay leaves
6 tablespoons all-purpose flour
6 cups reserved chicken stock
¼ cup heavy cream
Salt

Heat a large wide stew pot or Dutch oven over medium heat. Add the butter and oil. Once the butter is melted, add the carrot, celery, garlic, and bay leaves. Cook until the vegetables are soft, about 8 minutes. Stir in the flour. Continuing to stir to coat the vegetables, cook for 2 minutes to remove the starchy taste. Slowly pour in the chicken stock, 1 cup at a time, stirring well after each addition. Reduce the heat and let the sauce simmer until it is thick enough to coat the back of a spoon, about 15 minutes. Then stir in the heavy cream, and add salt to taste. Set the pot aside.

DUMPLING DOUGH

2 cups all-purpose flour
1 tablespoon baking powder
1 teaspoon salt
1½ teaspoons sugar
½ teaspoon freshly ground black pepper
¼ cup lard, at room temperature
⅔ to 1⅓ cups heavy cream

In a large bowl, sift the flour with the baking powder, salt, sugar, and black pepper. Using your fingers, work the lard into the dough until it is crumbly; then stir in the cream until the dough comes together. The dough should be thick, like a very moist biscuit dough.

TO FINISH

Freshly cracked black pepper
Chopped fresh flat-leaf parsley

Pour half of the sauce into another large wide pot, and set both pots over medium heat. Divide the reserved shredded chicken equally between the two pots and bring up to a simmer. Using two small spoons, carefully drop the dumpling dough into the pots. The dumplings should cover the top of the sauce but should not be crowded. Reduce the heat to medium-low, cover, and let the dumplings poach for 6 to 9 minutes, until they are firm and puffy. Serve immediately, garnished with freshly cracked black pepper and chopped parsley.

Morels & Ramps with Eggs on Toast SERVES 4

The abundance of morels and other mushrooms in the spring was another way the woods provided for early mountain dwellers.

Not long after chef Ian Boden had moved to Staunton, Virginia, from New York City, he got a phone call from a young woman he'd recently met. "I called him and said that my grandpa had some mushrooms, did he want to buy them?" his wife, Leslie, recalls. Ian laughs. "She pulled up with a McDonald's bag filled with the most beautiful mushrooms I'd seen. I was paying a fortune in New York for morels not like the likes of these."

"And I said, Granddaddy will take five dollars for them to play the scratch Lotto," Leslie finishes, grinning.

Ian created this simple dish, in keeping with the traditions of gathering mushrooms and ramps in the spring. It is also delicious made with chanterelles, which grow wild in parts of the Appalachians.

To clean wild morels, mix warm water and a handful of salt in a large container until the salt dissolves. Submerge the morels in the salt water for 15 minutes. If there are any bugs in the morels, this will force them out. Remove the morels from the water and pat them dry with a clean towel.

1 pound morel mushrooms, cleaned, stems trimmed
7 tablespoons butter
20 ramps, trimmed, greens and bulbs separated
Salt and freshly ground black pepper
1 cup heavy cream
4 large, thick slices rustic bread
4 large eggs

Cut any overly large mushrooms so that all are roughly the same size.

Place 1 tablespoon of the butter in a large skillet set over medium heat. When the butter is foaming, add the ramp bulbs and cook until they start to soften, about 1½ minutes. Then add the cleaned morels, another 1 tablespoon of the butter, and a healthy pinch of salt. Reduce the heat to medium-low and allow the morels to cook for 3 minutes or until just tender, stirring occasionally.

Add the heavy cream and gently simmer until the cream has reduced by about half, about 15 minutes. Add the green ramp tops and 2 tablespoons of the butter to the morel mixture. Let simmer about 3 more minutes, stirring to make a pan sauce. Season with salt and a healthy amount of freshly ground black pepper. Set aside.

While the ramp tops are simmering, toast the bread.

While the bread is toasting, in a skillet that is large enough to accommodate 4 eggs, melt 1 tablespoon butter over medium heat. Crack the eggs into the skillet, and cover. Let cook for 4 minutes for just-set sunny-side-up eggs, or cook to your preference. Remove the lid and season with salt and pepper.

To serve, butter the toast with the remaining butter.

Place one slice of toast on each of four plates. Top the toast with the creamed morels and ramps, and lastly one fried egg. Add another turn of black pepper.

Venison or Beef Hand Pies

MAKES I DOZEN

Half-moon-shaped hand pies are usually filled with a sweet dried apple or peach filling, but they were such a handy thing to pack inside a miner's lunch pail that some enterprising wives and mothers filled the pastries with meat. This can be made with lean grass-fed beef instead, but since venison has a tang to it, I'd suggest adding just a teaspoon of apple cider after the sorghum syrup if that's what you use.

DOUGH

2¼ cups all-purpose flour, plus more for dusting
1 teaspoon kosher salt
½ teaspoon baking powder
¾ cup skim milk
½ cup lard or solid vegetable shortening

FILLING

2 tablespoons olive oil
1 pound ground venison
1 cup finely chopped green cabbage
¾ cup shredded carrot
½ cup diced onion
½ tablespoon Spanish smoked paprika
½ teaspoon freshly grated nutmeg
1 teaspoon ground allspice
Dash of cayenne pepper
½ teaspoon kosher salt
⅓ cup warm water
1 tablespoon tomato paste
½ tablespoon sorghum syrup
Ginger Bean Chowchow (page 160), for serving (optional)

Make the dough: The dough needs to rest for 2 hours before you roll it, so begin with plenty of time. In a bowl, mix the flour with the salt and baking powder. In a small saucepan set over low heat, heat the milk until bubbles appear around the edge of the pan, and then remove it from the heat.

In a large bowl, combine the hot milk with the lard. Stir with a fork until the lard is nearly melted—there should be some pea-sized pieces of lard left.

Add the flour mixture and stir with a fork just until a shaggy dough forms. Transfer the dough to a lightly floured surface and knead until smooth. Roll the dough to form a wide log about 6 inches long, wrap it tightly in plastic wrap, and refrigerate until chilled, at least 2 hours.

Prepare the filling: Heat the olive oil in a large skillet over medium heat. When the oil is very hot, crumble the venison into the pan. When it begins to brown, stir in the cabbage, carrot, onion, paprika, nutmeg, allspice, cayenne, and salt. Continue to cook over medium heat, stirring occasionally, for about 6 minutes, until the onions are transparent and the other vegetables are al dente.

In a small bowl, quickly mix the warm water, tomato paste, and sorghum together until dissolved. Pour this liquid over the meat mixture and continue to cook, stirring, until it is absorbed, about 30 seconds. Transfer the mixture to a bowl and allow it to cool while you prepare the crusts.

Make the pies: Preheat the oven to 400°F.

Remove the dough from the refrigerator and cut it into 12 equal pieces; put 6 back in the refrigerator. Form each of the remaining 6 pieces into a ball. Then, on a lightly floured surface, roll out each ball to form a 6-inch round (the dough will be thin). Brush water over the lower edge of each round. Mound about ¼ cup of the filling on the lower half of each round. Fold the upper half of the round over the filling to make a half-moon, leaving a ½-inch border; press the edges together to seal.

Use a lightly floured fork to crimp the edges, and pierce the top of each pie with a fork. Use a spatula to transfer the pies to a large, lightly floured baking sheet. Repeat with the remaining dough and filling.

Bake for 25 minutes or until the crusts turn golden. Remove and allow to cool until they can be handled before biting in.

Serve with Ginger Bean Chowchow.

Roasted Root Vegetable Salad with Bacon & Orange Sorghum Vinegar

SERVES 4

Delicious root vegetables love the cool of both spring and fall in the mountains. Gardeners love the twin harvest. The root cellar is where such vegetables were stored in plenty of mountain homesteads, although some folks kept them in baskets and bins in a cool, dark place in the house. In fact, folks with larger houses might close off "the front room," as the living room was more commonly called, to conserve on heat when the weather got cold. That room might then become an ad hoc fruit and vegetable cooler.

My mother kept the Christmas fruit in the front room until company came, but not vegetables. We ate them too fast then—boiled, buttered, and salted or eaten raw with salt. Today I make this lovely salad first in the spring, then again as autumn splashes the hills with the colors of the carrots and beets.

3 medium yellow beets, trimmed and scrubbed
3 medium red beets, trimmed and scrubbed
2 large carrots, cut into 1½-inch pieces
1 teaspoon olive oil
Salt
4 red radishes, thinly sliced
½ small red onion, thinly sliced and separated
   into rings
4 slices bacon, cooked
Orange Sorghum Vinegar (page 232), to taste
Drizzle of bacon grease, to taste

Preheat the oven to 400°F.

Wrap up the yellow beets in a large piece of aluminum foil. Do the same with the red beets, and place both packets on a baking sheet. Roast until the beets are tender at the center when pierced with a knife, about 1 hour.

Meanwhile, on a separate baking sheet, toss the carrot pieces with the oil. Season with a sprinkle of salt. Roast the carrots for about 25 minutes, until tender and caramelized.

When the beets come out of the oven, carefully open the packets to release the steam, and let the beets cool. Once the beets have cooled, gently rub the skins off (this works well with a towel, but they will stain the fabric) and cut the beets into wedges.

To assemble the salad, lay the red beet wedges on the bottom of a large shallow serving bowl. Lay the roasted carrots on top, and then the yellow beet wedges. Throw in the sliced radishes and red onion. Break up the bacon slices and scatter the pieces on top. Season with salt and drizzle with the Orange Sorghum Vinegar. Toss ever so gently. Give it a taste and determine if a drizzle of bacon grease is needed. Serve.

English Pea Salad with Cream Dressing SERVES 4

I grew up eating my mother's version of a lovely light salad that's traditionally made with fresh green peas—which she called "English peas"—and cream dressing. She re-created it for us using the frozen peas available in the city. And then she read a recipe for pea salad with canned tiny peas and shredded cheese and probably pimentos and I can't remember what all because after she'd made it a couple of times, she stopped: none of us would eat more than a bite or two. She never went back to the original, and it faded from my memory until I came upon chef Travis Milton's riff on this church supper staple. One taste and I was off to try to re-create my mother's different but kin version. I like to eat this with a small spoon, as I did once upon a time, and I wish I still had the small, square hobnail glass dishes she served it in.

½ cup heavy cream
½ teaspoon apple cider vinegar
¼ teaspoon honey
Salt
2 cups fresh or frozen peas
½ cup thinly sliced small radishes
¼ cup minced green onions
Freshly ground black pepper

About an hour before you are ready to make the salad, make the dressing by pouring the cream into a pint jar with a lid. Add the vinegar, honey, and a few pinches of salt. Screw on the lid and shake the jar steadily for 1 minute. Then allow it to sit at room temperature for about an hour. The dressing should thicken but still be pourable.

Bring 2 cups of water to a boil in a saucepan and add the peas. Allow to boil, uncovered, for 1 to 2 minutes, until just barely tender. Drain and rinse immediately with cold water until the peas are no longer warm. Drain thoroughly, and then pat them dry with paper towels.

In a medium-sized bowl, toss the peas with the radishes and green onions. Then add the dressing, using a rubber spatula to get it all from the jar. Add plenty of freshly ground black pepper. (Some may want additional salt, but I like the clean, light flavor without it.) Chill, covered, for at least 30 minutes before serving.

Mama's Mashed Potatoes

SERVES 6

My mama, like most mountain women I know, always referred to potatoes as Irish (said more like "Airsh") potatoes to differentiate them from the sweet potatoes we also loved—but the term also provided a linguistic clue to our region's history of immigrants and settlers.

When I first wrote about my mother's mashed potatoes in the late 1980s, fine restaurants were serving "wild rice medley" as the starchy side dish. Not long after, mashed potatoes began to make a comeback: chunky, "smashed," garlicked, peppered, lobstered, and made with Yukon Gold or another "new" variety. They were often delicious, always interesting. I've enough Irish and German in my background to ensure I've never met a potato I didn't like. But my mom's pure and simple recipe nevertheless remains the best to me.

She used the round-faced potato masher with a waffle grid. I've tried other mashers and methods, but this masher is the one that creates the perfect balance of creamy and fluffy. I often find them in secondhand stores; if you locate one, press the face of the masher hard against your palm to make sure it is sturdy enough.

1 tablespoon salt, plus more to taste
6 medium russet potatoes (about 3 pounds)
8 tablespoons (1 stick) butter at room temperature
1 cup half-and-half or whole milk

In a large saucepan with a lid, dissolve the 1 tablespoon salt in about 2 quarts of water. Cover and bring to a boil over high heat.

Peel and quarter the potatoes. (If you are using larger potatoes, you may need to cut them into 6 pieces, each about the size of an egg.) When the water boils, add the potatoes to the pot and cook, covered, until they break apart easily when pierced with a fork. This can take from 15 to 25 minutes.

Drain off the water, reserving the potatoes in the pot. Toss the butter in with the potatoes and re-cover. In a small saucepan over medium heat, or in the microwave, heat the half-and-half to a warm state.

Use a potato masher to mash the potatoes and butter together in the pot, mashing vigorously through all the potatoes four or five times, until smooth. Pour in the warmed half-and-half and mash through once more to blend. Taste and add salt if needed; then beat vigorously with a large wooden spoon for about a minute to fluff. Serve immediately.

VARIATION

If you have good buttermilk, you can substitute it for part of the half-and-half, using ½ cup buttermilk and ½ cup half-and-half. But don't heat the buttermilk—just allow it to come to room temperature before adding it.

The Shack's Sweet & Savory Banana Pudding SERVES 8

When Ian Boden set several small mason jars of his banana pudding in front of a group of us one night at his Staunton restaurant, The Shack, I picked up my spoon to have just one polite bite. It's a mercy that after that first bite I didn't convert that spoon into a weapon to fight everyone else at the table for every last jar. Luckily, Ian had a few more in the back.

The hypnotizing goodness of this pudding lies in the earthy banana bread and the seesaw back and forth between its miso salty smack and the classic pudding sweet.

PUDDING

4 egg yolks at room temperature
½ cup sugar
Pinch of salt
4 cups heavy cream
1 packet (¼ ounce) powdered gelatin
2 whole vanilla beans, halved lengthwise

BANANA BREAD

4 tablespoons unsalted butter, melted and cooled, plus more for greasing the pan
2 overly ripe bananas
3 ounces red miso paste
1 large egg
⅓ cup (packed) light brown sugar
⅔ cup all-purpose flour
⅓ cup buckwheat flour
½ teaspoon baking soda

ASSEMBLY

1 cup crushed vanilla wafers
4 bananas, peeled and sliced

Make the pudding: Whisk the egg yolks, sugar, and salt together in a large bowl. Set aside.

Pour ¼ cup of the cream into a small bowl. Sprinkle the gelatin over the cream and stir with a fork until incorporated. Let sit for 5 minutes.

Pour the remaining 3¾ cups cream into a saucepan and whisk in the gelatin-cream mixture. Scrape the seeds from the vanilla beans into the cream. Heat over medium-low heat, bringing the cream to a point just under a simmer, whisking every so often to incorporate the gelatin.

Remove the pan from the heat and very slowly drizzle the cream into the egg mixture while whisking constantly. Pour the mixture through a fine-mesh strainer set over a clean bowl, and transfer it to a refrigerator to chill. For the first hour, whisk the pudding every 15 minutes to incorporate any skin that forms on top. Then cover the pudding with plastic wrap after the last whisk, pressing the wrap directly onto the surface. Let chill for 3 hours. It will be about halfway set at that point.

Make the banana bread: Preheat the oven to 300°F and lightly grease a 1-pound (8½ × 4½-inch) loaf pan with butter.

Peel the bananas and place them in a blender along with the miso, egg, and brown sugar. Blend until the ingredients are combined and smooth. Set aside.

Mix both flours and the baking soda together in a large bowl. Gently stir the banana mixture into the flour until just incorporated, and then drizzle in the melted butter. Be careful not to overmix, as that would result in a less tender bread.

Pour the batter into the prepared loaf pan and bake for 30 to 35 minutes. The bread is done when a toothpick inserted into the center comes out moist but not wet. Turn out on a rack and allow to cool completely. Use your hands to break into coarse crumbs.

Make the banana pudding: In either individual mason jars or a single large baking dish, arrange alternating layers of pudding, bread crumbs, bananas, and vanilla wafers, starting with pudding on the bottom and ending with wafers on the top. Be sure all the banana slices are completely covered by pudding to prevent browning. Refrigerate, covered, for 4 hours or overnight before serving, so that the pudding can finish setting.

Florida Slone's Gingerbread

MAKES 14 TO 16 SCONE-SIZED BREADS

The cookbook written by mid-19th-century cook, caterer, and pastry shop owner Malinda Russell contains over a dozen recipes for types of gingerbread. In some communities in eastern Kentucky, politicians well into the 20th century paid local cooks to bake gingerbread to be given away on election day at the polling grounds, each vying for the better treat to trade for votes. Knott County, Kentucky, celebrates gingerbread's social and political impact in the region with a festival each fall honoring a different local family's special gingerbread recipe. The first so honored was Florida Slone's.

The Slone family roots are German, and Florida Slone's recipe has echoes of *Lebkuchen*. The small breads are not nearly as sweet as contemporary American gingerbread, and to the uninitiated may, at first bite, seem a bit crumbly and dry—but then the spices and the winey flavor of the black walnuts start to work on your mouth and suddenly you can't wait to have that next bite.

Pretty, merry, brown-haired Deborah Slone laughs when I ask if I can print her grandmother's recipe. "I hope so," she says, suggesting there's a bit of a story there.

When Florida was a toddler, she had a fever that she barely survived. It left her with a speech impediment, and she was marked as being unable to go to school. "But when she was in her sixties," Deborah told me, "she went to the Hindman Settlement School and learned how to read and also got her driver's license." Over the years, as Florida experimented with her beloved gingerbread recipe, she would write down new versions and share them. "There's no other recipe that she copied down that much," Deborah said. "It's the one thing she liked to make, and we know also that what she wrote down was really meaningful to her because writing was something she didn't do until she was sixty-four or sixty-five. There's nothing that reminds me so much of her as her gingerbread."

GINGERBREAD

4 to 5 cups all-purpose flour, plus more for shaping
½ tablespoon baking soda
2 tablespoons ground ginger
1 teaspoon ground cinnamon
½ cup sugar
½ cup black walnut meats
4 tablespoons butter, melted
½ cup sorghum syrup
½ cup honey
2 large eggs, beaten
½ cup whole milk
1 teaspoon vanilla extract

GLAZE (OPTIONAL)

½ cup powdered sugar
1 tablespoon warm water

Preheat the oven to 400°F. Line two large baking sheets with parchment paper.

In a large bowl combine 4 cups of the flour with the baking soda, ginger, cinnamon, and sugar, stirring until fully blended together. Stir in the black walnut meats. Set aside.

In a medium bowl beat together the melted butter, sorghum syrup, honey, eggs, milk, and vanilla until fully blended.

Make a well in the center of the flour mixture and pour the liquid mixture into it. Use a large spoon or floured hands to fold the flour into the liquid, a handful at a time. Pat the flour in, turning the bowl and the dough to incorporate it gently. You want the dough to hold together well enough that it can be shaped, but not be stiff and dry. You may need to use additional flour to get the right consistency. (If you do, don't worry about adding more baking soda as the amount here is adequate.)

When the dough holds together in the bowl, coming away from the sides without sticking, turn it out on a lightly floured surface and gently pat it into the shape of a fat log (but not really rounded on the bottom), about 14 inches long and 4 inches wide.

Use a sharp knife to cut off pieces about 1 inch thick, and lay them on the prepared baking sheets with about 2 inches between them. (You can pat them lightly to make them more in the shape of rectangles, but they will spread out a bit while baking in any case.)

Bake for 10 minutes, and then turn the baking sheets in the oven. Bake for 6 to 8 minutes more, until the cakes are turning golden.

If you'd like to glaze them, whisk together the powdered sugar and warm water in a small bowl while the cakes are baking.

Remove the cakes from the oven and transfer them to racks to cool. If you are using the glaze, apply it over the tops of the cakes while still warm; their heat will help loosen the glaze.

These are good warm out of the oven but actually get better by the next day, so once they are fully cooled, transfer them to a container with a lid or a sealable plastic bag and store at room temperature.

Messing with Greens

Winter in the mountains begins with the first bowl of soup beans, corn popped later to fuel the crisp early night with conversation. In good years, the fun of getting cozy seems to last until Little Christmas, the end of the holidays on January 6. Ah, but then the slow slide into cabin fever begins. It's not that winter doesn't have its pleasures in the mountains—it's just that it sticks around too long.

That may be why mountain dwellers seem to have an absolute passion for wild spring greens—the more pungent, the better. That's why they start scouting the landscape in the first warm days, for the telltale signs of ramps, most famously, but also for branch lettuce and then creasies. It's why they look for early poke and pick its tiny, tender leaves. And that love of greens extends as long as it can, right through the last of the fall mustard and kale in the garden. Each green has its own distinct flavor and texture, and certain greens are cooked one way while others are best made another. While there are plenty of methods for cooking these greens, they can largely be grouped into three families: lettuces for killing, sallet, and pot likker.

LETTUCES FOR KILLING

Families take to the woods to gather up a mess (meaning enough to feed everybody) of greens and come home to fry up a skillet of bacon. The cooked bacon is crumbled, to be added with chopped green onions on the finished dish, and the hot bacon grease is used to dress the crisp greens, also doused with cider vinegar, a dose of salt, and black pepper.

Branch lettuce is one of the favorites for killing. It gets its name because it can be found along the edges of icy mountain springs, or branches, in the earliest spring. Not actually a lettuce, it's a variety of *Saxifraga* with toothy, fuzzy leaves that offer just a bit of resistance when you bite, and a taste that is tart and cleansing. Of course killed, or kilt, lettuce—so called because the hot dressing wilts or "kills" the greens—can be made with any crisp garden salad green. Even in the city, I knew that spring was in the air when my mother announced that killed lettuce was for supper. She used the best iceberg lettuce she could find; these days I gravitate toward mâche and arugula mixed with young romaine. My mother would make a skillet of cornbread and that would be our meal—something primal and reviving in that big bowl of hot dressed greens.

SALLET

Sallet isn't salad. A sallet of greens in the South is made by cooking particular fresh greens fairly quickly in a skillet of hot bacon grease. In the mountains, we make sallet with a variety of wild greens. The most famous of these is poke sallet, of course, and if you have the album by Tony Joe White that spells it "Polk Salad," my guess is you shouldn't blame that Louisiana boy. That prissy spelling was likely fotched on by a record label on one of the coasts, bless its heart.

"Poke" is short for pokeweed, a wild and profuse plant with leaves that are edible only in the very early spring, and only if cooked properly. It's a bother to prepare, but we bothered because the taste—similar to spinach, but brighter and tangier—is one a body begins to crave. Poke is said to have tonic and reviving qualities, and while I can't make any such health claims for it, I know I always feel pert after eating a mess. We harvested only leaves smaller than your hand, and no other, potentially lethal, part of the pokeweed was consumed. After rinsing them well, we boiled the poke greens in a big pot of water for 3 minutes uncovered, and then thoroughly drained the water. We'd repeat the process, and some folks boiled and drained as many as four times. I rinsed the leaves after the second draining, then shook and patted them dry with a tea towel. The "mess" was then cooked in bacon grease in a skillet with chopped-up green onion until everything was tender, and then eaten with cornbread.

Poke was not the only wild green to get the "sallet" treatment. Dock, purslane, lamb's quarters, and in some parts of the mountains, tiny new fiddlehead ferns are favorites. When my parents lived in Detroit during World War II so my daddy could work in the factories, my mother gathered dandelion and other wild greens from the median of a boulevard. She told me she couldn't find kale or mustard in the grocery, but the tender greens cooked with bacon provided a taste of home.

Creasy greens, known elsewhere as "land creases," are a type of mustard that grows both wild and cultivated in the mountains. Similar in flavor to watercress, creasies are both strong in taste and firm in texture, so while some folks these days eat them snipped raw into salad, the preferred way of dealing with them in southern Appalachia was to cook them into sallet. They shrink in the cooking considerably, so it takes a mighty big amount to feed a family, and that's why beaten eggs were often scrambled into the skillet.

Sochan, or sochani, is another wild spring green, particularly beloved by the Cherokee. Growing profusely along creeks and rivers, when it comes into maturity, this coneflower in the sunflower family will bear bright yellow daisy-like flowers. But the edible leaves of the plant are gathered when young and tender, well before bloom time, in the early spring. Sochan leaves should be rinsed well and then covered with water and simmered until tender before draining well. They can then be made into sallet. The green is also good in stews, and the Cherokee often added it to a pot of hominy.

Once a pungent mountain secret, deliciously garlicky spring ramps now show up in restaurants all around the country, and there is some worry that they are being badly harvested to meet this demand. Old-timers knew that ramps should not be pulled from the ground, root and all, but harvested with a sharp knife, cutting the bulb a bit above the rootstock and leaving that root to spread and regenerate a new crop the next spring. Many folks cooked the chopped-up ramp leaves and bulbs as described for sallet. But generally they were combined with potatoes and/or eggs as described in Country Ham, Ramps & Taters (page 61).

POT LIKKER

Greens are not only a spring tonic in the mountains; they provide vitamins, minerals, and flavor in the early part of winter. Collards thrive in the sandy soils and hotter climate of the Deep and coastal South, but they are very rarely among the greens preferred for growing and eating in the southern Appalachians. The Scots-Irish brought kale to the region and that sturdy leaf was ballast in the pot. Mustard and turnip are also prized— sometimes added to the kettle for bite to kale's more mineral tang, or cooked alone. Hardy characters, all three can sometimes be found in the long-harvested garden plot, poking up through the snow.

This sturdiness calls for a long slow braise with a chunk of pork for seasoning. Like Soup Beans (page 154), a bowl of greens might serve as the center of a wintertime supper. Beloved sometimes even more than the tender greens, the rich broth, called pot likker, marries the essence of the greens with the umami of the pork, and is best consumed sopped up with absorbent cornbread. (Schisms exist over whether the best method to do so is to dunk a wedge or crumble it in. I am ecumenical and appreciate both.)

Killed Lettuce SERVES 4

The defining part of this dish is that the greens—and the chopped green onions that are mixed with them—are not cooked, but are tossed with vinegar and hot bacon grease to wilt them. In that general rubric, variations exist. My mother tossed the raw lettuce and onions in vinegar and then poured on the bacon grease. Sheri Castle's grandmother cooked the vinegar and grease together with a bit of sugar. A friend of my family made hers by tempering a beaten egg with the hot grease and vinegar and then cooking it to make a thick dressing. My mother once killed a bowl of vinegared lettuce by pouring on ladlefuls of hot, pork-seasoned pinto beans. A number of restaurant chefs serving killed lettuce these days like to top the dish with a soft-cooked egg so the runny yolk can become a part of the dressing.

Here are proportions and directions from my family's kitchen to get you started. Serve this with cornbread to sop up the dressing.

8 cups torn crisp salad greens (in bite-sized pieces)
2 whole green onions, finely chopped
4 bacon slices
¼ cup apple cider vinegar
Salt and freshly ground black pepper

Rinse and thoroughly dry the greens, and then toss them with the green onions in a large bowl.

Fry the bacon in a skillet over medium heat until very crisp, and remove from the skillet to drain. Remove the skillet from the heat. Immediately pour the vinegar over the lettuce and toss, then pour the warm bacon grease over that, tossing again. Add salt and pepper to taste. Crumble the bacon over the greens and serve immediately.

Sallet SERVES 4

Any sturdy spring garden green—new kale, mustard, turnip greens, or spinach—can be cooked in bacon grease to make sallet for either a main course or a side dish. As you will want to harvest whatever is available in either garden or the landscape when it is young and tender and cook it right away, the amount of greens may vary a good bit, and their variety and age will also affect cooking times or call for some variations, so a specific recipe is less helpful than this basic one.

2 tablespoons bacon grease (from 2 to 3 slices of
    bacon) or olive oil
¼ cup chopped whole green onions (optional)
1 pound fresh sturdy greens, chopped or torn
    (6 to 7 cups loosely packed), washed and drained
    (see Note)
Salt and freshly ground black pepper
Crumbled crisp-cooked bacon, for garnish (optional)
Vinegar, for serving
Hot sauce, for serving

In a large skillet, heat the bacon grease over medium-high heat until shimmery-hot. Add the green onions and cook for 1 minute, stirring (if using—otherwise you can serve raw green onions on the side).

Carefully add the first batch of greens to the hot grease (the water on rinsed or parboiled greens will cause the grease to pop). Use tongs or a spatula to stir and toss the greens while they cook. As soon as they wilt down and there is room, add more. Depending on the type of green and the degree of initial tenderness, the cooking time may vary from 3 to 10 minutes. Taste to see when they are done. If the greens are still a little too firm, you can cover the pan, remove it from the heat, and let them steam for a couple of minutes. Add salt and pepper to taste. Garnish with crumbled bacon, if using, and pass the vinegar and hot sauce on the side.

NOTE: Poke must be boiled and drained of its water at least twice, as described on page 55, to be edible. Sochan needs to be parboiled to tenderize the leaves. Other tender greens can simply be rinsed thoroughly (often it requires more than one drenching to get rid of grit on foraged or fresh-picked greens). Drain, but do not aggressively dry the greens; the leftover water helps them cook.

Braised Greens & Pot Likker

SERVES 4 TO 6

Groceries now sell packaged "southern" greens or braising greens that are rinsed and torn into bite-sized pieces and include a mix of different kinds of leaves. If you're new to pot likker greens, this is a good place to start.

¼ pound salt pork, or 1 ham hock
2 pounds hardy greens, such as kale, mustard, or turnip
2 teaspoons salt, plus more to taste
Ground white pepper, to taste
1 tablespoon sorghum syrup (optional)
¼ cup apple cider vinegar (optional)
4 to 6 slices sweet white onion, or 8 to 12 whole green onions, trimmed, for serving

Fill a pot with 2 quarts of water, set it over high heat, and add the salt pork. Bring it to a boil, turn down to a simmer, and cover to make a broth while you clean the greens.

Rinse the greens well, perhaps several times, to remove any dirt or grit. Strip the leaves from the stems and tear them into bite-sized pieces. Some folks discard the stems, but I like to trim off the bottom and chop them into ½-inch-long pieces to throw in the pot.

When the greens are prepped, add them to the pot, a handful at a time, pushing them down with a wooden spoon. Add the salt. For a more complex flavor, dissolve the sorghum in the vinegar and stir that into the pot.

Turn the heat to low, cover the pot, and let everything simmer for an hour. At that point, test the greens to see if they are silky, and test the pot likker to see if you want to add some white pepper or need more salt. If the greens are still resilient, cover and cook longer, until they almost melt in your mouth.

Remove the salt pork and serve the greens with their pot likker. My mother always served them with a slice of sweet white onion or a trimmed green onion on the side. I do the same, and you should, too.

Spring Ramp Pot Roast SERVES 6

On those early days of spring when it was too beautiful to not open the windows but too cool to be comfortable when she did, my mother would put a chuck roast in the oven and let it braise low and slow, keeping the kitchen both airy and cozy. Maybe that's why I was craving beef this spring, just when the dogwoods bloomed and the ramps came in. So glad that I was, as a handful of the ramps, chopped and mixed with onion and the meat, produced drippings of lip-smacking delight. There was more than enough to sauce the meat and soak the cornbread. (Be sure your chuck roast is well marbled and has some fat for the best braising and drippings.)

If you don't have ramps, you can make a blend of half green onions and half garlic, coarsely chopped, in their place. English Pea Salad (page 48) and Redbud Caper Deviled Eggs (page 302) make fine springtime sides. You can also make this in a slow cooker; see Note on page 60.

1 tablespoon kosher salt
3½-pound bone-in chuck roast
4 cups warm water
1 tablespoon sorghum syrup, plus more for the pan juice (optional)
2 teaspoons sweet smoked Spanish paprika
2 tablespoons olive oil
½ large yellow onion, sliced ¼ inch thick
10 ramp bulbs, coarsely chopped
8 to 12 small new potatoes, unpeeled
Salt and freshly ground black pepper
2 tablespoons cornstarch
¼ cup cold water

Preheat the oven to 325°F.

Rub the kosher salt into the chuck roast.

Pour the warm water into a bowl, and whisk in the sorghum syrup and paprika until dissolved; then set aside.

Heat the oil in a large Dutch oven (see Note) set over high heat, and when it is very hot, add the roast and brown it on both sides (this takes about 6 minutes per side). Remove the pot from the heat, transfer the roast to a plate, and deglaze the pot with the sorghum mixture. Return the roast to the pot.

Spread the onion slices evenly over the top of the roast and sprinkle the ramps among them.

Cover the pot, place it on the center rack in the oven, and braise for 1½ hours. Turn the roast over, cover again, and braise for 1½ hours more, but now check on it every half hour or so. The roast is done when the meat will pull apart easily with a fork, but before it falls apart or shreds. Remove the pot from the oven, and turn the heat up to 425°F for roasting the potatoes.

Lift the roast from the pot, allowing the juices to drain back into the pot, and set it on a cutting board to cool slightly, tenting it with foil to keep it from drying out. The roast may come apart in sections, and this is fine.

Defat the pan juices, reserving about 1 tablespoon of the fat. Set the pan juices aside. Halve the potatoes and lay them cut side down on a baking sheet. Drizzle the reserved fat over them, then flip the potatoes so the fat coats both sides and the cut sides face up. Season with salt and pepper, and then roast for about 20 minutes. Turn the potatoes over and roast for another 5 minutes, until both sides are crisply browned and the potatoes are cooked through.

(recipe continues)

When the chuck roast is cool enough to handle, remove the bone and any large pieces of fat and arrange the sections of roast on a warmed serving plate. You can remove the cooked, soggy onions and ramps for the sake of looks, but I much prefer to leave them for flavorful eating, and so far so does everyone who sits at my table. Place the roast in a warm place, like the back of the stove, while you make the gravy.

In a saucepan, bring 2 cups of the reserved pan juices just to a boil. While they are heating, whisk the cornstarch into the cold water to dissolve. When the pan juices just begin to boil, slowly add the cornstarch mixture, stirring as you do. Bring back to a boil and boil for about 1 minute, stirring constantly, until thickened. Taste, adjust the seasoning with salt, pepper, or sorghum as desired, remove from the heat, and cover to keep warm until you are ready to serve the roast.

When the potatoes are ready, arrange them around the roast pieces and serve, with the gravy passed on the side. If you have made Real Cornbread (page 120), my favorite thing is to split open a small wedge, lay it on my plate, crust down, and pour gravy over the top.

NOTE: You can make this in a slow cooker, too. Reduce the warm water from 4 cups to 1 cup and the smoked Spanish paprika from 2 teaspoons to 1. Mix the sorghum and paprika into the 1 cup of water. Brown the roast on both sides in a heavy skillet first, and deglaze the skillet with the seasoned water. Set the roast in the slow cooker, turn it on low, add the deglazing mixture, cover the roast with ramps and onions, and braise for 8 hours. In the slow cooker, this roast makes more than 2 cups of pan juices, so you will have an intensely flavored cup or so to flavor another dish.

Country Ham, Ramps & Taters

SERVES 2 AS A SIDE DISH

Technically not a green, ramps are such a part of the spring foraging cycle that they seem to serve the same reviving purpose. This dish—a savory, satisfying mix of garlicky-oniony ramps, tender potatoes, funky country ham, and eggs mixed up like a mountain country carbonara—appears on the table with a mess of poke or creasy greens, the whole making supper when served with cornbread.

You can ramp up this basic recipe just about any way you like. If you love your ramps and want more of that intense flavor, add a half dozen whole ramp bulbs to the skillet in addition to the chopped ones. You can also increase the eggs and turn this into a ramp frittata, following the usual method for making one. Some people add cheese to this. (I don't know why.)

When ramps are finally exhausted, you can make this dish with an equivalent amount of chopped green onions. It's not as potent, but it's delicious alongside a mess of winter greens, as described on page 54, or Soup Beans (page 154).

⅓ cup country ham scraps, with fat
Olive oil or bacon grease, if needed
½ pound new potatoes, sliced about ⅓ inch thick
6 small ramp bulbs with about 1 inch of greens attached, chopped
Salt
2 large eggs, beaten

Remove as much fat as you can from the ham scraps, reserving the fat, and chop the ham meat.

In a large heavy (preferably cast-iron) skillet that has a lid, render the reserved fat over medium heat, pressing down on the fat while it's frying to release the oil. You want to coat the bottom of the skillet liberally, and if you don't get enough grease from the ham fat, you can augment it with a splash of olive oil or bacon grease after you remove the remaining pieces of ham fat.

Add the potatoes to the skillet in a single layer. Fry on high heat for about 3 minutes to brown them. Then turn the potatoes over and sprinkle the chopped ramps over them. Cook, stirring occasionally, and when the potatoes are glistening, add the reserved ham scraps. (You can chop the scraps into smaller bits, if you like.)

When the ham begins to sizzle, cover the skillet and reduce the heat to medium. Cook for 10 to 15 minutes, stirring occasionally to keep from sticking, until the potatoes are tender.

Taste before adding any salt. Country hams are salty by nature and vary by degree, so you may not need any additional salt.

Remove the skillet from the heat and set it aside for a few minutes to cool. Then pour the beaten eggs over the potatoes and toss to just cook and coat. This is not so much a scrambled egg dish as it's a mountain version of spaghetti carbonara with potatoes instead of pasta. Immediately after stirring in the eggs, spoon the mixture onto plates and serve.

Colcannon serves 6

My mother insisted that there be mashed potatoes on the table whenever she served cooked kale greens, and further thought you were foolish if you didn't put a little of each on your fork together for each bite, followed close by a nibble of green onion. When I encountered my first recipe for colcannon, I understood why. It was the Irish in us.

This rich recipe was inspired by the colcannon served at Main Street Meats in Chattanooga, a dish so sustaining it will almost make you forgo their heavenly hamburger. Almost.

1 bunch kale (about ¾ pound), stemmed and
    chopped
9 tablespoons (1 stick plus 1 tablespoon) unsalted
    butter
¼ head green cabbage, thinly sliced
1 medium yellow onion, halved and thinly sliced
4 garlic cloves, thinly sliced
1 bay leaf
⅛ teaspoon ground mace
⅛ teaspoon ground white pepper, plus more to taste
⅛ teaspoon ground mustard
Pinch of cayenne pepper
½ teaspoon salt, plus more to taste
⅓ cup light beer
½ cup chicken broth
2 pounds red-skinned potatoes, quartered
½ cup heavy cream
¼ pound bacon, crisp-cooked and chopped

Place a large bowl filled with ice water next to the stove. Bring 4 cups of water to a boil in a large saucepan; add the kale and return to a boil. Reduce the heat to maintain a simmer and cook for 3 minutes. Then drain, and plunge the kale into the ice water to stop the cooking. Drain again, and transfer the kale to paper towels to dry.

Melt the 1 tablespoon butter in a large Dutch oven set over medium heat. Add the cabbage, onion, garlic, bay leaf, mace, white pepper, mustard, cayenne, and the salt. Cook, stirring often, until the onions are soft, about 8 minutes.

Add the beer to deglaze the pan, and stir until evaporated, about 2 minutes. Add the chicken broth and reduce the heat to medium-low. Cook until the liquid is reduced by about half, about 5 minutes. Remove the bay leaf.

Stir in the blanched kale, and when it is warmed, remove the pot from the heat. Add salt and white pepper to taste. Cover and keep warm while preparing the potatoes.

Cover the quartered potatoes with cold water in a large pot. Place over high heat and bring to a boil. Salt the water generously, and then turn the heat down to a simmer and cook until the potatoes are tender, about 15 minutes. Drain the potatoes, setting the empty pot aside, and mash them in a large, sturdy bowl until they begin to have a creamy consistency.

Pour the cream into the empty potato pot, add the remaining stick of butter and a few pinches of salt, and warm over medium-low heat until melted. Combine the butter mixture with the potatoes and continue to mash until smooth.

To serve, divide the potatoes among bowls. Top each with some of the cabbage mixture and garnish with the bacon.

Kale Potato Cakes SERVES 6

Leftover mashed potatoes were often the base for potato cakes at our next meal. My mother seasoned hers with onion chipped small and plenty of pepper, but I like to add other ingredients for a hearty main dish. And I like these so much that I don't wait for leftovers, but make them from scratch. Serve them with Old-School Tomato Gravy (page 218).

3 pounds russet or Yukon Gold potatoes
Salt
1½ pounds kale
Olive oil
3 whole green onions, finely chopped
5 ounces Asiago cheese, shredded
Freshly ground black pepper
4 eggs, beaten
Old-School Tomato Gravy, for serving

Peel the potatoes, quarter them, and place them in a large saucepan. Cover with cold water, add a teaspoon of salt, place over high heat, and bring to a boil. Then turn the heat down to a lively simmer and cook until potatoes are tender, 15 to 20 minutes.

While the potatoes are boiling, rinse the kale well, remove the stems, and coarsely chop the leaves. Heat about a tablespoon of olive oil in a wide heavy skillet and add the kale, a few handfuls at a time, with a couple pinches of salt. Sauté until just wilted. I like the kale al dente, with a little resiliency, but you may prefer to cook it to a softer stage.

When the potatoes are done, remove the pot from the heat and drain them. In a large sturdy bowl, mash the potatoes until they have a creamy consistency (a few small lumps allowed).

Combine the kale with the potatoes. Add the green onions and the cheese. Taste the mixture and add salt as needed (Asiago can be very salty and additional salt may not be desired). Add pepper to taste. Add the eggs and mix thoroughly. Pat the potato-kale mixture into cakes approximately 3 inches in diameter and about ½ inch thick.

Preheat the oven to warm.

Pour olive oil into a heavy skillet until about ¼ inch deep and place it over medium heat. When a bit of the potato mixture flicked into the skillet dances, add 3 or 4 patties (don't crowd the skillet). Fry, turning the patties over when they are crisp and golden, cooking them for about 3 minutes a side. Be careful, adjusting the heat to keep them from burning and adding oil when necessary. When they are golden on both sides, transfer them to a rack lined with paper towels to drain. Then keep them warm in the oven while you fry the remaining patties.

Warm the tomato gravy and pass on the side with the warm kale potato cakes.

Buttermilk Cabbage Soup with Black Walnut "Pesto" SERVES 6

Cabbage is a green you can keep in the root cellar deep into the winter, and it is often sliced thin and sautéed in butter or bacon grease as a sturdy side for a cold-weather supper. This soup pairs it perfectly with tangy buttermilk and the fragrantly earthy black walnuts that fall in abundance in the autumn. Black walnuts are a bear to get to, their outer husks staining hands a deep purplish black, the inner shells so hard that it breaks the nut meats inside to crack them. But they are so beloved and flavorful that mountain families would spend long winter evenings peeling, cracking, and picking black walnuts by the fire.

If you don't have or don't like black walnuts, you can make the "pesto" with pecans. It will be great, but just different.

This makes a delicious winter supper when served with Lisa Donovan's Pimento Cheese Nabs (page 86) and a Spiced Pickled Peach (page 220) on the side.

PESTO

6 tablespoons black walnut pieces
4 teaspoons apple cider
Salt

SOUP

1 small (1 pound) head green cabbage
2 tablespoons butter
1 medium white onion, diced
Salt and freshly ground black pepper
3 cups chicken broth
3 cups whole-fat buttermilk at room temperature

Prepare the pesto: In a small heavy skillet over medium heat, toast the black walnut pieces, shaking the pan, until they just begin to turn golden, about 3 minutes. Be careful not to burn them.

Put the toasted walnuts in a blender, add the cider and a large pinch of salt, and pulse until a loose, grainy paste is formed. Remove the pesto from the blender and set it aside.

Make the soup: Split the cabbage in half, remove the core, and cut each half into 4 wedges. Slice the wedges into thin strips.

Melt the butter in a Dutch oven over medium heat, and sauté the onion until it just begins to soften, about 4 minutes. Add the cabbage and a few pinches of salt, and stir well to coat with the butter.

Add the broth and bring to a lively simmer. Cover and simmer for 10 minutes or until the cabbage is tender.

Remove the pot from the heat and stir in the buttermilk. Return it to very low heat and warm it slowly, stirring as you do, so the buttermilk doesn't curdle.

Serve the soup in individual bowls with a tablespoon of the black walnut pesto in the center of each serving. Pass the salt and pepper for additional seasoning.

Salt of the Earth

There is no beginning to this history, but one place to start is with salt.
—CATHERINE VENABLE MOORE, "O BEULAH LAND"

Rich Valley Road, the asphalt two-lane into Saltville, Virginia, runs through a wide valley along the base of Clinch Mountain. I slow down as much to savor the glide as for safety, and in slowing, I note what is happening roadside. The closer I get to town, the closer it seems that the small frame and brick houses sit to the road, their porches facing it.

I come from porch-sitting people, so it pleases me to see most of these are occupied. Wearing clothes that still speak of work—jeans and overalls, apron and housedress— the older folk on them have earned the right to sit idle at noonday. Even in the yard of a single-wide—flower-bordered, well kept, yet porchless—three iron-haired men have arranged their lawn chairs out front in proper porch order: not clumped conversationally to face one another, but turned in a single line to the road, the better to see who is passing by. Raised in the vernacular, I don't wave but lift two fingers from the 11 o'clock position on the steering wheel and give a short nod as I pass, receiving same in return.

While porches in this valley would have been availed of an evening, or after church on a Sunday, such midday midweek idleness would not have been common in the past. In its peak years, the salt mining industry in Saltville required three shifts of workers daily and provided livelihood for both town and country dwellers. And well before salt was discovered here by colonial entrepreneurs in the 1700s, this was a lively, active place. The salt licks made a rich hunting ground for the Native Americans who came to seek the diverse game that flocked in abundance to satisfy their salt need. And before the deer, elk, bear, and buffalo, the salt drew huge prehistoric beasts: mammoths, mastodons, musk ox, the giant ground sloth whose bones have been found in local archaeological excavations.

And before those enormous creatures? These mountains were the site of activity of seismic proportions. What we call the Appalachian Mountains was once part of a larger chain on the ancient supercontinent of Pangea. When that continent split apart, the mountains came asunder, too, leaving sister peaks in what is now Morocco, while this section drifted on to slam and shift and shape into North America with these peaks, then steep as the Andes, running up its eastern side. Those shifts were not gentle when

tectonic plates crashed and collided, creating sharp peaks and high plateaus. At one point a whole oceanic plate crashed in and under, storing in spots a secret wealth of salt water beneath the ground, the Iapetus Ocean.

I see the record of all of this at the Museum of the Middle Appalachians in the quiet, almost deserted downtown of Saltville. In a large, softly lit room the huge skeleton of a woolly mammoth shares space with a tabletop diorama of the town and surrounding valley. The table lights up salient points in the town's historical geography when buttons are pressed.

The museum has a smaller space for rotating exhibits. When I am there, that room is full of quilts handmade by women from the town, a different sort of history told in scraps and imagination and impossibly small stitches. And in a large, sunny third room, the story of the first people who lived here—shown with flints and arrows, beads and feathered apparel—shares space with that of the latest. The early history of a 20th-century company town is told in photographs and artifacts, presented with fond nostalgia by those who lived here and their descendants.

Salt sparked the first extractive industry in the southern Appalachians. Its processing required the harvesting of timber, then the excavation of coal, to keep the evaporative furnaces burning. In time, those resources were exported out as well, and that became a defining moment in the history of the region.

Salt is also a defining ingredient in the foodways of the southern mountains. At some point in the ancient processing of carcasses in the salt/hunting regions, the flesh came in contact with the mineral and magic was born. Not exactly the immortality of the Fountain of Youth that the early Spanish explorers came here seeking in the 1500s, but an alchemical extension of viability. Salt curing was the way that early hunter/gatherers prolonged the edibility of meat to get through the winter. Salt curing is what fueled the industry created by the colonists who came later to make their fortunes by shipping salt downriver to the meat-packers in Cincinnati, Louisville, Knoxville, Nashville, and as far away as New Orleans.

Is it any wonder that salt came to define many of the core foods of the region? Lip-puckering country ham and salt-cured pork. Sour corn and pickle beans. Melon served always with a sprinkle of salt. The ubiquitous Cheese Nabs in the glove box that no mountain trucker leaves home without. Salty slow-simmered kale and pinto beans. Jerky, kraut, and pickles of all kinds. Salt is the element that enabled life and nourishment through the harsh, stark winters of the mountains, winters that helped create a cuisine that was in one sense distinctly Southern and at the same time distinctly its own.

Much to chew on as I make my way to the museum gift shop, so no wonder that what I gravitate toward is a spiral-bound volume with a soft yellow paper cover amid the many "official" histories. It's the *Saltville Centennial Cookbook*. I am most intrigued by the evocative names of the more savory, salt-laced dishes, and the stories they conjure up: Dead Man's Soup, Bert's (Big Mama's) Cat Head Biscuits, Brain Croquettes, Parsnip Skillet, Dr. Finne's Baked Doves, Hungarian Soup (Hunky Soup), Paprika's (*sic*) Csirke (Chicken), Hunter's Goulash, Chicken and Dumplings (two versions), Heirloom Scalded Lettuce, Old Fashioned Hash. Clearly there is history here as well. Delightfully, the children, grandchildren, and friends tell a good bit of that history as this cookbook is studded with old black-and-white photographs and laced with memories of the women, and a few men, who turned these dishes out, day after day.

"There are few people in the Town of Saltville who have never eaten any of Granny Blackwell's cooking," I read.

"After retiring from Olin with 42 years of service, Ralph enjoyed fishing as often as possible."

"She was a generous person and worried over people who were in need. She liked to travel and ride the bus."

———

Such fragments remind me of summer evenings as a child. Lying on the grass down in Corbin with my cousins, lightning bugs flashing in the dark around us, we caught such pieces of the conversation my parents, aunts, and uncles were having on the porch above. From them we formed imagined pictures and stories of the past, our people.

We were all—my father, mother, sister, me—born in Corbin, Kentucky. But when I was about a year old and my sister twelve, my father got word of work in the distilleries in Louisville and we moved. My parents lived in the city the rest of their lives, but they never fully left the mountains. Like most members of the various hillbilly diasporas of the 20th century, we went "up home" whenever we could. My father worked in the boiler rooms, a fireman and oiler, hard labor but it suited his athlete's need for a physical challenge. (He'd been a boxer as a young man. The folks in Corbin said he'd been a good one.)

He worked swing shift, and "on call," and picked up overtime when he could to compensate for the layoffs that were a part of the distillery process then. Whenever a

stretch of more than two days off came up, we'd make the four-hour winding drive to "see the folks." We spent every summer vacation of my growing up in those hills. The steeper and more winding the road became, the easier my father seemed to sit in his skin, to smile from someplace deep.

Summers up home were not lazy. There was always a little time on the lake for reading and cards, swimming and fishing, but there were also things to do and my parents were always willing to do them. My mother cooked with her aunts for the passels of cousins who showed up every night to visit and remember. She helped with the canning, strung beans and then threaded them up for shuck beans, cleaned and mopped and hung out wet clothes just as she did at home.

My dad loved any job that required muscle and took him outside. One summer he and my great-uncle Charlie built a garage from the foundation up, the sound of boards slapping and the two men talking and laughing riding like a melody over the rhythm of the locusts. They would come in the house still telling a story, riffing back and forth like jazz hipsters as they got tall iced tea tumblers from the cabinet, then filled them with spring water that came from the faucet. As they turned to go back out, my dad would grab the salt shaker from the table, pour some in his palm and some in Charlie's, licking it up on his way out the door. "A man needs to keep his minerals balanced," he told me when I asked why. "Work in the summer, you sweat 'em out, salt puts them back in." Salt and spring water: Hillbilly Gatorade.

We sweated, too, children playing hard or doing chores, women working in the steaming kitchen. Maybe that's why I remember salt so clearly as the taste of summer. We put it on our fresh cucumbers and onions, the tomatoes that accompanied every supper. We consumed it ravenously on crisp crackers topped with tangy baloney or Vienna sausages on the deck of the pontoon boat at the lake. My cousins and I poured tiny mountains in our palms and dipped tommy-toes, still warm from the garden, before dropping them into our mouths. My great-aunt Johnnie kept a saltshaker next to her as she sat on the porch slicing tart June apples to dry, for use that winter in stack cake and fried pies. The drying sweetened them, she told me, and I knew that to be true. So did salt, she said, as she sprinkled some on a crisp sour slice and popped it in her mouth, then made one for me. I wasn't so sure about that, but there was a mingling of flavor there that was both sharp and haunting.

Even dessert in the summer needed some salt. After supper I'd ride into town with Daddy and Charlie to a grocery store that stayed open late; it seemed just to sell the dark green melons they kept in the back in long tin tubs filled with ice water. We rushed home to slice the melon while it was still deep chilled, perfect half-moons of vermillion laid on yellowed plates with sweet flowers and tiny age veins around the edges. Nobody plunged in until the saltshaker made the rounds.

My cousin David ate cinnamon Red Hots on saltine crackers; we poured salted peanuts into our glass-bottled Cokes. Even ice cream, that pure sweet blend of milk and sugar, required salt. Not in it, but in the old crank freezer that Charlie and my dad would take turns turning. The ice had to be crushed just right, then layered with a handful of rock salt. Inevitably in the process, one of the women would caution, "Don't let that salt get high enough to seep into the cream," and then someone would tell the story of the time that happened. And then another story, and another one, as we sat patiently on the screened back porch and waited for the cream to ripen, just a little anxious that the first bite should be a sweet, not salty, one.

When these visits ended—summer vacations, long weekends—there would be a sadness in the leaving. Tears—salt again—were shed by the women and children. The men cleared throats, mopped sweaty foreheads with handkerchiefs that just managed to slip by their eyes. Someone would say, "Going back to the salt mines, Pap?" My dad would laugh and we'd drive away.

I don't know where my child's image of "the salt mines" came from. A cartoon? A book I'd read? In my imagination, they were far, far away, part of an exotic desert world of swirling sand and spices. I did not know then that salt had been "mined" just one county over from Corbin.

In the early 1790s, the first saltworks in Clay County, Kentucky, were started on Goose Creek. In 1807 the town of Manchester was incorporated there and the full-scale mining of salt began. The industry there peaked from 1835 to 1845 but continued for some time after. In 1862 the Union Army's leadership ordered all saltworks there destroyed to undermine the food supply of the Confederacy, even though their esteemed officer, Brigadier General T. T. Garrard, owned one of the biggest.

Three years later, in 1865, my paternal grandfather, David Franklin Lundy, was born. Clay County was not a peaceful place then, and that was true before the war and after. Violent feuds mark its history, but unlike the stereotypical stories of mountain feuds over moonshine or marriages gone wrong or cows gone astray, these were wars

fueled by the ambitions of the wealthy entrepreneurs who owned the salt mines and dictated the lives of those who worked in them. The most famous of these involved the prominent White and Garrard families, owners of the Upper Goose Creek Salt Works and Union Salt Works, respectively. Battles began as soon as the saltworks were established, and bad feelings and violence generated from them continued through the Civil War and on, as late as the 1930s.

Blood. Sweat. Tears. Salt is essential to each; each is a part of salt's story.

One of the earliest white settlements west of the Allegheny's Great Divide was made at Draper's Meadow, where present-day Blacksburg, Virginia, lies. Mary Draper Ingles was a young mother in the settlement when a hostile Shawnee raid occurred in late July of 1755. Several settlers were killed and a few taken captive, including Mary and her young son, Thomas. The natives led their captives north along the rivers until they arrived in the Kanawha River Valley of what is now West Virginia, just below present-day Charleston. There were natural salt licks there, and Mary and the other captives were forced to work the grueling tasks of harvesting and evaporating salt from the saline water bubbling up from the earth. When the party moved on, continuing to follow rivers, they may have come as far as the Big Bone salt licks in Kentucky. It was there or near there where Mary made her escape.

The legend of Mary Ingles's capture and escape comes in many heroic versions and not all of them are based on fully established fact, but there are a few things we know. She walked more than 500 miles home by following the rivers she'd come up, subsisting on the likes of black walnuts, berries, sassafras, and frogs. She arrived at the end of November, nearly starved and almost naked, at the homestead of a friend, Adam Harmon, near present-day Eggleston Springs, Virginia. Mary and her husband, William Ingles, were reunited and eventually had four more children while establishing a home, tavern, and ferry on the New River. Mary lived to be eighty-three, dying in 1815.

She also told her fellow settlers about the salt.

———

"Come on past the S-curve and you'll see the farm on the right," Lewis Payne tells me over the phone. "Look for the cows and horse under the tree and turn right up that drive. When you see the Dr. Seuss tree, make a left and you can park just beyond. That's J.Q. Dickinson Salt-Works."

I am wondering how he knows the cows will be there, and what a Dr. Seuss tree just might look like, as I drive down the Kanawha River Valley, south of the small town of Malden, West Virginia. It's less than a mile from Malden, and there are quite a few other curves in the alphabet before I get to S. When I do, though, there are the cows and a horse, just like Lewis said. Beyond them there's a tall, kind of goofy-looking scraggly pine that provokes me to laugh.

As I park, Lewis walks up, a boyish-faced, smiling man wearing a light blue oxford cloth shirt and chino pants, just as he does in photos on the J.Q.D. website. J. Q. Dickinson Salt is the Southeast's first entry in the burgeoning world of artisanal culinary salt. Established in 2013, the company's crisp, nuanced crystals had, by the spring of 2014, found their way into some of the best restaurant kitchens in the country. Fans include chef Sean Brock, who gets a ten-pound shipment monthly, and Baltimore's master of charcuterie, Spike Gjerde, who uses J.Q.D. exclusively at his Woodberry Kitchen. Ian Boden of The Shack in Staunton, Virginia, uses it as a finishing salt, noting, "I really like the crystal structure . . . not super hard like *sel gris*. It's pretty soft and tender."

Lewis and his sister and cofounder, Nancy Bruns, are the seventh generation in the Dickinson family to be working this land. Harvesting its salt is a tradition with roots going back to the very start. Lewis leads the way to one of the oldest buildings on the sixty-acre property: the tall, narrow company store/office where yellowed records dating to the early 1800s are stacked in dust-covered books in a storeroom. He tells me that not long after Mary Ingles found her way home, those who heard her story began making the trek to the Kanawha Licks to harvest the mineral. By the end of the 18th century, the first commercial furnace had been fired to process the salt water that naturally percolated to the surface. Early in the 19th century, the first wells were dug to tap into the ancient ocean beneath. By 1815 there were fifty-two furnaces operating in this narrow river valley, owned by the first industrialists to "mine" the southern Appalachians. William Dickinson was one of them.

Lewis tells me that the earliest records show that slaves were employed at the saltworks. They weren't "owned" but were "leased." It was assumed for a long time that there were few slaves then in the mountain South, and that this was one of the great reasons why so many Appalachian southerners fought for the North in the Civil War, why Kentucky remained a border state, refusing to secede, why West Virginia broke away from Virginia and became its own state. To be sure, there was strong anti-slave sentiment in the region, but not because there were no slaves.

In fact, slaves and, later, freed blacks were responsible for a good bit of the labor

in the early salt industry in the southern Appalachians, as well as labor for building railroads, driving livestock, and ultimately in the coal mines. Before the Emancipation Proclamation, business owners would pay slave owners to lease the men and women who were deemed "property." These early workforces also included indentured whites, who were leased in the same way from those who owned their contracts or controlled their lives in other ways. Davy Crockett's father indentured his twelve-year-old son to a man he owed money to, and the adolescent Crockett served out the debt driving cattle from East Tennessee to Virginia. Booker T. Washington worked in a salt-packing house in the Kanawha Valley following Emancipation. There's a modest monument to him now in Malden.

We walk to a corroding old salt furnace down by the river, its rusting, slightly menacing hulk like something out of a story about orcs or trolls. The tall two-story house that William Dickinson's family lived in sits up on a rise behind us, empty and deteriorating, its wide porch overlooking the scene. Many of Dickinson's industrial peers lived as far as they could from the wood-fired, then coal-fired, iron cauldrons along the river. Filled with salt water, they ran day and night to rapidly evaporate the water and leave the valuable mineral behind. Kanawha salt was known by its red color, an indication of the strong presence of iron. The stench from the fires and the mineral evaporation was intense, but the location of the salt licks along the river highway was an economic boon. Barrels of salt would be loaded onto flat boats made from trees felled nearby, their trunks lashed together on the bank. It was a worker, usually a slave, who rode the boat to Cincinnati or Nashville, selling the salt for the best price he could get, and selling the lumber from the boat, too. He would use a bit of that money to buy a horse or a mule, and return "home."

Kanawha salt was used in the meat-curing industries in Porkopolis, the name Cincinnati bore for a while, and in Nashville. Sometimes it went to Louisville or Knoxville, or as far downriver as New Orleans. In 1851 "The Great Kanawha Salt" was chosen the best in the world at the world's fair in London. Hundreds of wells were producing more than 3 million bushels of salt annually.

Then in 1861, a disastrous flood wiped out most of the saltworks along the river. That, plus the war, effectively put an end to the "salt making capital of the East." Dickinson's family continued to produce salt, however, up until 1945. A black-and-white photo on the website shows twenty-two men (and one dog) in the crew in 1940, a few years before the operation closed.

Today, Nancy and Lewis are writing not only a new but a very different chapter in the family story of salt. "We want to create something sustainable with our salt business," Nancy says. "Sustainable in many ways."

Nancy has long been interested in all things culinary. For several years she and her husband, Carter, operated a popular restaurant and catering business in western North Carolina. They sold it and moved to South Carolina in 2008 when he decided to go back to school for his master's degree in U.S. history. Carter's thesis was on industrialization in the Kanawha Valley, "and suddenly he was studying the history of my family," Nancy says. "At some point I asked him why they'd stopped manufacturing salt in the Valley. Was it all gone? When he said no, things began to fall in place."

Nancy and Lewis decided to partner on the project to revitalize the family business, but in a very different way than their ancestors would have recognized: no black iron kettles or fossil fuels needed. J.Q. Dickinson Salt is evaporated using solar power generated in a series of greenhouses leased from cousins who also have a nursery business on the property. The saline water from the wells is kept in holding tanks first, so the iron can settle out. (J.Q.D.'s Kanawha salt is snow white, not a trace of red in it.) The water is then evaporated in the first two greenhouses, the salt crystallized in the third. The process has been one of trial and tasting, Lewis says with a grin. "Nancy is quality control. I'd say, 'Hey, this is good.' She'd say, 'It could be better.' She knew what she wanted and she kept us fine-tuning until we got it and the process down."

The process now yields about four ounces of salt for each gallon of brine. They plan to produce 7,000 pounds of salt annually. As we walk through the peaceful greenhouses, a young woman is currying the salt with a long-handled rake. I am taken by the elegant beauty of the wooden rakes, small hand paddles, and scoops that are used for the process. It turns out they have a double purpose. Wood is used because metal would leach traces into the brine that could turn the salt bitter. But Lewis says they also use these specific tools because each is handmade regionally and he and Nancy are hoping to encourage local economies.

I look up the tool company, Allegheny Treenware, and discover that the West Virginia owners/artisans, Sue and Stan Jennings, met in 1984, working underground in the coal mines. When the mines closed, they tried a number of jobs before taking a chance on their passion, wood carving. Their risk paid off and now their products are sold all around the country, including from the J.Q. Dickinson online catalog.

Nancy and I have tea together a few weeks later and she tells me that while she knows J.Q.D. will, by its nature, remain a small business, she likes the far-reaching possibilities of just such connections. She says she especially likes knowing the saltworks complements the changes afoot to support local food and food-related economies. In addition to the treenware, J.Q.D. markets mini saltcellars, salt bowls, and salt pigs made by a West Virginia potter. Even the lids they use on their jars are made in West Virginia.

"And one of my favorite things is our *nigari*," she says. The oily-feeling, magnesium-rich liquid left after the salt is harvested is the substance used to coagulate soy milk and make tofu. Nancy says they are marketing it to health food stores and chefs, noting that "It also makes a beautiful ricotta. I'd love to have a local cheese maker start using it for that."

A month or so later, I discover a gem of a restaurant tucked surprisingly in a tiny old mountain town in Giles County, Virginia. The Palisades occupies an old general store in a community that once thrived as a tourist destination for the wealthy visiting its hot springs. Those days are gone, though, so I am astonished to see a fine-dine restaurant in a mostly shuttered downtown, doing a respectable business midweek. I understand why when I taste the food. Pickled plums that pucker and kiss. A sustaining salad of tangy local greens mixed with tender hominy, field peas, and crisp bacon and topped with smoky, salty kernels of popcorn. The best trout I've ever eaten—raised locally, covered in a savory biscuit crust. Thinking nothing could top that, I am surprised by the simple dessert of a drop-dead-ripe local peach, sliced and accompanied by a lightly sweetened homemade ricotta and mascarpone. I make a note to call the owner, local girl Shaena Muldoon, and chef Kevin White later. I scribble a note to remind myself about the ricotta with *nigari*. I pause with pen in hand and turn to my friend and say, "There's something I know about this town but I can't remember it." He says, "Eggleston Springs?" And then it comes to me: Mary Ingles's homecoming.

Later that night, I look up *nigari*. I find that translated from the Japanese, the word means "bitter." The liquid residue of making salt from which *nigari* is derived, is itself called "bittern" in English. I sit with that for a moment and then decide that this seems a good place to end this story of Appalachian salt. At the point where the bittern begins to turn to something sweet.

Mary's Sweet & Salty Reward

SERVES 4

Mary Draper Ingles arrived in what later became Eggleston, Virginia, in the cold of November. She'd been living on black walnuts and little else for much of her harrowing journey, so I'm not sure she'd have wanted anything much to do with them or, for that matter, with salt. However, I've based this grown-up fruit, cheese, and nut dessert on her memory and on a dish I was once served at the Palisades Restaurant. The savory nature makes this a perfect accompaniment to a dessert wine or, if you're like me, a neat shot of good bourbon. (That's something I bet Mary might get behind.) This recipe also works well with soft, ripe pears, and can even be made with a good-quality jarred peach or pear, drained, but one that has been packed in juice, not sugared syrup. If you'd like to make your own ricotta, the J.Q. Dickinson Salt-Works website has a wonderful recipe for one using their *nigari*: www.jqdsalt.com/fresh-ricotta-cheese.

4 ripe medium to large peaches
½ cup fresh ricotta cheese
¼ cup Spiced Sorghum Black Walnuts (recipe follows)
Sorghum syrup, for drizzling
Flaky salt, for finishing (optional)

Peel, pit, and slice the peaches, and arrange each one in a fan shape on a dessert plate. Place 2 tablespoons of the ricotta in the center of each plate. Sprinkle the black walnuts around the edge of the cheese. Drizzle the sorghum over the top, and sprinkle with salt, if using. Serve, encouraging folks to fork up a dollop of ricotta, syrup, and black walnuts with every peach slice.

Spiced Sorghum Black Walnuts

MAKES ½ CUP

This is adapted from a recipe for glazed pecans that Sheri Castle developed for a previous book of mine, *Sorghum's Savor*. In that recipe Sheri used cayenne and freshly ground black pepper instead of ginger. Feel free to glaze pecans or English walnuts if you don't like or don't have black walnuts, and to experiment to your taste with the spices.

½ tablespoon butter, melted
1 tablespoon sorghum syrup
¼ teaspoon salt
¼ teaspoon ground cinnamon
¼ teaspoon ground ginger
½ cup black walnut pieces
1 tablespoon coarse raw sugar

Preheat the oven to 350°F. Line a baking sheet with parchment paper.

In a medium bowl, stir together the butter, sorghum, salt, cinnamon, and ginger until smooth. Add the black walnuts and stir gently but thoroughly until the nut meats are fully coated. Spread the nuts in a single layer on the prepared baking sheet.

Bake for 12 to 15 minutes, stirring every 5 minutes and checking in the final round so they don't burn. When the nuts are ready, most of the glaze will be sticking to them and the lot will be a dark brown, but not blackening.

Remove the baking sheet from the oven and immediately sprinkle the sugar over the nuts, tossing lightly to coat. Allow the nuts to cool on the baking sheet, breaking apart the clumps as soon as they are cool enough to touch. The glaze will harden as it cools. Store any glazed nut meats you don't use in a jar with a tight lid—if you don't eat them right off the baking sheet.

Lisa Donovan's Pimento Cheese Nabs MAKES ABOUT 26 NABS

Acclaimed pastry chef Lisa Donovan, formerly of Sean Brock's Husk in Nashville, grew up traveling with her family, as her dad was in the army. "I think there's a biological imperative that has us seeking a sense of place," she said. "I'd wandered the whole planet wondering where my place was. It wasn't until I went to southwest Virginia that I felt, 'This is it.' When I connected with my mountain grandmother about baking, I realized I did a lot of things instinctively that were also what she did."

With that in mind, I asked Lisa if she'd create a recipe for every mountain pickup truck driver's glove compartment emergency ration: cheese nabs. (Note that these are salty, but in the mountain South, any packaged cracker snack—even the sweet ones, or the ones filled with peanut butter—are called "cheese nabs.")

When she sent the recipe, she wrote, "They may seem a bit labor intensive, but I promise they are worth every bit of 'freeze,' 'set,' and 'hurry up and wait.'" People, that woman does not lie.

You will need a stand mixer with paddle and dough hook attachments, and you will need to start this recipe a day before you want to eat the nabs. Just put the pimento cheese together after dinner one evening and start the crackers the following morning.

PIMENTO CHEESE FILLING

½ cup mayonnaise (Duke's brand preferred)
3 ounces sharp cheddar, finely shredded
3 ounces mild cheddar, finely shredded
1 (2-ounce) jar diced pimentos, strained
1 teaspoon Worcestershire sauce
1 teaspoon finely grated yellow onion
¼ teaspoon cayenne pepper

CRACKERS

2 teaspoons leaf lard, frozen
2 cups all-purpose flour (King Arthur brand preferred), plus more for rolling
1 tablespoon active dry yeast
1 teaspoon sugar
¼ teaspoon kosher salt
¼ teaspoon baking soda
¼ teaspoon cream of tartar
⅔ cup warm water (about body temperature)
Coarse sea salt
1 egg whisked with 2 tablespoons water

Prepare the pimento cheese filling: Mix all the ingredients together in a medium-sized bowl. Cover and refrigerate overnight.

Make the crackers: Cut the frozen leaf lard into small cubes, about the size of peas, and return them to the freezer while you mix the dry ingredients.

Put the flour, yeast, sugar, kosher salt, baking soda, and cream of tartar into the bowl of a stand mixer that has been fitted with the paddle attachment. Mix on low speed to combine. Work in the lard to make a crumbly mix.

Remove the paddle and fit the mixer with the dough hook attachment. Start the mixer on low speed and slowly add in the warm water. Once the water is added, increase the speed to medium and mix for 3 minutes. Turn the mixer off and cover the top of the dough snugly with plastic wrap while it's still in the bowl. Let the dough rest for 30 minutes.

Use lightly floured hands to remove the dough from the bowl and then form it into 2 balls. Wrap each ball in plastic wrap and gently flatten them into disks. Let these chill in the refrigerator for 40 minutes.

Line two baking sheets with parchment paper. Unwrap one dough disk and place it in the center of one of the baking sheets. Use a lightly floured rolling pin to roll it out to a ⅛-inch thickness. Top it with a second piece of parchment paper and place it in the freezer. Repeat this process with the second dough disk and baking sheet. Let freeze for 2 to 3 hours.

Remove one of the baking sheets from the freezer, and gently remove the top layer of parchment paper. Use a 2 × 2-inch biscuit cutter (or a knife) to cut out an even number of squares from the dough, cutting directly on the parchment-lined baking sheet. Pull gently on the squares to separate them. Remove any dough scraps remaining from cutting. (If you have enough scraps, you can reroll, freeze, and cut again.) Use a fork to score each square with 3 rows of 2 holes each, and then sprinkle the squares lightly with coarse sea salt. Return them to the freezer, and repeat this process with the second portion of dough. Let the crackers freeze while the oven preheats.

Preheat the oven to 375°F.

Remove the baking sheets from the freezer and bake the crackers for about 5 minutes. The crackers will be pale and about 75 percent baked at this point. Transfer to wire racks to cool.

Puree the chilled pimento cheese in a blender until smooth. Line a sheet pan with parchment paper. Spread the cheese out on the lined sheet pan and top it with a second piece of parchment. Roll the cheese evenly into a ⅛-inch thickness. Freeze it for 2 hours.

Remove the cheese from the freezer and use a 1 × 1-inch cutter to cut out an even number of squares. (You'll need half the number of cheese squares as of the crackers you've made.) Return the pan to the freezer for 15 minutes. (If the cheese gets too warm to handle when you're cutting it, just pop it back in the freezer for about 5 minutes.)

Meanwhile, heat the oven to 375°F again.

To assemble the nabs, remove the cheese from the freezer and use a knife or narrow spatula to pick up a cheese square and place it between two crackers, making a sandwich.

Place the sandwiched crackers on the prepared baking sheet. Brush the tops with the egg wash and sprinkle with coarse sea salt. Bake for 5 minutes, until the crackers are cooked through and have developed a sheen. Remove them to a wire rack and allow them to cool to room temperature before serving. The cheese nabs will keep in an airtight container at room temperature for 4 to 5 days.

Pepperoni Rolls SERVES 6 FOLKS
FROM "OFF" OR 3 WEST VIRGINIANS

My daddy was not the only workingman to appreciate the restorative properties of a little extra salt. Coal
miners often took a slice of jerky or a tin of Vienna
sausages in their lunch pails. The Italian immigrants
who came to work in the north and central West Virginia coalfields often carried a stick of pepperoni and
a slab of fresh bread, and that gave rise to one of the
region's most beloved foods, the pepperoni roll.

Most everyone agrees that Giuseppe (Joseph)
Argiro was the former-miner-turned-bakery-owner
who decided one day to wrap the sticks of meat inside
yeasted bread dough and bake it all into a one-handed
snack. The recipe here came out of a conversation
with West Virginia cookbook author Kendra Bailey
Morris and southwestern Virginia chef Travis Milton.
Kendra noted that there needs to be just a hint of
sweetness in a good pepperoni roll and Travis offered
this recipe with sorghum syrup.

2⅛ teaspoons active dry yeast
1 cup warm water (110° to 115°F)
1 teaspoon sorghum syrup
2¾ cups all-purpose flour, plus more for rolling
1 teaspoon kosher salt
1 teaspoon olive oil
Nonstick cooking spray or oil
2-pound hunk of deli pepperoni, about 3 inches in
    diameter
4 tablespoons butter, melted

Combine the yeast with the warm water and the
sorghum in a small bowl. Stir, and let stand for 5
minutes.

Combine the flour, salt, olive oil, and yeast mixture in
the bowl of a stand mixer fitted with the dough hook.
Mix on low speed to combine, and then gradually
increase the speed to medium. Continue to mix until the
dough begins to pull away from the sides of the bowl,
about 5 minutes. The dough will be sticky.

Spray a large bowl with cooking spray or oil it. Use
floured hands to remove the dough from the mixing
bowl and transfer it to the greased bowl; cover the bowl
with a damp towel. Let the dough sit in a warm place
for 45 minutes to rise.

Prepare the pepperoni while the dough rises: After
removing any exterior casing, cut the pepperoni in
half lengthwise. Then cut each half into 9 long sticks.
You should end up with 18 sticks weighing about
1½ ounces each.

Lightly spray or oil a baking sheet. When the dough is
ready, use floured hands to remove the dough from the
bowl and transfer it to a floured surface. Cut it into 6
equal portions and roll them into balls. Place the balls
on the prepared baking sheet. Spray or lightly oil the
top of each ball of dough and cover them lightly with
plastic wrap. Let sit for 20 minutes.

Preheat the oven to 350°F.

Uncover the dough. Using floured hands, remove
one dough ball and place it on a floured work surface.
Either roll or stretch the dough into a round that is
roughly 8 inches in diameter. Be careful not to make the
dough round too thin; if it is, it will be hard to roll up
the pepperoni.

Place 3 pepperoni sticks crossways on the dough round,
leaving about 1½ inches between them and the same
distance between them and the edge of the dough. Take
the dough edge closest to you, fold it over the first
pepperoni stick, and then proceed to roll it up, so that
the pepperoni sticks alternate with a layer of dough.
Return the roll to the baking sheet, setting it with the
seam side down. Repeat this process with the remaining
dough balls and pepperoni sticks.

Brush the rolls with the melted butter and bake for 30 to
35 minutes, until golden brown and cooked through.
Remove from the oven and brush with any remaining
butter. Let cool completely before serving.

Miner's Goulash SERVES 6

Like the *Saltville Centennial Cookbook*, countless 20th-century Appalachian community cookbooks contain at least one recipe for goulash. These dishes, which were adopted and adapted (sometimes dramatically), reflect the wave of Hungarian immigration that occurred in the U.S. between 1870 and 1920. Significant numbers of these newly landed Hungarians came to the coalfields of West Virginia, eastern Kentucky, southwest Virginia, and Pennsylvania looking for work. Many were initially exploited as strike breakers and met with animosity and sometimes outright violence. As tensions ultimately ebbed in the workforce, domestic connections were made as well, recipes exchanged, and changes made to reflect the provisions, and tastes, of the region.

Paprika, with its plangent bitter bite, is the primary seasoning in goulash, so it is of utmost importance to have a fresh jar of Hungarian paprika. You can serve this over noodles, or try it as I recommend, ladled into a wide well in a mound of Mama's Mashed Potatoes (page 50).

Any piece of fresh pork with a nice edge of fat and connective tissue will work for this, but if the meat you have doesn't give you enough fat for rendering, you can use bacon grease or lard to brown the meat.

1½ pounds boneless pork shank
Salt and freshly ground black pepper
½ tablespoon apple cider vinegar
1 teaspoon sorghum syrup
¼ cup sweet Hungarian paprika
1 medium onion, coarsely chopped
2 garlic cloves, crushed
3 medium parsnips, medium diced
1 large carrot, medium diced
1 medium red bell pepper, stemmed, seeded, and
   medium diced

Trim the fat from the outer edges of the pork and place the pieces of fat in a large Dutch oven over medium-low heat to render. Fry the fat until browned on all sides, pressing down with a metal spatula from time to time.

While the fat is rendering, cut the meat into 1-inch chunks. When you have enough grease to cover the bottom of the Dutch oven, remove and discard the chunks of fat. Add the meat to the pot and season it liberally with salt and pepper. Turn the heat up to medium-high and cook, occasionally stirring lightly, until you've browned the meat on all sides.

Add ½ cup of water to the pot and stir with a spoon or spatula to loosen any crust on the bottom. Stir in the vinegar and sorghum. Sprinkle the paprika over the meat and stir to incorporate it. Then stir in the onion and garlic. Turn the heat down to a low simmer (barely bubbling, but bubbling), and cover the pot. Cook for 1 hour, checking occasionally. The liquid should not be evaporating and getting lower; in fact, as the juices in the meat are released, it should be increasing slightly. If not, then turn the heat a little lower or splash in some more water.

After 1 hour, add the parsnips, carrot, bell pepper, and ¾ cup of water. Stir, and turn the heat up slightly until the liquid begins to bubble. Then turn it down to the previous slow simmer, cover, and cook for another hour. Taste, and add salt if needed. Remove the pot from the heat, but leave it covered to keep warm while you cook noodles or potatoes to go with the stew.

Swing Shift Steak SERVES 2

My dad worked swing shift most of my life, and my mother, like many salt, railroad, coal, mill, and factory wives, adjusted our household schedule around his. When he worked 7 to 3, we gathered of an evening at the round oak table in the dining room, and platters of vegetables, hot cornbread, and meat would appear. On other shift days, supper and breakfast might merge into a meal that was a bit of both.

One of the fundamental building blocks in my mother's repertoire for such revolving mealtimes was the inexpensive and quick-cooking eye of round steak. She would pound the steaks with her heavy metal waffle-faced potato masher, then season and quick-fry them, keeping them surprisingly juicy even though well done. (Yes, they have a little chew to them, but we were a family of ruminators in more ways than one.) She would serve them with potatoes, biscuits, and vegetables for dinner, or with eggs in the morning.

My favorite of these meals was served to my dad and me late at night, before he picked up his lunch sack, kissed "his girls" goodbye, and went off in the dark to work. For those supper/breakfasts, my mother would fry the steaks and make a quick gravy that she served over soft rye bread laid to the side. She rarely joined us at the table in the kitchen where these meals were served, preferring to stand next to the stove, sipping coffee, smoking, and smiling.

(You may increase to serve four, though, you won't need to increase the flour for the gravy.)

2 eye of round steaks, each about ¾ inch thick
Salt and freshly ground black pepper or lemon
    pepper
3 tablespoons all-purpose flour
¼ teaspoon sweet smoked Spanish paprika
Vegetable oil or lard
2 pieces soft rye bread
½ cup whole milk

Lay the steaks on a cutting board. Using the tenderizing (pointed) face of a meat mallet, lightly pound each side. You do not want to pound the meat super-thin or to make holes through it. You want to thin it to about ½-inch thickness and make plenty of shallow ridges to hold the seasoning and flour. Flip the steaks over and do the same to the second side, then repeat for each side.

Lightly salt and liberally pepper each steak, and rub them lightly to help the seasoning sink in.

In a wide, shallow bowl or on a plate, blend the flour, paprika, and a generous pinch of salt well. Dredge each steak in the flour, coating both sides and using your fingertips to gently press the flour into the ridges, just to make sure the coating sticks. Reserve the remaining flour.

Set an amply sized, heavy, lidded skillet over high heat and add enough oil to slick the whole pan. (You can use lard, but an oil with a higher smoke point is easier to work with.) When the oil is hot but not smoking, add the steaks and brown them quickly on each side (this takes about 2 minutes per side). Turn the heat down to low, cover the skillet, and let the steaks cook for about 5 minutes, until just cooked through.

Lift each steak, allowing a little of the juices to run back into the skillet, and place it on a warmed plate. (If you would like to serve the steaks on rye toast, this would be the time to put the bread in the toaster.)

Sprinkle 1 tablespoon of the reserved seasoning flour into the skillet, and stir quickly to flavor it with the juices. Scrape the skillet to loosen the crust, and add 2 tablespoons of water to the juices to help scrape up the browned bits. Slowly stir in the milk, using the back of the meat spatula or a wide spoon to flatten any lumps as you do. When the flour is incorporated with no lumps (there will be solid flecks of the meat's breading, but no large lumps of flour), turn the heat up to medium and bring it to a boil, stirring steadily all the time. When the gravy just begins to thicken, remove it from the heat and add salt to taste.

Place the toast or piece of bread on the plate next to the steak, and cover with the gravy. Serve.

Smoked Oyster Stew for Two

SERVES 2

While fresh oysters were a holiday treat in mountain towns with a railroad depot, tinned smoked oysters could be found in many larders year-round. Inexpensive and packed with protein and iron, they were a salty, nourishing, high-energy addition to the miner's lunch box. Like tinned Vienna sausages, they provided a salty tang, and a can of either eaten with a sleeve of saltines was a fine meal at work or on a day spent fishing. Smoked oysters also made a memorable addition to the simple potato soup that constituted many a late-night supper for a husband and wife after the second shift, eating while the children slept.

Look for naturally smoked oysters that are packed in pure olive oil for this recipe, as you will be eating the oil as well as the oysters. They may cost a little more, but they're worth it.

½ teaspoon salt, plus more to taste
2 medium baking potatoes, peeled and medium diced
6 to 8 ounces naturally smoked oysters in olive oil (tin sizes vary)
1 small yellow onion, medium diced
2 cups whole milk
Lemon pepper, to taste

In a small saucepan, dissolve the ½ teaspoon salt in enough water to cover the potatoes and bring to a boil over high heat. Add the potatoes, stir, and bring back to a simmer. Cover, and cook until the pieces are tender when pierced with a fork, about 5 minutes. Drain, and return the potatoes to the pan. With the back of a fork, lightly smash about a third of the potatoes, leaving the rest in cubes. Cover to keep warm.

Drain the oil and juices from the oysters into a small skillet or sauté pan set over medium heat. (Set the oysters aside for later.) Sauté the onions in the oil until they soften, about 4 minutes. Add the onion mixture to the potatoes, season with salt to taste, and stir to coat. Cover and let sit for 3 minutes to let the flavors mingle.

Add the milk to the potato mixture, and heat it over medium-high heat until barely bubbling, stirring as you do. Continue to simmer, stirring, for 3 minutes; then add the oysters and any oil or juices still in the tin. Stir for a minute. Then remove from the heat, cover, and let sit for a few more minutes.

Add plenty of lemon pepper and salt to taste, then serve. This can be served with oyster crackers, of course.

Palisades Hominy Salad

SERVES 4

Hominy, bacon, and greens, oh my! That makes for a fine salad, but topping it all with "croutons" of salty, sweet, and smoky popcorn vaults this dish, as served at the Palisades Restaurant in Eggleston, Virginia, into the realm of the sublime.

TOMATO VINAIGRETTE

¼ cup red wine vinegar
1 tablespoon tomato paste
1 tablespoon ketchup
½ teaspoon kosher salt
½ teaspoon sugar
¼ teaspoon freshly ground black pepper
¼ cup extra-virgin olive oil

SALAD

1 (14.5-ounce) can hominy, undrained
1 red bell pepper, seeded and medium diced
1 jalapeño chile, seeded and minced
4 thick bacon slices
1 small red onion, cut into ½-inch-thick rounds
2 cups lightly packed fresh arugula

POPCORN

1 teaspoon (packed) light brown sugar
½ teaspoon sweet smoked Spanish paprika
¼ teaspoon kosher salt
⅛ teaspoon onion powder
1 (1-ounce) pack plain microwave popcorn (about 4 cups when popped)
2 tablespoons butter, melted

Make the vinaigrette: Whisk together the vinegar, tomato paste, ketchup, salt, sugar, and black pepper in a small bowl until smooth. Then whisk in the oil to incorporate.

Prepare the salad: Bring the hominy and its liquid to a simmer in a small saucepan over medium heat. Cook until heated through. Drain off the liquid and pour the hominy into a bowl. Stir in all but 2 tablespoons of the tomato vinaigrette. Cool to room temperature, stirring occasionally, about 20 minutes. Then stir in the bell pepper and jalapeño.

Cook the bacon in a large skillet over medium-low heat until very crisp, about 12 minutes. Drain the slices on paper towels, reserving the fat in the skillet, and then crumble them. Pour off all but 2 teaspoons of the fat from the skillet, leaving the browned bits undisturbed. Return the skillet to the stove and heat it over medium-high heat. When the fat sizzles, arrange the onion slices in a single layer in the skillet. Cook, turning them over once, until lightly browned in the center and charred along the edges, about 2 minutes per side. Separate the slices into rings.

Make the sweet and smoky popcorn: Stir together the brown sugar, paprika, salt, and onion powder in a small bowl. Pop the popcorn according to the package directions, and pour it into a large bowl. Drizzle with the butter, sprinkle with the brown sugar mixture, and toss to coat.

Assemble the salads: Divide the arugula among four serving plates. Drizzle with the remaining 2 tablespoons tomato vinaigrette. Top with equal portions of the hominy mixture and the charred onions. Sprinkle each salad with bacon and about ½ cup of the popcorn. (Serve the rest of the popcorn on the side.) Serve at once.

Rösti SERVES 4

The power of salt to season is nowhere clearer than when it graces hot, crisped potatoes. The best I've ever had were served to chef Edward Lee and me when we landed at The Hütte Swiss Restaurant after a roller-coaster ride down the two-lane-with-coal-trucks-roaring-by that leads into the tiny Swiss-Appalachian village of Helvetia, West Virginia. Giddy, we may have ordered everything on the lunch menu. All of it was good, but what we could not get enough of was the perfectly balanced crisp and tender, sublimely salted rösti.

This recipe is my homage. The secret is in the squeezing, essential for the quickly browned crust with tender potatoes inside. Oh . . . and maybe a little credit to the bacon grease. Serve this with "Clabber," Chive & Caper Tater Sauce (page 96) and Helvetia-style Honeyed Applesauce (page 243).

Rösti is traditionally made as a single "cake" in a wide, heavy skillet, but if you are concerned about breaking the cake when you flip it, do what I often do and fry in four individual patties.

2 pounds russet potatoes
1 tablespoon kosher salt
Freshly ground black pepper
3 tablespoons bacon grease
"Clabber," Chive & Caper Tater Sauce, for serving

Peel the potatoes and grate them on the large holes of a box grater. Lift a handful of grated potatoes and squeeze it over a bowl or the sink to drain off as much liquid as possible. Drop the squeezed potatoes into a bowl and continue until all the potatoes are squeezed.

Sprinkle the salt over the potatoes and add black pepper to your taste. I like a lot, some like less. Toss to distribute the seasoning.

Place a wide, heavy skillet over medium heat and melt the bacon grease in it. It should cover the bottom of the pan, about ⅛ inch deep. When it begins to shimmer, flick a piece of grated potato into the hot grease. If it sizzles instantly, add the rest of the potatoes, a spatula or spoonful at a time. Do this gently as you don't want the grease to bounce and burn you.

When all the potatoes are in the pan, use the back of the spatula to gently press down and form them into a compact round "cake."

Cook until the underside is a deep, crispy brown and the top potatoes are turning translucent; this takes 10 to 15 minutes. Keep an eye on the potatoes while they are cooking and turn the heat down to keep them from burning, if needed. Conversely, if the top potatoes are translucent but the bottom is not crisply brown, turn the heat up a bit to quickly darken it.

Gently move a spatula underneath the potato cake and around the skillet to loosen it, and then lift the whole cake, turn it over, and slide it back into the pan. (If this seems awkward, you can remove the cake to a large plate, place another plate over the top, and, holding the plates together, invert them, flipping the cake over. Then slide the cake, uncooked side down, back into the pan.)

Cook the second side for 7 to 10 minutes, until brown and crisped. Remove the rösti from the pan, let it drain briefly on paper towels, and then serve it immediately on a warmed platter. Pass the "Clabber," Chive & Caper Tater Sauce.

"CLABBER," CHIVE & CAPER TATER SAUCE MAKES 1 3/4 CUPS

Clabber milk was a common ingredient in the homes of folks who had a dairy cow. Fresh raw milk left out would naturally ferment and sour, creating a tasty and nourishing ingredient, similar to Greek yogurt. Clabber milk was frequently eaten for breakfast or as a snack with some sweetening and cinnamon sprinkled on top. It also was used as an ingredient in baking and in making sauces such as this one. If you favor raw milk, you can try to make your own clabber by leaving a bowl out on the counter, covered with cheesecloth. It's universally recommended that you not use pasteurized milk because it will simply spoil. Clabbering is unpredictable, though, so I use plain whole-milk Greek-style yogurt to make this sauce. It's great for potatoes of all kinds, from chips to rösti to Perfect Potato Salad (page 301).

You can substitute ½ cup of buttermilk for the equivalent amount of yogurt to make a yummy buttermilk dressing for salads or chicken wings.

1 cup plain whole-milk Greek-style yogurt
½ cup mayonnaise
3 tablespoons minced fresh chives
1 tablespoon minced brine-packed capers
   (try the Redbud Capers, page 302)
2 teaspoons juice from caper jar
½ teaspoon apple cider vinegar
Salt

In a small bowl, mix the yogurt, mayonnaise, chives, capers, caper juice, and vinegar together. Taste, and add salt according to how you are going to use the sauce (less if a dip for salty chips or on top of well-salted rösti, a bit more if dressing potato salad or a baked potato). It can be served immediately, but is best if covered and refrigerated for at least an hour.

Old-Style Vanilla Ice Cream

MAKES ABOUT 3 PINTS

It took forever, it seemed to us children, for my father and Uncle Charlie to hand-crank ice cream to firmness in its salt-and-ice bath. The men seemed to enjoy that time, though, the steady rhythm of the crank setting the pace for their stories and jokes. Finally it would be time, and everyone would return to the porch, screened safe from mosquitoes. Soon there was only the steady sound of spoons scraping bowls.

There are two recipes here, one with raw eggs in an uncooked cream base, and the other made with cooked custard, which is what the USDA strongly recommends. There is a risk of salmonella from raw eggs, but I would make it with well-washed eggs fresh from a good farm. I am not advising you to do the same, but I offer the recipe here because this is how it would have been done in the mountains.

These are recipes to be made in an old-style churn machine with a canister that sits in a tub of salt and ice. The consistency of the ice you use in the freezer bucket is key to the quality of the finished cream. You want crushed ice, not cubes, but also not fine snow ice. The ice you buy in bags at the grocery is usually too chunky, so when you get it home, wrap the bags in towels and whale away with a hammer for a bit to get ice that is roughly the size of peas.

UNCOOKED CREAM BASE

2 large eggs, cold
1¼ cups sugar
3 cups heavy cream, cold
2 cups whole milk, cold
2 tablespoons vanilla extract
¼ teaspoon salt

In a large bowl, beat the eggs to a light froth; then add the sugar and beat until the mixture stiffens. Add the remaining ingredients and mix until thoroughly blended. Pour into the freezer can, place in the refrigerator, and chill for 30 minutes. Follow the directions for freezing at right.

COOKED CUSTARD BASE

8 large egg yolks
4 cups sugar
4 cups half-and-half
2 whole vanilla beans, halved lengthwise
2 teaspoons vanilla extract

In a large bowl, whisk the egg yolks and sugar until thoroughly blended.

Pour the half-and-half into a heavy saucepan. Scrape the vanilla beans to extract the seeds, and then add both seeds and scraped pods to the half-and-half. Heat the mixture on medium-high heat, stirring occasionally, until it's steaming but not boiling.

When the half-and-half is hot, remove the vanilla pods and pour a few tablespoons of the hot liquid into the egg mixture, stirring as you do. Continue to slowly add the half-and-half in small increments, stirring until all has been added and the mixture is thoroughly blended. Return the mixture to the saucepan and heat it gently, stirring constantly, until the temperature reaches 160°F.

Remove the pan from the heat, pour the custard into a bowl, and chill until very cold. If possible, chill the freezer can as well. When the custard is fully cooled, stir in the vanilla extract and pour the mixture into the freezer can. Follow the directions for freezing.

FREEZING

Ice
Rock salt

Place the chilled canister in the ice cream machine and pour a good couple of inches of ice into the freezer bucket evenly all around the canister. Sprinkle a handful of rock salt evenly over this. Then add more ice, then more rock salt, until the layers reach just below the freezing canister's lid. End with ice. There will be a plug in the bottom of the machine that the water from melting ice can pour out of, and you'll want to add more ice around the canister as it does melt.

Crank until the ice cream is stiff and can hardly be cranked more. If you're using an electric machine, it will automatically stall out. It's good to have more than one person cranking, both so her/his arm doesn't get worn out and also to double-check if the cream really is that hard near the end or if the cranker is just tired. Even if it feels done, give the crank one or two final pushes for good luck.

Carefully take the canister out of the freezing bucket and wipe away the water with a towel before carefully opening the lid. Remove the paddle.

Put the lid back on quickly so the ice cream stays super-cold. Drain off any excess water from the freezer bucket and place the canister back in, packing salt and ice around it again, but this time only an inch or so of ice before adding more salt. Wrap the whole thing in a quilt and let it sit for an hour or two, if you can stand it. You can also put the canister into a freezer to cure, if you'd like.

This ice cream is best consumed just after sundown.

Salty Dogs: Chili Buns and Slaw Dogs

Childhood summertime in the mountains meant tying an emerald June bug to a string and letting it fly around your head, catching lightning bugs at dark and putting them in a jar to light your dreams, or piling in the Studebaker and going to the closest custard stand for a chili bun or slaw dog. Everything except the Studebaker is still a part of summer in the mountain South—especially the custard stand, which is often what a drive-in restaurant is called, even if it doesn't serve custard.

There's the Dip Dog in Marion, Virginia; the Frosty-Ette in Sand Gap, Kentucky; Skeenies Hot Dogs in Charleston, West Virginia. Pal's Sudden Service all around East Tennessee; the King Tut Drive-In in Beckley, West Virginia; and the Frosty Bossie in Coeburn, Virginia. These are just a handful of places my friends and I have frequented. All such serve ice cream treats, some make a mean burger, and the Sterling Drive-In in Welch, West Virginia, makes a deep-fried sub with chicken salad, cranberry sauce, and bacon as its filling. Really. But the aficionados know that what you really come for begins with chili on a hot dog bun.

The first thing to understand is that neither the chili bun nor the slaw dog, aka West Virginia Hot Dog, are quite the same thing as what the rest of the world calls a chili dog.

A chili bun is just that: Chili. On a bun. It has no dog. A slaw dog does, along with the chili, but it also has . . . that's right, slaw.

Compact and quickly consumed, chili buns seem to have sprung up in the pool halls of southeastern Kentucky around the Depression era, but a formally researched history has yet to be done. In the breach, I like to claim their inception for my hometown of Corbin and note that our earliest oral history of chili buns involves iconic poolrooms, The Fad and Nevels. By my early childhood in the 1950s, the best buns in town were being made at the Dixie.

It was in the early 1960s that the chili bun moved out of shady poolroom culture (where "nice" women and little children were not allowed) and into the burgeoning drive-in custard stand scene. There it met the West Virginia Hot Dog, which many claim had its origins at the Stopette Drive-In outside of Charleston, West Virginia, during the Depression, when wieners and cabbage were cheap eats.

Chili bun chili is called "chili sauce" in West Virginia hot dog culture—a finely grained aggregate of ground beef, spices, and something to make it all hold together—

and dogs with such sauce and slaw on top are now served throughout the South, sometimes called North Carolina Dogs, but not when anyone from West Virginia is in earshot.

Here are the rules: Buns should be soft, not toasted. Either can be dressed with bright yellow ballpark mustard and chopped white onion, but ketchup, pickles, and/or kraut are largely frowned upon. Hot sauce—favored brands are Crystal, Tabasco, and Texas Pete—may be liberally applied by those who wish for more heat. Jalapeños? Well, now you're talking schisms.

Chili Bun Chili, aka Chili Sauce

MAKES ENOUGH FOR 5 CHILI BUNS
OR 8 SLAW DOGS

———

Chili Bun cognoscenti swear their favorites have a secret ingredient. Plenty of Corbin folks trade a recipe, said to be the Dixie's original, that contains crushed cornflakes. I prefer the taste and texture of saltines. My mother believed the crucial spice was probably a couple of twists of pool chalk. I side with those who make chili bun chili with flat beer for the liquid. I'm not sure it makes the chili better, but it makes the cook mellow.

1 cup flat beer or water
1 pound lean ground beef
1 garlic clove, minced
1 teaspoon salt
6 saltine crackers, finely crushed (⅛ cup)
1 tablespoon tomato paste
2 teaspoons New Mexico ground red chile or cayenne pepper
1 teaspoon ground cumin
¼ teaspoon ground cinnamon

Put the beer and ground beef in an unheated medium saucepan. Use your fingers to gently rub the beef until it makes a slurry with the liquid. You don't want chunks or lumps. (Some folks use a potato masher to get the right texture.)

Stir in the garlic, salt, and cracker crumbs and place the pan over medium-high heat. Bring the mixture to a boil, stirring to keep it from sticking to the bottom of the pot.

Turn the heat to medium-low and continue to cook, stirring frequently to prevent sticking, until the liquid has largely evaporated but the mixture is still very moist, about 4 minutes. The chili should be a finely grained aggregate that holds its shape on the spoon.

Stir in the tomato paste. Remove from the heat and stir in the ground chile, cumin, and cinnamon. Cover and let sit for 5 minutes before serving.

Slaw Dog Slaw

MAKES ENOUGH FOR 8 SLAW DOGS

———

Chop the cabbage into small pieces, but don't use a grater or food processor because that releases too much juice and makes the cabbage too tart.

3 cups finely chopped cabbage (about half of a small head)
¼ teaspoon salt
Freshly ground black pepper
¼ cup mayonnaise
2 teaspoons whole buttermilk or milk

In a medium bowl, season the cabbage with the salt, and add pepper to taste (more is better). Thin the mayonnaise with the buttermilk, and mix it well with the cabbage.

To make the chili buns: Lightly paint the inside of a hot dog bun (see Note below) with yellow mustard. Pack 3 or 4 heaping teaspoons of chili sauce into the bun, starting with a spoonful in the center and smoothing it in with the back of the spoon. Add more, moving out to either end and smoothing lightly as you go, until the bun is filled. (You're not making a sloppy joe; the chili should be firm in the bun.) Top with chopped white onion to taste. Pass hot sauce on the side.

To make the slaw dogs: Heat hot dogs by submerging them in boiling water for 5 minutes. Paint the inside of the hot dog buns with yellow mustard, and sprinkle in chopped white onion to taste. Drain the dogs and pat dry. Place them in the buns and cover each with about 2 tablespoons chili sauce, then about 2 tablespoons slaw. Pass hot sauce on the side.

NOTE: When buying buns, check the sugar content in the nutrition information. Some buns have as much as 4 grams. That's way too sweet. Pick a bun with 2 grams of sugar.

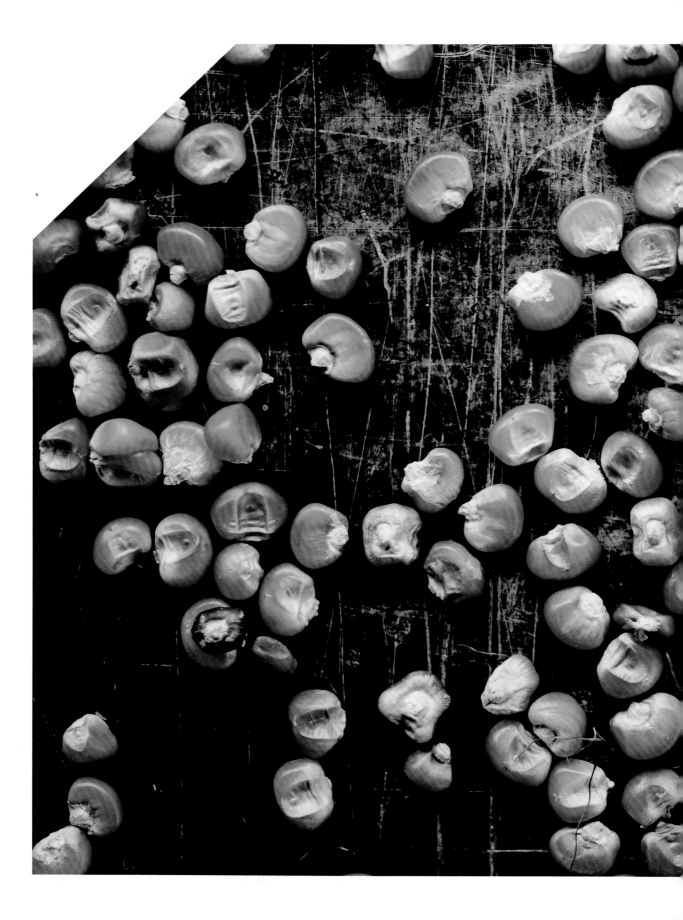

Corn

I get lost a few times on my way to Snowbird, North Carolina. The kind of lost where you don't even see a turn and the two-lane you're on becomes one and then gravel, so you circle back and there, plain as day, is your turn where you are sure it was not. It's the kind of lost where you feel as if the mountains are watching and considering before they decide to invite you in.

It doesn't seem a full-on fancy to imagine these long, contemplative mountains as knowing and protective. During the Cherokee removal of the 1830s, the infamous Trail of Tears, the mountains of Graham County sheltered many of the native people who hid rather than be forced from their ancestral lands. When the former Cherokee lands were seized and put up for sale, those Cherokee who could bought back their land through the agency of a few sympathetic whites such as Colonel Will Thomas. The Cherokee who stayed or returned to this place from the West—Junaluska walked back from Oklahoma to settle here, where the town of Robbinsville now sits—kept to many of the older traditions. The Snowbird community of the Cherokee, who live in the deep valleys of these mountains now, is said to have the highest number of full-blooded Cherokee and the greatest number of Cherokee speakers in the Eastern Band.

I am headed to the banks of Little Snowbird Creek for the annual Fading Voices Festival, held on Memorial Day weekend each year. For a few miles it feels as if I'm being enfolded into immensity; then the land opens out into a long, wide valley and I see on the left the gray stone Snowbird Baptist Church, and across the road on the right, a field that backs into trees running along the creek. Pickups and cars are parked on the edge of the field near the road, and families pour out of them, dressed for a picnic. A rowdy game involving lacrosselike sticks is just finishing in the field, and the shirted and shirtless young men who've played intensely are now joking and jostling one another on the way to find cold drinks.

There's a stage set up where veterans from many wars will later be honored, as will Miss Snowbird, a young woman wearing a traditional-seeming beaded crown and the long calico dress adopted by Cherokee women in the missionary era, along with sleek glasses and a great big watch. Bluegrass, rock, country, and gospel singers will take the

stage at various times throughout the day, but the first focus of the annual gathering is a mound-building ceremony, a ritual wherein people from the community—and anyone else—may place a little dirt on an ancient mound and offer a prayer. People talk quietly, warmly with one another as they walk away from the mound, toward the river and the picnic. I realize there's no cell phone in sight, no teenager texting, no child lost in a game of electronic blips and bleeps.

Along the river, under the trees, booths have been set up to shelter demonstrations of traditional craft making. There are booths with more contemporary crafts for sale and tables filled with food. A young mother is making jewelry out of corn and commercial beads as her children splash in the creek behind her. "Bead corn," she names it, and tells me it's ancient, a grass that grows bearing just one kernel, not a cob. The kernels are shaped like tiny onions; their dark gray has an opalescent sheen, like a land pearl. I read later that there is a Cherokee legend that says that where the people shed their tears on the forced march to Oklahoma, this singular corn sprang up, a kernel for each tear, a sign that the Creator had not forgotten them. I am reminded of the words of Cherokee poet Marilou Awiakta, from the end of the poem "I Offer You a Gift":

Against the downward pull,
against the falter
of your heart and mine,
I offer you a gift
a seed to greet the sunrise—
  Ginitsi Selu
Corn, Mother of Us All.
  Her story.

———

Corn is everywhere in the food booths at Snowbird. Sochan, the wild spring green with a pronounced mineral tang, simmered here with fatback, is served piled on flat corn cakes, hot off the griddle. There are two kinds of bean bread, one with pintos baked into a cornmeal batter in a pan, the other more like a tamale, the beans speckled through a cornmeal mush wrapped in its husk and baked. Chestnut bread is actually a dumpling of cornmeal and chestnut flour mush and chopped chestnuts, with a taste that is distinctly sweet. There is more conventional contemporary fare including something like a sloppy joe made with ground buffalo, hot dogs, and the "Indian tacos" you can find at state fairs and ball parks, with highly seasoned meat and beans piled on a grease-glistening disk of puffy white flour. But the longest lines are at the booths for the genuinely traditional foods. One of the most popular: bowls of tender simmered hominy, brown beans, and black walnuts in a grayish broth. My first taste tells me this needs meat, needs salt, but after a bite or two I catch its subtlety. It tastes of the earth. It tastes nourishing.

I hear a low *thump, thump, thump* and head to a demonstration booth where two silver-haired women wearing long calico dresses sit in straight-back chairs, watching a young girl in cut-offs and a red halter top determinedly pounding dried corn with a pestle that's maybe five feet long; its wide, heavy top gives each pounding stroke more weight. This is how the Cherokee have been grinding corn into meal since before Europeans invaded their land. History tells us that the women took turns, a communal process, and both corn and meal were stored in a place where everyone had access; anyone could have some whenever they were hungry.

————

"Cornbread Nation" is a term coined by New England–based food writer John Thorne (and borrowed, with his blessing, by the Southern Foodways Alliance as the title of its multivolume anthology of distinguished southern food writing). In his classic of American foodways, *Serious Pig*, Thorne notes that corn, which natives introduced to the Europeans who landed on their shores, was a political and sociological world apart from the domesticated grains the settlers had known in Europe. Those grains required cultivation of large fields over time, and by many hands, leading to the feudal system of lords and serfs, followed by that of landowners and tenant workers. "Those who owned the fields and the mills that ground what was grown in them owned the culture," Thorne wrote.

The corn of the New World required none of that. A single settler could sow corn in quickly turned but uncultivated ground with maybe a fish head for fertilizer, beans and squash for nitrogen and protection. Within a matter of months, new ears could be harvested before they were fully ripe and pulverized into a rough bread, while a season's harvest could be carefully stored to last until the next one. Corn could be made into bread, grits, hominy, mush, pudding, succotash. It could be popped or eaten fresh off

the cob; it provided fodder for animals. The shucks could serve as tinder, fill mattresses, be turned into brooms or play pretties. Cobs could be turned into pipes or jellies. Of course, corn made amazing liquor.

And it made for remarkable mobility. The Cherokee ground (nixtamalized, but we'll get to that) cornmeal and parched it for flavor and storing. They carried this high-level nutrient in pouches and could travel long distances without stopping for food, simply reaching in for a handful of meal, pausing at a stream for water. The pioneer questing for a better place could pack the meal from the harvest in one gunnysack, seed for the next in another, and set off in search of a new homestead.

Corn, Thorne says, "had an immediate and subversive effect on the newborn American character," leading to a country founded on an ethos of self-reliance and a fierce independence. "What corn gave the small landholder in self-sufficiency it gave double in self-esteem."

How it must have seemed to those second sons, indentured prisoners, and, later, newly freed men and women arriving in these mountains to suddenly have in their hands literal seeds to such independence. And while corn was ultimately supplanted as the meal of daily bread in the rest of North America where more expansive fields could be cultivated for wheat, it has held on as the mountain South's defining food. Cornbread in Appalachia is both sustenance and communion, nutrition and identity.

The Cherokee shared not only seeds but also their knowledge of how to utilize corn with the newcomers. Corn eaten with beans ups the protein from each. The pairing of grains and legumes shows up in most indigenous cultures; it may be deep body knowledge. Less intuitive, perhaps, is the process of nixtamalization, which all Native American people practiced. Nixtamalization involves soaking the corn in an alkaline solution—the Cherokee used ashes dissolved in water—making the otherwise-bound niacin in corn available to the body for absorption. A corn-based diet without this process—or an additional protein—can lead to pellagra. This happened in parts of Spain and Italy when corn was introduced there by traders but the nixtamalization process was not adopted. Pellagra showed up later in the South as people stopped treating corn with lye, as poverty narrowed the larder to little more than corn and fatback. But pioneer women in the mountains adopted the process, and lye pots on open fires outside the house were used for putting up hominy well into the 20th century. Gristmills eventually dotted the region, and corn—both as ground meal and as liquid pleasure—became a commodity to be bought and sold as well as family sustenance.

Jack Dellinger brushes leaves off the seat of a plastic chair outside his family's gristmill and proffers it. Cane Creek rushes through a forest of tall trees, unruly rhododendron, and ferns. When I made the turn at Bakersville, North Carolina, to follow the road four miles to Dellinger Grist Mill at Hawk, the late morning was sunny and dry. But as the road began to move alongside the creek, the air cooled and became noticeably damper. The green scrim flanking the two-lane became so deep and intense that now, sitting in it, I imagine that if we are too long talking, moss may cover my shoes, a strand of kudzu may work its way up my leg.

Jack wears a zippered windbreaker, jeans, hiking boots, and a merry grin, looking a good bit younger than his eighty-four years. The mill looks well preserved, as well. The building is over a hundred years old, but the family milling business has been at this site since 1867, when Jack's great-grandfather Reuben Dellinger arrived. Reuben was the son of Henry Dellinger, who built a gristmill and sawmill in Avery County and taught his son the trade. Henry was the first generation of the family born in America, his father having come from Germany in 1750. When Reuben's young wife, Mary, was killed in an accident at the family mill, Reuben left his holding and moved to Hawk, but continued the family business. As did his son, David. As did his son, Marvel.

But when Marve passed away in 1955, the mill was idled. None of Marve's seven children wanted to be a miller. Jack, one of the seven, had used the GI Bill to become an electrical engineer and was long gone. He eventually became a computer programmer for NASA, working on the Apollo mission before he retired and moved with his wife to Florida in 1997. But then the old mill and the home place called to him.

"I grew up right there across the road," Jack says, nodding toward the sharp rise that starts just beyond the narrow asphalt. His voice is so soft that I have to lean forward a little to hear him over the caroling of the creek.

"We bought nothing from the store except coffee, salt, and pepper. This was in the 1930s. I was born in '31, and there were seven of us. And right over there was the molasses furnace. We used to make thirty gallons a season, and my mama's molasses cookies were the best you'd ever eat. She had a two-acre garden right beside the house, and then there was a two-acre potato patch. We had an oat field to feed the horses, and behind the oat field, we had a wheat field.

"Now that mountain over there where we lived goes up at a fifty-, sixty-degree slope back beyond the house, and up that slope, we had a ten-acre cornfield. All flint corn, and that crop had to be enough to last us until the next one. And I'd dread the morning that always came when my daddy would say, 'Jack, after breakfast, saddle up that horse and go on up to start plowing that field.' It took two full weeks to finish, and I learned to hate that cornfield with a passion. When I got grown enough to git, that's what I did. And this mill sat here idle for forty-two years, because I had run away from that cornfield up there."

In 1997, though, Jack paid a visit to the old home place. "I came back up here and you couldn't even see the old mill from the road. There was forty-four acres of lumber hadn't been cut since I don't know when. And the wheel was leaning precariously and all covered in poison ivy. And I got this crazy notion, 'Lordy, I'd sure like to see that wheel go. I believe I'll cut this timber and then I think I'll restore that old gristmill.' Three years and a ton of money later, that's what I'd done."

The mill was placed on the National Register of Historic Places in 1998 as the last gristmill of its kind in North Carolina, distinguished not just for its longevity but because of its waterwheel, one of the first metal alloy wheels made by Samuel Fitz of Hanover, Pennsylvania.

"The wheel comes apart so it was shipped in eight five-hundred-pound chunks," Jack said. "The closest railroad was the Southern and it stopped in Morgantown, which is thirty-eight miles as the crow flies, but of course, you don't go as the crow flies.

"It took Reuben and his four boys about four years total to get this thing up and running," Jack says, proudly adding, "I use the same wheel and grinders today."

We walk around the mill and Jack points out details. Inside he shows me the grinding stone and says, "When a grain of corn falls down between these stones, it's like a million little scissors take to it. You can adjust the distance between the stones while running and you can tell if you need to by the feel of the meal as it comes out. Every corn is different, you know.

"When I was growing up, every family up here had a cornfield, and everybody believed their corn was the best. Mountain people are funny about their corn, and every family would have their own meal sacks. Used to be a big yellow cherry tree right there and they'd hook their horses to it and wait until their meal was ground, wanted to be sure it was their corn."

Jack grinds Hickory King currently, selling bags of cornmeal, polenta, and grits so delectable that a group of Charleston, South Carolina, women drive up every summer to get their year's supply for shrimp and grits, he tells me. I believe him. I've bought a bag of his cornmeal at a craft store in nearby Spruce Pine, and the flavor of the bread it makes is buttery and tangy. Divine.

He says he'd like to start grinding some of the older heirloom corn, and has been thinking about asking some neighbors, the Woody family, if they'd be interested in growing it for him. "If anybody could do it right, it'd be a Woody," he offers. "Daddy always said you could put a Woody on a big flat rock about a mile square and in about three months he'd be making a good living.

"I sure wish I could still grow my own corn, though." Jack laughs. "Isn't that something? Run away from the cornfield and now come back."

————

Jack Dellinger describes a day at his father's mill in the 1930s with people tying their horses to the yellow cherry tree to wait for their meal to be ground. We can be sure there was conversation shared and connections made under that tree. Mills predated courthouses and even the general store in most small Appalachian communities, and served a similar function as the gathering place where community was woven. The miller knew without asking whose crop had been a bad one in any given year and often saw that as an opportunity to find ways to proffer help without embarrassment.

The miller *also* knew when a homesteader grew and ground more corn than the family could reasonably use in pone and mush in a season. If you were a trustworthy stranger needing a little tot of something to tide you through the winter, the miller might be the man to tell you who best to ask. Through most of the history of the southern Appalachians, making whiskey and other spirits was not only legal but common. Orchards were planted to make hard cider, wine was made from native grapes, and cordials from other fruits. Whiskey was made from rye, and sometimes wheat, as well, but fine corn likker was the mountaineer's art.

Corn was both sustenance and a potential cash crop, but it was far more lucrative—easier to ship and commanding a greater price—to distill it than to sell plain kernels or meal. Because of its value, even when legal, a still might be hidden to deter theft, but over time most everyone in a community—not just the miller—would know whom to ask if they wanted to buy or trade. And that sort of community knowledge continued right through Prohibition into the modern age.

It's an irony worth some amusement that the part of the country known for the quality of its home-distilled spirits is also full of dry counties and townships. "Dry" means it's still not legal to sell spirits there, but it certainly doesn't mean they aren't imbibed. And the illicit distillery still weaves a web of connection in some mountain communities.

Lora Smith was born and raised in Corbin, Kentucky, the same town I was born in some thirty-five years before her. Her grandfather told her about a legendary bad batch of hootch brewed up in that town before either of us came along. A fuel additive in the liquor gave anyone who drank it a case of "jake leg," a paralysis that could be temporary or permanent. The flop-foot limp it provoked in even a mild case was a telltale sign of anyone who'd been sipping from such a batch. Lora's grandfather told her that men all over Corbin were crippled, or walking with such a gait, and a raid seemed imminent, yet never materialized. In fact, neither did the sheriff nor the county judge for several days, and when they finally did appear, they were walking jake leg as well.

Lora wrote about moonshine in a story for *Punch* magazine a couple of years ago, noting that whenever a proposition arose to legalize liquor in Corbin or other mountain towns, an unlikely alliance between temperance-minded church people, who flooded the polls, and prosperous bootleggers—who bribed the *rest* of the folks going to vote—kept legal liquor out. So it was that when she was growing up, one of the same families who made and sold liquor in her dad's day was still doing so in hers. And it was a rite of passage for the youth in her community to know which road to turn up out past Woodbine to find the makeshift wooden booth where a Swofford would sell you a pint without you even having to leave the car.

"Beyond catching a buzz," Lora wrote, "bootlegging was one way small towns created a culture of insiders and outsiders. You either knew where to buy alcohol or you didn't. It was a crooked kind of belonging, but the shared experience kept us connected to community memory and site-specific places in our county. By keeping a secret, we defined an identity."

In 2006 Corbin ended a century of Prohibition by voting to go "moist" (meaning restricted service of alcohol in restaurants), and in 2012 the town went wet (allowing package liquor sales) by a mere 98 votes out of 1,676. It was part of a trend across the region as small-town boosters realized that alcohol sales generated higher revenues and were more attractive to both visitors and locals.

Buttermilk Brown Sugar Pie

MAKES ONE 9-INCH PIE

Pies were the Mother of Invention because necessity required that they be made from whatever was on hand. In the summer there was no dearth of fruit that could be gathered—often by small children who would eagerly do the work for just reward later. In the winter dried apples, peaches, and squash could be simmered into a filling for the hand or fried pies beloved in the region. Vinegar pie was as tasty as, and easier to come by than, one made with lemon, and apple cider could be boiled to make a tart and tangy filling. Buttermilk was enough to turn a simple custard filling into a more complex delight. And using cornmeal as the thickener in these simple pies added character as well as flavor.

My cousin Michael Fuson introduced me to brown sugar pie. It was his favorite, he told my mother when his family moved from Corbin to Louisville and he began spending time in her kitchen. "Well, honey, then I'll make you one," she said. That my mother could make brown sugar pie was news to me. Mike was as generous as a homesick teenage boy could be and allowed me an ample slice before consuming the rest on his own. It was, I thought, one of the loveliest things I'd ever eaten. But then I made a version of my own with buttermilk instead of cream, and the sum of these two pie parts was greater than the whole of all pies put together.

Single unbaked pie crust (use your favorite recipe or
    ¼ batch of Emily Hilliard's Pie Crust, page 238)
1½ cups (packed) light brown sugar
¼ cup very finely ground cornmeal (see Note)
½ teaspoon salt
3 large eggs, at room temperature
4 tablespoons butter, melted and cooled to room
    temperature
¾ cup whole buttermilk, at room temperature
1 teaspoon vanilla extract

Preheat the oven to 350°F. Place the crust in a 9-inch pie pan and refrigerate it while making the filling.

In a medium bowl, combine the brown sugar, cornmeal, and salt.

In a large bowl, beat the eggs until frothy. Beat in the melted butter. Add the dry mixture and stir vigorously until the brown sugar is dissolved. Add the buttermilk and vanilla.

When all is well combined, pour the mixture into the pie crust and bake for 45 minutes, or until the center is set (no longer liquid, but still tender to the touch).

Allow the pie to cool until just barely warm before slicing. I like to drizzle about ½ tablespoon of buttermilk over my slice.

NOTE: If your cornmeal is not very fine, you can whir it in a blender until it is a little denser than flour. If it is mostly fine but not fully so, you can sift it to remove any larger pieces.

David Bauer

Farm & Sparrow bakery is located in Candler, North Carolina, just ten miles from bustling tourist- and hipster-filled Pack Square in Asheville, but a world apart. Down a rough-paved two-lane, Farm & Sparrow's "headquarters" occupies the garage of a nondescript ranch house. Two white delivery vans sit in the driveway, and one of them looks rough. Having slipped its gears one rainy afternoon, it met the creek in an ugly mash-up that ended its use as a vehicle. Ever resourceful, David Bauer—owner, miller, and chief bread baker—turned the van into a storage room for sacks of wheat berries and corn.

David has an unruly thatch of coal-black hair, dramatic black eyebrows, and sometimes a bold black beard. But everything else about him—his hands, his white T-shirt and gray britches—has a pale dusting of flour. The dust is not like a recent splash one might brush off, but a patina, seeming embedded in fabric and skin.

David Bauer was born in 1980 in Wisconsin, attended the University of Minnesota, and believed he was on the path to becoming a professional musician. "Then all at once, the band broke up, my girlfriend and I broke up, the job I'd had ended, I finished college," he tells me with a rueful grin. "I was at a loss about what to do."

The idea of working the earth appealed to him, so he found a gig as an intern with a farming family in the north country, and there he helped to build an oven and fell in love. "It was a pretty cold, wet winter and I stayed by that hearth. I just stuck close to it. It became like a friend."

Fascinated by his fascination with the hearth, he connected with the North House Folk School. Baking bread struck a chord for David and pretty soon he found a niche baking for restaurants . . . really good restaurants. In fact, David soon reached what many in the restaurant world would have considered the pinnacle of a career: the offer of a job baking for Thomas Keller's French Laundry and Bouchon in California's Napa Valley.

"But I was interested in milling, in heirloom grains," he says. Through friends who shared those passions, David heard of a bakery with a great oven for sale in the Blue Ridge Mountains of North Carolina. He laughs.

"I know it sounds crazy, but all I knew about this part of the world was what I saw when my band played Dollywood once. But I knew I loved that oven. So I said no to Bouchon and came down here. I kind of liked the idea of going someplace I knew nothing about."

That first oven was in the tiny town of Marshall. It was 2006. "I had nine hundred

FARM+ SPARROW

HRW

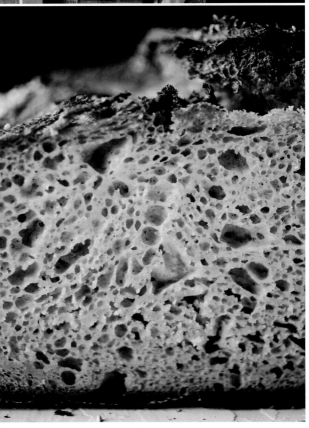

dollars and bought some grain and a small stone mill. The first couple of years here, I didn't sleep. I had no money. I baked all the time. I really wasn't thinking so much about business."

But David tapped into a blossoming market for artisan breads in nearby Asheville. When he found the property in Candler, he leveraged a rural initiative loan to buy it and expand. The garage houses the custom-built oven and a stone mill shipped from Austria. It also smells like heaven with bread cooling, fragrant freshly ground flour and cornmeal, and baskets and bins of grains—particularly corn.

In 2008 there was a wheat crisis, with the berries declining dramatically in quality while rising in price. David asked a local heirloom corn farmer, John McEntire, to grow an heirloom wheat, Turkey Red, for him, and then an heirloom rye. He began working with more mixtures of the grains in his breads. Working with and learning from McEntire and Anson Mills's Glenn Roberts, David says he was soon captivated by heirloom corn. And, he says, the southern Appalachians was the perfect place to explore this passion.

"This region is the nexus of wheat, rye, and corn. People grew all three and we use all three in our breads (along with spelt and buckwheat), but at this point, we're using so much corn, more than any other bakery in the country." The Grit Bread, in which the foundation of wheat and cornmeal is augmented by the addition of heirloom grits, is incredibly moist; the fermented grits absorb liquid and expand, becoming fat and a little springy, with a flavor and texture not unlike cheese. David tells me, laughing, "We still get a call about every other week from some vegan who's bought our Grit Bread and is sure we've put cheese in it."

While Farm & Sparrow uses red wheat grown in northern Ohio, the corn and other ingredients are grown by fifteen farmers right around the bakery. That gives David leeway to encourage experiments, and when we talk he has a farmer growing a patch of Tennessee Red Cob, a corn developed around Knoxville in the late 1800s. He shows me a quart bag of kernels he culled from the pounds and pounds of harvest because they had a different look, an opalescent shine that was distinctive enough to catch his eye and attention. David plans to plant these and see if he can develop a different strain.

"My favorite thing about the old grains is that they're still kind of wild. They're still doing stuff in the field; they're not stuck in history," he says. "And the thing I love about corn—this whole thing about independence, having the freedom. As a baker, when you're using corn, you can control the flavor of the bread from the seed. That's what I end up telling new bakers who come here to see what we're doing. For us, being here, corn is the key. It's corn that will set you free."

Perfect One-Eyed Jack SERVES 1

I can't claim this delicious breakfast dish for the southern Appalachians exclusively, but if you have a slice of incredible bread, like that made by David Bauer at Farm & Sparrow bakery outside of Asheville, North Carolina, I can think of nothing finer to do with it. In the summertime, it's delicious with a thick slab of the broadest ripe tomato from the garden. In the winter, it's lovely with a dollop of Old-School Tomato Gravy (page 218) on the side. It's best served as an over-easy egg with a still runny yolk for drenching the toast. It's simple to make, but doing it correctly elevates it from tasty to perfection.

This recipe is for one. Enlarge it to fit your needs around the breakfast table, but make sure you have enough room in the pan for both the slice of bread and its removed "hole."

1 slice rustic white bread
1 tablespoon unsalted butter
1 large egg
Salt and freshly ground black pepper

Use a biscuit cutter or a sharp knife to make a hole in the center of the slice of bread that's large enough to accommodate an egg—about 2½ inches in diameter. Leave the cut-out "hole" in the slice of bread for now.

In a skillet that's large enough to accommodate the bread, melt ½ tablespoon of the butter over medium heat. Place the bread in the butter, sliding it around the pan a bit to soak it all up. Let this toast for a minute or so, until the bread is just beginning to turn golden on the bottom but not browned.

Remove the bread from the skillet, turn the heat a little bit lower, and add the remaining ½ tablespoon of butter to the skillet. Remove the "hole" from the slice and return the bread to the pan, toasted side up and centering on the melted butter. Crack the egg into the hole, and toast the punched-out piece of bread alongside.

When the white of the egg turns solid on the bottom, gently flip the one-eyed-jack to cook the other side of the egg, just long enough for it to set. Enjoy immediately, seasoned with salt and pepper to taste.

Beans

In the parts of my lifetime spent living and eating outside the South, I've learned that there are places where folks don't know beans about beans. They don't know the velvety beauty of the white acre cream pea or the mineral tang of the earthy red clay pea, nor ever heard of the Whippoorwill nor the Turkey Crowder.

Many such folks think that lima beans only come in the size of a nickel, tasting brackish no matter how much butter you lavish on them, not suspecting that they range down to dime size, and the smaller they get, the sweeter and creamier. Nor have they heard of that mountain favorite, the speckled butter bean, mottled purple and green and when tasted with cream and butter, like eating the soul of the earth.

When I first encountered Frances Moore Lappé's seminal work *Diet for a Small Planet* as a vegetarian-dabbling young hippie in 1971, I understood immediately and instinctively her primary point: combining beans and grains in a meal increases the nutritional value of each and gives the body a whole protein. That's why almost all indigenous cultures in the world have at the core of their diet a combination of legume and grain. In the mountain South, those fundamental building blocks were cornbread and meaty, bean-filled green beans in warm weather, and in the winter, soup beans (pintos) and dried green beans, called "leather britches" or "shuck beans." But while Lappé's work provided the nutritional reason for our love of beans, there is more to say about their survival, in remarkable variety, in the region. Growing beans is an Appalachian art; describing them tells a mountain story.

————

The long summer sojourns I spent with my family in Corbin, Kentucky, were a lesson in beans. My great-aunt Johnnie's were white half-runners, narrow but full. She could grow 'em, my mother said, but not cook 'em, so when she could, my mom would take things over at the stove, knowing how much white bacon was enough, when to add the salt, when to tuck the small potatoes into the pot. My cousin Jessie's husband, Jim, planted their beans on a sunny slope and her pot was speckled with pinkish, squared-off seeds. They were almost my mother's favorites, but Ethel's, she said, might be the best.

Half-runners again, but these were planted across the creek from Johnnie's patch, and those beans were both meaty and sweet to a degree I've never tasted in another. Even my mother's beans could not measure up.

There were multiple pots of green beans to choose from at the two family reunions every summer at Levi Jackson State Park. My mother didn't need to see who brought what pot to know Ethel's beans. She could recognize them on sight and silently but knowingly point me to the right one to start filling my plate.

It was farmer and renowned seed saver Bill Best who explained to me that the story of my different family beans was about much more than styles of cooking. Bill has explained quite a few things to me, as he is a scholar and philosopher, as well as husband of the land. For more than forty years he worked as an administrator and professor at Berea College, where his wife, Irmgard, was director of student accounting. Bill taught modern dance and was a swim coach. He was also a groundbreaker in establishing modern Appalachian studies. His first book, *From Existence to Essence*, published in 1999, is still considered a fundamental text in understanding what it means to be a modern Appalachian in a larger culture that does not share the same values. He has made it his life's work to clarify the dissonance between the truth of Southern mountain life and culture and the dismissive way it is perceived and portrayed by the dominant world "outside."

In short, Bill teaches that American culture has evolved to largely value the acquisition of things: cars, tech devices, supper from the latest chef to make headlines. Appalachian culture instead places a higher value on connections. Beans are a perfect example of that as we value them not only for taste and nutrition, but also for less tangible reasons. We pass seeds from generation to generation, sharing their names and stories to connect us to our origins. We plant our preferred pole beans in the corn so the former may use the latter's stalks to twine up, a connection of crops. The bean plant replenishes nitrogen sapped from the soil, connecting us to the earth. We see the thick strings down the sides of the beans we prefer not as a nuisance, but as an opportunity to gather on the porch willing hands of all ages, the older women teaching children how to pull the zipper gently down one side, then the other. As we work, we share gossip and memories connecting us to our family, our community, and our history. Bill notes that being intangible, such treasures of a culture of connection are virtually invisible to the citizens of a culture of acquisition and so mountain culture gets cast, at best, as quaint and anachronistic; at worst, ridiculous or perverse. Bill urges us to look past such assumptions, to dig deeper for the truth. He also grows some mean beans.

The sixty-acre farm where Bill and Irmgard live is about twenty minutes from the center of the small college town of Berea, Kentucky. It's in a narrow, fertile valley that stretches long at the foot of Robe Mountain on the verge of the Cumberlands.

In the greenhouse, a number of different heirloom beans are coming along. Beans cross-pollinate with too much ease, and while Bill is growing some beans for eating, and some for selling at the Lexington and Berea farmers markets, he is also growing-out beans purely for their seeds, to continue their specific heirloom strain. Bill tells me that the differences my mother and I tasted from Johnnie's pot to Jessie's to Ethel's were as much, maybe more, in the beans themselves as in the cooking. And even, he says, if Johnnie and Ethel had planted from the same initial seed but on different sides of the creek, with different soil and shade and aspects to the sun, in a matter of just a few growing seasons, those seeds might have changed enough to produce two distinctly different green beans. There's magic in that, Bill says, and again, it's the magic of connection: from one season to the next; from mother's hand to son's to grandchild's; from one mountain holler to another; from the past to the present and now, hopefully, to the future.

Bill has collected and cataloged more than seven hundred heirloom beans since the mid-1960s. And while Bill receives seeds and stories from people all across the country, he says at least three-quarters, maybe more, of the beans have their roots in southern Appalachia.

Their names and provenance are a mix of poetry and history: the Gallahar, sent to Bill from a woman in Minnesota whose grandfather grew them in Clinton, Tennessee; Lena Mae Nolt's Holy Land from Casey County, Kentucky, and Rose Beauty from Estill County; the Case Knife with the long, large pod that gives it its name and similarly, the Pink-Tip Greasy or the Spangler with a pink and yellow mottled skin; the Logan Giant, beloved in West Virginia; the Doyce Chambers Greasy Cut-Short from Haywood County, North Carolina.

Bill grew up in Haywood County in the mountains of North Carolina, on the Liner Creek part of the Upper Crabtree community. In the 1940s and 1950s, as most of the rest of the country became increasingly dependent on the marketplace to provide food for the family table, the Bests continued, as their kin and neighbors did, to rely on their garden for sustenance.

"For us, as families whose only livelihood was subsistence farming supplemented by a little hunting, trapping, and ginseng digging, gardening was not merely a hobby," Bill remembers. "Good gardens ensured eating well until the next ones started yielding."

From the very beginning, gardening was a lesson in connections, not only to the earth but also to family. His Grandmother Sanford was a cook and gardener beyond compare, Bill says, and she was the drive behind the workforce that was her family. She rose earlier than the roosters, waking them to crow and rouse everyone else. She planted multiple gardens, taking advantage of the varied locations and terrain of a mountain homestead. "If you look, you'll see that a lot of mountain gardeners do that," he says. "She planted vegetables along the fence by the road, too, in case anybody hungry was passing by. They could just reach over and take what they might need."

As the oldest, Bill helped his mother plant the green beans each summer to fill the table year-round. His mother canned the beans they grew. They also picked quantities to dry to make shuck beans. And along with gathering beans for eating immediately and storing to eat later that year, Bill and his mother took in enough bean seeds to save and guarantee a good crop for the following year.

His father was an influence as well, encouraging in his son the desire to learn and experiment with new techniques. Bill's father was the first in their community to plant hybrid corn; Bill grew hybrid corn for a project in the tenth grade, setting a North Carolina one-acre production record in 1951 and winning a trip to the National 4-H Club Congress in Chicago. Is it any wonder, then, that Bill Best grew up with a passion for planting things?

His life as a farmer, Bill notes, was the laboratory for his own understanding of the larger issues of his Appalachian heritage. "I ordered seeds from the slickest catalogs," he confessed. But the tomatoes Bill got from catalog seeds seemed tough and tasteless compared to the ones his mother had grown. And the beans? Bland and definitely not the tender, delicious varieties he had known as a boy. It was Bill's mother, Margaret Sanford Best, who heard him complain about such things and, in the mid-1960s, started him on saving with the gift of several bags of seeds she had saved from her garden.

It was not unusual for a woman to be passing on the seeds, Bill notes: "Up until recently, when it's become a sort of popular thing, it has largely been women who have saved seed, because it was largely women who planted the gardens for the family and tended them."

————

If you stay on the interstates and major highways, it is possible to drive through much of West Virginia, eastern Kentucky, and the adjoining parts of southwestern Virginia and eastern Tennessee and never see the jaw-dropping devastation that the extraction

of coal has wrought. More than five hundred mountains have been destroyed by the now most common method of "mining," mountaintop removal. But coal companies don't do their work next to the interstates, and the state officials who work with them don't run main highways past the vast gutted wastelands of blackish gray slag gouged by heavy machinery.

One dramatic exception to hiding the scars of industry in the region is the corridor of I-64 that runs between Ashland, Kentucky, and Charleston, West Virginia, a route I took many times when I lived in Louisville in the 1980s and '90s, and that in my memory is always shrouded in an industrial belch of emissions, its edges flanked by huge concrete and metal holding tanks and the dystopian constructions of chemical plants and refineries. I remind myself that these are visible signs of jobs for people who want to stay in the region. I have had many conversations with folks from "off" who don't understand why anyone would.

The out-migration of southern Appalachians searching for work in industry has long been a part of the region's story. It's why my parents and sister went to Detroit during World War II and ended up in Louisville shortly after I was born. It's why the late

Appalachian poet and activist Don West's family left the mountains of north Georgia to work in the textile mills of Atlanta. It's why there are Appalachian communities in Bakersfield, California; Chicago; Dayton; Columbus; Toledo; and Cincinnati. It's why several of the Appalachian-rooted heirloom seeds Bill Best has been sent over the years came from gardeners in Oregon and Washington. The lumber industry attracted mountain timber men and their families to migrate there in the last century. They took the seeds from their gardens as a way to stay connected to the places they loved but left behind. And knowing they would face stark working conditions and meager pay, they took seeds to keep themselves alive. This was true as well for those who migrated from agrarian homesteads to the coal camps and cities of the mountain South.

Writing of the coal camps in West Virginia at the beginning of the last century in *Life, Work, and Rebellion in the Coal Fields*, historian David Alan Corbin notes that well into the 20th century, the majority of miners in Appalachia planted gardens and kept cows, pigs, and poultry. Not only was gardening a continuation of the prior life of subsistence farming, but it came naturally to the European immigrants from nonindustrial countries and the black miners who had frequently been sharecroppers.

While a miner might tend his garden before his shift or on a day off, the garden was largely the purview of the miner's wife and daughters, and of any sons not old enough yet to mine. Corbin quotes one miner who boasted that his wife and daughter "worked harder in the fields than any man ever did and that's why we grew more stuff in the [company] towns than farmers on their farms."

These were not "hobby gardens," but a crucial part of a mining family's survival and well-being. They decreased a miner's debt to the company store and provided fresh vegetables—as well as meat and milk from the livestock—to compensate for the poor wages and to tide the family over in times of no work. Contrasting the southern Appalachian coal town to those elsewhere, Corbin notes that a union organizer in 1896 wrote: "There does not exist the hunger and suffering that is found in [other coalfields]. Every available spot of ground seems to have received attention from the plow or spade, the house resembles the homes of the market gardeners. . . . They raise all the vegetables they require and this assures them that the wolf shall be kept from the door."

As I make a winding drive through the hills flanking the Ohio River, I realize I am seeing that same tradition, still thriving a century later. In the rural and residential stretches between strips of metal warehouses and concrete factories, small frame houses and neat single-wides perch on hills with gardens rising up at a steep slant behind them. When the passage opens to flatter valleys and the gardens root in level land, I find myself thinking that there is still something about them that makes me see them as distinctly *mountain*. And then it hits me: They all have trellises or long stick teepees or extra-tall fences rising in the air and covered in green. Runner beans. Pole beans. Appalachian heirloom cornfield beans.

————

Like many a mountain son or daughter, Bill Best began to plant the seeds his mother saved for him. And he saved his own. In 1973 he was the youngest member of the brand-new Lexington, Kentucky, farmers market. That's two years after Chez Panisse opened in Berkeley, California, and quite a few before Alice Waters would be heralded for bringing on the local food and gardening movement across the country. ("What's that lady in California who's had such success with school kids in gardens?" he asked me one time, wanting to give Waters props for her teaching.)

Customers who had moved to the bluegrass city from the mountains needed no convincing about his beans, even though Bill's heirlooms were priced significantly higher. "A lot of folks would come buy a bag of my beans, and then a bag of those other beans from commercial seed. I finally asked why and they said they mixed the two, the cheaper ones for bulk, but mine for flavor. After a while, the other growers saw what I was getting and raised their prices, and then folks were just buying my good beans."

Some of his customers began to bring Bill seeds of their own—prized tomatoes and family beans—and he began to grow them out for seed. A scholar at heart, he also recorded their stories—family names and place of origin, of course, but also the anecdotes and memories that were, in Bill's estimation, as much the nourishment as the bean itself. In those stories, he found insights, commentary. "There's lots of different beans people will refer to as a Preacher Bean," he tells me. "The preacher would eat at one house one Sunday after church, and then another the next. Sometimes it was a circuit preacher, going from one town to another. Oftentimes a family would give the preacher a handful of their best bean seeds as a present to take away. And the preacher would take those seeds to the next house the next Sunday and give them to the folks there. And they might give him some of their seeds, and he'd take them on." Then, drily, he continues: "Same thing happened with politicians, when they were making the rounds. But nobody thought enough of them to call their seeds Politician Seeds."

Bill began to meet other seed savers and they began to swap. Pretty soon, he'd started an archive in a chest freezer. In 1988 an article in a rural regional magazine about his bean-saving ways brought in eighty-six letters from people in six states who were interested in sharing seeds. He answered them all and the seed saving grew like Jack's beanstalk. Bill and his son Michael established the not-for-profit Sustainable Mountain Agriculture Center to formalize the process of sharing and selling, and to further the study of heirloom seeds. In 2003 the Southern Foodways Alliance honored him for this work with the Ruth Fertel Keeper of the Flame Award.

For over thirty years now people who have heard about Bill's work have been sending him their seeds in the mail or handing them to him at the farmers market. The seeds come in medicine bottles or in those miniature jam jars you get with room service in hotels. Irmgard says the most popular package is a cardboard check box bound with duct tape.

Here's what's special about these beans, why they matter to such folks who care about food and flavor: Beans mutate easily. In the old days, a gardener or farmer would note the plants in his or her crop that had desirable characteristics. These were not typically the characteristics that a seed company looks for when selecting plants or hybridizing for commercial purposes. Disease resistance and early yield are universally positive attributes, but while commercial growers have a primary interest in ease of harvesting, shipping tolerance, and shelf life, home growers were far more interested in flavor and tenderness.

Like his mother, Margaret, Bill is passing the literal seeds of his cultivation to his son Michael. Operations for The Sustainable Mountain Agriculture Center will move to Michael's place in Cookeville, Tennessee, where he is a professor in the School of Environmental Studies at Tennessee Tech University. Like his dad, Michael grows and sells heirlooms. "He's always got tomatoes at the Chattanooga farmers market way before me," his dad confides, and by the smile around the corners of his mouth, I know he thinks that's an awful good thing.

As I drive away from Bill and Irmgard's farm, a packet of Nickel Bean seeds on the seat beside me, I dream of green beans. I imagine fat, fragrant green pods corrugated with hearty white, pink, ivory, yellow, or brown seeds. I see beans simmering in a slow pot on the back of a stove. And next to it, I see an empty black skillet that is waiting impatiently until it's time for cornbread. I fantasize sopping.

Shuck Beans or Leather Britches

SERVES 8 TO 12

"Leather britches" or "shuck beans" refers to the method of preserving certain types of green beans by drying them in their pods. Rehydrated and cooked, the skins take on the texture of silk and nearly dissolve on the tongue, while the beans are tender, rich, and velvety.

Shuck beans were traditionally strung on thread and hung in a dry place out of sunlight until they fully dried. The beans shrivel and curl as they dry, and the story goes that they looked like leather britches that had gotten wet and then dried out, hence that name. Shuck beans, which is what my family and many folks call them, or shucky beans, as others say it, refers to the fact that they were dried "in the shuck." (Beans that were popped out of their shuck, or pod, were called "shell-outs" or "shellies.") And in a very few parts of the southern Appalachians, shuck beans are referred to as "fodder beans."

When the beans are dried, they can be put away in cloth or paper bags (some folks put in a dried pepper to keep out insects), or in more modern times, stored in jars or tins or plastic bags. Some folks freeze them in airtight bags, but they will keep a couple of years if tightly enclosed and stored on a shelf out of sunlight.

Beans were preserved this way to provide much-needed protein through the long mountain winters. Remember that part about protein, because we'll come back to it in a minute. The commonly accepted folklore of the mountain South says this was a tradition among the southeastern tribes, and contemporary Cherokee people continue to make shuck beans, as do other southern Appalachians today. But it appears that the practice may have originated in Germany and been brought to the mountains by early settlers from the Palatinate, and then adopted by the rest of the people in the region. *Getrocknete Bohnen* is the term used in Germany to refer to any number of dried beans, including whole green beans strung on thread and dried exactly as described here. (See page 33 for more to this story.)

Whoever started it, mountain people universally embraced the dish, and today, long past the need for preserving every morsel from the garden to get through the winter, southern Appalachians still dry green beans. Many folks like to do it the old way with the *ristra*-like strings of beans hung on an enclosed porch, in the attic, or in an out-of-the-way corner. You can also dry beans the way many do apples, by spreading them on a large screen or sheet strung taut between sawhorses. Back in the day when cars had a ledge under the back window, some folks would spread towels and dry the beans there. A few folks dry beans in an electric dehydrator, but most of us who've had such will tell you that they just don't seem to taste as good.

And taste brings us to protein. The green beans the early settlers dried were fat and full of beans—the source of the meaty flavor that gives this dish its body. Shuck beans were made with beans at the end of the harvest season, often the last beans from the vine.

So, for truly tasty shuck beans worth your time and effort, I would encourage you to grow or look for someone growing an heirloom pole bean with strings. If you live somewhere that they grow greasy beans or cut-shorts, you've hit the jackpot. Heirloom half-runners are also good. And again, only bother with pods that are fat and full of beans.

Five pounds of green beans will make about 4 cups of dried shuck beans, and when they are rehydrated in cooking, that will make about 8 servings. That's the proportion I give in the recipe, but you may dry fewer to see if you like them the first time, or you may dry lots more.

Beans can vary according to type and degree of dryness, so cooking times and some measurements can vary as well. These instructions tell you best estimates of time, what to look for, and how to adjust for variables. Shuck beans can be cooked ahead, refrigerated, and warmed right before serving if you need to time your meal precisely.

In many mountain families, shuck beans are a traditional part of the feast for Thanksgiving, Christmas, and/or New Year's. In my family, though, they were a much-beloved winter supper, served only with plenty of hot Real Cornbread (page 120) and sliced raw onion on the side.

(recipe continues)

4 cups dried shuck beans

2 ounces seasoning meat, such as salt pork or ham hock

1 teaspoon salt, plus extra if needed

If the beans are still on the thread, cut the knots at both ends and slide them off, discarding the thread.

Break the whole beans into smaller pieces, and as you do, pull off any strings you may have missed when they were fresh. Place the beans in a colander and rinse them lightly to rid them of any dust that may have settled while drying. Transfer the beans to a large pot and add 2 quarts of water (if you're cooking more beans, just press them down with your hand and make sure there's enough water to cover them by an inch).

Place the salt pork or other seasoning meat in the pot. Bring the water to a rapid boil, then turn the heat down to a lively simmer and cover the pot. You want there to be bubbles among the beans, but not to let the water bubble hard enough to rattle the lid. Cook for 3 hours, checking the water level often and adding boiling water if the level falls below the beans. Remember that the beans will be buoyant for some time, so use a large spoon or spatula to press down to see what the actual water level is. Be careful to not let the pot boil dry!

After 3 hours, test a bean (the actual bean) to see if it breaks open easily and is tender inside. The skin may be a little tough, but the inner part of the bean should be soft, not chalky. If not quite there, cover and cook a little longer, testing every 10 to 15 minutes. When a bean tests ready, add 1 teaspoon salt, turn the heat up to a lively boil, and partially cover the pot. Cook for an additional 30 minutes at a lively boil. During this time, you are letting the beans finish tenderizing and also reducing the amount of liquid in the pot. You want the cooking water to evaporate enough so that the beans are just starting to come out of the liquid but are not stranded and dry on top.

Test another bean and this time you are looking for a fully creamy interior. The pieces of the pods will be translucent and feel like silk. If you think the beans need to cook longer, lower the heat back to a lively simmer and continue cooking and testing until they are done. Then remove from the heat, fully cover the pot, and let rest for 20 minutes.

Taste the beans and add more salt, if needed. The amount of salt will vary depending on how salty the seasoning meat is. Remove the salt pork and serve.

Soup Beans SERVES 8

Any number of dried beans make delicious bean soup, but if a mountain person says they want a bowl of "soup beans," you know they are talking about meaty, rich pintos. The smell of the first winter pot of soup beans simmering on the back of the stove filled our house with warmth and a sense of great comfort. My mother would serve them with a skillet of golden Real Cornbread (page 120), the sliced sweet white onion or trimmed green ones that were essential with every bite, and a jar of chowchow or pickle relish for those who wanted a dollop on top. Soft, salty brown beans are still one of the finest tastes I know. This is how my mother made them, and I do still.

1 pound dried pinto beans
½ pound salt pork
1 small onion
1 garlic clove
2 teaspoons salt

The night before, sort the beans to make sure there are no small rocks, twigs, or clumps of dirt. Rinse them well in a colander, then put them to soak in a big bowl with cold water at a level a couple of inches higher than the beans. Leave them at room temperature overnight.

When you are ready to cook, skim off and discard any skins or funky beans that have floated to the top. Put the beans and any soaking water into a heavy pot with a lid, and add more water to reach about an inch above the beans. Nestle the salt pork into the beans.

Peel the onion and garlic clove, and nestle them into the beans as well. Bring the water to a boil on high heat, then turn it to a simmer and cover the pot. Cook the beans at a simmer until they are very soft and tender. Depending on the age, and therefore the dryness, of the beans, this can take from 1 to 2 hours.

Remove the seasoning meat, the onion, and (if you can find it) the garlic from the pot and stir in the salt. Allow the beans to simmer, covered, for another 15 minutes or so to let the salt soak in. Taste, and add more salt if needed. Serve hot. I like to crumble my cornbread in the bowl and pour the beans over it.

VARIATION
You can also make a meatless version of soup beans by substituting 3 tablespoons of olive oil and 2 teaspoons of smoked Spanish paprika, sweet or mild, for the salt pork. Some mountain cooks like to flavor the beans—cooked with or without meat—with a couple teaspoons of peanut butter.

Succotash SERVES 6

Coming from a Narragansett term for "broken corn kernels," "succotash" is most commonly applied today to a dish of frozen or canned lima beans and corn. But in the mountain South the possibilities for delicious variations on this basic theme are much broader. This is not so much a matter of kitchen sorcery as it is a reflection of the variety of beans and corn available from the garden, depending on the season.

The small green limas called "butter beans" and beloved throughout the South are grown in mountain gardens, but there are also striped and speckled, purple, red, and mottled butter beans as well. These are simmered until tender and then fresh corn, cut and scraped from the cob, is added to the pot to provide the beans company and produce a milky sauce.

The same can be done with fresh green beans cooked from scratch, but at our house the green bean version was always a dish made with leftovers (see page 156). If you can find small, fresh butter beans or peas at your farmers market in the summer, that's what you will want to use. If you simply can't find fresh, then frozen baby lima beans will do, but the corn should be fresh on the cob so you can "milk" it. The corn should be white or pale yellow and not be one of the super-sweet hybrids.

2 cups shelled fresh butter beans
4 ears fresh corn
Salt and freshly ground black pepper
3 tablespoons butter
¼ cup chopped green onion, white and green parts

Put the beans in a saucepan, add water to cover them by 1 inch, and bring to a boil. Partially cover the pot and turn the heat down until they are cooking at a lively simmer. Cook until done—meaning that the inside of the bean is perfectly creamy but the outside is still whole. The time will depend on the size and the freshness of the beans and can be anywhere from 10 to 40 minutes. You may need to add more water to keep the beans just covered as they cook.

While the beans are cooking, shuck and "milk" the corn as in the directions for Skillet Corn (page 117), and set aside.

When the beans are done, drain off any excess cooking water, reserving ¼ cup of the cooking liquid. (If you don't have ¼ cup left over, add water or milk to make ¼ cup.) Lightly salt the warm beans.

In a large skillet or saucepan, melt the butter over medium heat. Add the green onions and cook, stirring, until they just begin to soften, about 3 minutes. Add the corn with all its milky juices and the cooked beans. Add the reserved cooking water from the beans. Cook, stirring gently, for about 10 minutes, until the corn is just tender. Salt and pepper liberally and serve immediately.

Mountain Green Beans & Taters

SERVES 6 TO 8

I understand why folks from "off" are often bewildered by how long I say to simmer a pot of fresh green beans. It's because I am not talking about the skinny, soulless, beanless beans found in most groceries. In the mountains, we still grow green beans that are fat and full of tasty meaty beans, and we cook them low and slow to coax out their distinct flavors and to help the body access all that nutrition.

At your farmers market look for vibrant pods that are lumpy and filled with beans inside. If you're in the mountains, any variety of greasy bean is prized. (They are called that because the outer surface appears shiny, as if greased.) If the grower is growing from heirloom seed, a white half-runner is delicious (although commercially bred ones are becoming tough). If you can find McCaslan beans, their aroma while cooking is intoxicating. Outside the South, Romano or Italian green beans are often your best bet for finding a pod with ample fat beans. Beans with strings seem to have better flavor, as well, and the ritual of stringing and breaking them for the pot is as good as twenty minutes of zazen.

Leftover green beans can be mixed with fresh corn the next day to make a quick succotash. If you've made Skillet Corn (page 117) for the first meal (always a good idea!), combine any leftovers in one pot and gently heat until just warm. If you're adding fresh corn, cut the kernels off the cob and press out the milk as for skillet corn and add both to the beans. Add a bit of water, if needed, and simmer for 5 to 15 minutes, until the corn is cooked to your liking.

2 pounds green beans
¼ pound salt pork
½ teaspoon salt, plus more for seasoning
16 golf-ball-sized new potatoes

Prepare the beans for cooking by removing the strings and snapping them into pieces about 1 inch long.

Place the beans in a large lidded pot and add enough water to just cover them. Nestle the piece of salt pork in the center of the beans. Add the ½ teaspoon of salt to the water.

Bring the water to a boil on high heat. Reduce the heat to a lively simmer, cover the pot, and cook until the beans (not the green pods, but the beans themselves) are tender. This takes about 1 hour, and you may need to add water to keep the beans from cooking dry. Check the pot often.

Taste the broth and the beans and add additional salt if needed. Place the potatoes in the pot, pushing them down into the broth. Cover, and simmer for 20 to 30 minutes, until the potatoes are tender enough to break apart easily when pierced with a fork. Remove the salt pork and serve.

VARIATION

To make a meatless version, substitute 2 tablespoons of olive oil plus 2 teaspoons smoked Spanish paprika, sweet or mild, for the salt pork. You may want to add more paprika for a meatier effect when you taste and adjust the salt, but do so sparingly as it also has a slightly bitter edge.

Buttermilk Cucumber Salad

SERVES 4

The absolute best summer supper is a pot of Mountain Green Beans & Taters (page 156), a bowl of Skillet Corn (page 117), and a platter of sliced tomatoes and cucumbers straight out of the garden. When they are small, tender, and just picked, cucumbers are mighty fine with just a dash of salt. But this inspired treatment from my friend Chris Bryant is so good, I could make a full supper just on this and a slab of hot cornbread.

Be sure to seek out full-fat buttermilk, not the reduced-fat kind, which is just too wimpy to work. If you can't find full-fat buttermilk, you can substitute plain full-fat yogurt, but the search for the buttermilk really is worth the effort.

The only cucumbers I peel are the ones from the grocery, which have been waxed. Garden-fresh ones in season have thin, tender skin that adds color and texture to the dish.

2 cups thinly sliced cucumbers (about ¾ pound)
½ cup very thinly sliced sweet onion
1 cup whole buttermilk
1 tablespoon chopped fresh dill (see Note)
1 tablespoon apple cider vinegar
1 teaspoon kosher salt
1 teaspoon sugar
½ teaspoon freshly ground black pepper

In a medium bowl, combine the cucumbers with the onion, buttermilk, dill, vinegar, salt, sugar, and black pepper. Cover, and refrigerate the salad for as long as 20 to 30 minutes to allow it to marinate and chill completely.

NOTE: Chris encourages improv, suggesting substituting basil, cilantro, mint, or tarragon for the dill if the meal warrants, and he even suggests that occasionally jalapeño or banana peppers are just the ticket.

Ginger Bean Chowchow

MAKES ABOUT 9 CUPS

This recipe was developed to accompany a magazine story about Appalachian seed saver Bill Best. The green beans make a surprisingly crisp yet hearty variation of mountain folks' favorite sweetly spiced relish. The ginger reflects Bill's dry, sharp sense of humor.

You will need to marinate the vegetables overnight before covering them with the hot vinegar the next day, and then the vinegar will need to cool. The chowchow can be served then, but it's even better chilled. It sounds funny to serve beans on beans, but a big tablespoonful of this on top of a bowl of soup beans served with cornbread is a pure delight.

2 cups diced fresh green beans
2 cups baby lima beans, fresh or frozen (thawed if frozen)
2 cups small-diced fennel bulb
1 cup small-diced green tomato or tomatillo
½ cup finely chopped sweet white onion
3 tablespoons kosher salt
3 cups distilled white vinegar
¾ cup sugar
1½ tablespoons coarsely chopped fresh ginger
1½ teaspoons fennel seeds
¾ teaspoon celery seeds
¾ teaspoon mustard seeds
¾ teaspoon whole black peppercorns
5 garlic cloves, halved

Fill a large bowl with ice water and place it next to the stove. Bring 3 cups of water to a boil in a large saucepan; add the green beans and lima beans and return to a boil. Reduce the heat to maintain a simmer, cover, and cook for 5 minutes. Then drain, and plunge the beans into the ice water to stop the cooking.

When the beans are cool, drain and return them to the (empty) bowl. Add the fennel bulb, green tomato, and onion to the beans. In a separate large bowl, whisk the salt into 4 cups of water until dissolved, then pour this over the vegetables. Cover and refrigerate overnight.

The next day, drain the vegetables and discard the brine.

Combine the vinegar and sugar in a large pot. Bring to a gentle simmer over medium-low heat, stirring to dissolve the sugar. Add the ginger and simmer for 5 minutes. Add the fennel seeds, celery seeds, mustard seeds, and peppercorns and continue to simmer for 10 minutes. Remove from the heat and add the garlic. Let rest for 5 minutes, and then strain the infused vinegar through a fine-mesh sieve into a bowl.

Pour the infused vinegar back into the pot and add the vegetables. Simmer gently, stirring often, until the vegetables begin to soften, about 10 minutes.

Using a slotted spoon, transfer the vegetables to a container (or containers) with a tight-fitting lid, such as a canning jar. Pour the liquid over the vegetables and let stand at room temperature until cool. Then cover and refrigerate for up to 1 month.

Shelley Cooper's Speckled Butter Bean Cassoulet with Rabbit Confit

SERVES 8

My great-aunts not only canned both chicken and squirrel meat in their broth, but also put them up covered in fat. This was a traditional means of storing meat before the invention of mason jars, the layers of fat sealing the meat from bacteria and salt protecting it from decay—it also intensified the flavors. *Confit* refers to that whole process, but in contemporary cooking, *confit* has come to mean as well the delicious technique of slow-cooking the meat in fat. The process tenderizes otherwise tough or stringy game and imbues it with the flavor of the seasoning.

Shelley Cooper makes her rabbit confit, which she shares here, for the Speckled Butter Bean Cassoulet she serves at Dancing Bear Appalachian Bistro in Townsend, Tennessee. The combination of the butter beans' creaminess and the rabbit is just divine.

The rabbit confit is a two-day process. The meat can also be used in lieu of chicken in Karl Worley's Roasted Chicken & Dumplings (page 40), and is delicious shredded and served on a plate with lots of tasty pickles. And if you're not up for rabbit, the Speckled Butter Bean Cassoulet is quite good with shredded chicken, pork, or even without meat at all.

You may serve this immediately, but the cassoulet is most tasty made a day in advance and reheated so that all the flavors can marry.

⅓ cup bacon grease
½ pound salt pork, cut into ¼-inch cubes
1 pound fresh chicken-apple link sausages, cut into chunks
3 small carrots, thinly sliced
2 medium yellow onions, medium diced
3 inner celery stalks, medium diced
4 garlic cloves, crushed and peeled
Salt and freshly ground black pepper
2 pounds fresh speckled butter beans
1 large tomato, chopped
2 quarts chicken stock

¾ to 1 pound shredded meat from Rabbit Confit (recipe follows)
4 fresh parsley sprigs
4 fresh thyme sprigs
1 bay leaf
2 tablespoons honey

Position a rack in the lower third of the oven and preheat the oven to 325°F.

Set a large Dutch oven over medium-high heat. Add the bacon grease and when it is just smoking, add the salt pork and sausage. Cook until browned, 6 to 8 minutes. Then add the carrots, onions, celery, and garlic and season with a few generous pinches of salt. Cook, stirring occasionally, until the vegetables are tender, about 10 minutes.

Add the butter beans, tomato, chicken stock, shredded meat from the Rabbit Confit, and a few pinches of salt. Take a second to tie the herb sprigs and bay leaf together with kitchen twine if you like, and add them to the pot. Cover the pot with two layers of aluminum foil, followed by the lid. Cook in the lower third of the oven for 2 hours.

Remove the pot from the oven and finish it off with the honey and salt and black pepper to taste. Spoon off some—only some—of the fat.

(recipe continues)

RABBIT CONFIT
MAKES ABOUT I POUND

½ cup kosher salt

¼ cup (packed) light brown sugar

¼ cup mixed chopped fresh herbs, such as parsley, thyme, and sage

Grated zest and juice of 1 lemon

Grated zest and juice of 1 lime

Grated zest and juice of 1 orange

1 whole rabbit (2 to 3 pounds)

12 cups duck or pork fat (can be either bacon grease or leaf lard, or both)

Combine the salt, brown sugar, herbs, and citrus zest and juice in a small bowl. Rub this mixture onto the rabbit. Transfer the seasoned rabbit to a large piece of cheesecloth and wrap the cheesecloth around it. Place the wrapped rabbit on a rack set in a jelly roll pan or roasting pan, and refrigerate for 24 hours.

Position a rack in the lower third of the oven and preheat the oven to 250°F.

Unwrap the rabbit, rinse it thoroughly, pat it dry, and nestle it into a large Dutch oven.

In a large pot, melt the fat gently over medium heat, and then let it cool for about 15 minutes. Carefully pour or ladle the cooled fat into the Dutch oven, covering the rabbit by about ½ inch. You might end up with some leftover fat, which is certainly not a bad thing.

Cover the Dutch oven, place it in the oven, and cook for 3 to 4 hours. While the rabbit is cooking, check the pot occasionally. The fat should not be simmering or boiling. If your fat gets too frisky, lower the oven temperature to 225°F or remove the lid and replace it with a layer of foil. The rabbit is ready when the meat is tender and can be easily detached from the bone.

Remove the pot from the oven and remove the lid. Let the meat come to room temperature, and then transfer it to a cutting board and shred it.

Remembrance of Jerry's Chili Past

SERVES 4

Of all the arguments over "true" recipes, none is more contentious than the one over chili. I will not enter the fray by declaring that my mother's chili was the best. I will simply say that when the nights get so long, and cold, and damp that it makes your heart crack, nothing soothes my soul so much as a bowl of Jerry Lundy's chili.

My mom's chili falls into the category some call "coal camp chili." That means it has tomatoes and plenty of beans—pintos, not canned kidney beans. In my childhood, my mother made every winter pot of chili from scratch and memory. There was no recipe. Here is what we know about my mother's chili: She cooked it in a cast-iron pot that was both deep and wide and seasoned over decades with both chicken fat and bacon. She used Mexene brand chili powder, but insisted on buying a new jar each winter so the spices would be fresh. She "doctored it," but just how remains a mystery.

I began trying to replicate the chili of my memory forty years ago and believe I've now almost got it right. When I make my memory of Mama's chili, I want it served up as she did: a sleeve of crisp saltines on the table, a tall glass of cold sweet milk on the side.

You are welcome to up the ante on any of the spices to please your palate. I pass Tabasco or another hot sauce on the side. If I use this chili for a Frito pie (chili poured over regular-sized corn chips and eaten with a spoon), I will garnish it with chopped white onion and grated cheese, but not when it's my memory I'm pleasing.

1 tablespoon bacon grease
½ medium yellow onion, medium diced
1 pound ground lean grass-fed beef
1 garlic clove, minced
1 teaspoon ground cumin
½ teaspoon ground coriander
¼ teaspoon New Mexico ground red chile or
    cayenne pepper

½ teaspoon salt, plus more to taste
2 cups cooked pinto beans, with about ½ cup
    cooking liquid
1 cup chopped canned tomatoes, with their juice

Melt the bacon grease in a Dutch oven over medium heat. Add the onion and sauté until just transparent, about 3 minutes. Crumble the beef into the pot, breaking it into small pieces no bigger than your thumbnail.

As the meat just begins to brown on the bottom, sprinkle the garlic over the top and then stir it in, turning the meat as you do. Mix the cumin, coriander, chile, and ½ teaspoon salt together in a small bowl, sprinkle the mixture over the meat, and stir it in.

When the meat is just browned, add the beans and the tomatoes. Bring to a simmer, stir, and then turn the heat down very low and cover the pot. Let the chili simmer for 30 minutes, stirring it occasionally to keep it from sticking and also making sure the pot is not drying out.

The juices from the meat, liquid from the beans, and juice from the tomatoes are usually enough to keep things juicy in the pot, but if needed, you may add more liquid in small increments. Bean liquid is best, tomato juices are next, but water is also all right. Just remember that you are not making soup, and so add liquid only if there's a danger of burning or sticking. The desired result is a thick meat-and-bean mixture with a little sauce.

Taste, and adjust the seasoning with salt if needed. You can serve the chili immediately, but it gets even fuller in flavor if you refrigerate it overnight and reheat it the next day.

The Third Sister

Until very recently, there were five regions that anthropologists considered "world food hearths," the places where early peoples first branched out from hunting and gathering and began to domesticate plants for food and develop the practice of agriculture. These regions also developed crops that have survived as primary modern food sources; they are Mexico (corn), Peru (potatoes), the Middle East (wheat and barley), Africa (soybeans and millet), and Southeast Asia (rice).

More recent study suggests that the eastern woodlands of North America, extending from the Mississippi River to the Atlantic Ocean, the Great Lakes to the Gulf of Mexico, may be a sixth world food hearth. This theory has been bolstered by archaeological findings in the Red River Gorge in the mountains of eastern Kentucky. Evidence of an early civilization there has already cracked the long-held myth that Kentucky was a hunting ground and pass-through for native peoples, but not a dwelling place. Seeds discovered at the site support the idea not only that people lived there, but that they cultivated several original crops, including sunflowers and sumpweed for oil, and goosefoot (a relative of quinoa), maygrass, erect knotweed, giant ragweed, amaranth, and little barley as starches.

They also cultivated indigenous squash, which still regularly graces our tables. Squash is the utility infielder of ancient crops. It could be bred to produce fleshy, soft-skinned summer squash or thick-skinned, vitamin-rich winter squash that could be stored through much of the cold season. Or it could be cut and dried. Its flowers and seeds are edible—the seeds by themselves, or ground to provide a thickening and flavoring for soup and stews. Hard-skinned squash with little flesh became gourds that could be hollowed out and dried to serve as bowls, dippers, and storage containers. Squash seeds and rind fragments found in eastern Kentucky date to about 3,700 years ago.

By the time Europeans first arrived in the Appalachians in the 1500s, squash was also being used as an agricultural tool. While the term was not necessarily used by all Native American tribes, the Three Sisters concept of companion planting was practiced widely, including by the tribes of the southern mountains. Corn, which evidence suggests came into the food chain about 1,400 years ago but was possibly grown and used for rituals some 400 years earlier, had become the primary "grain" for native peoples. Its stalks made a trellis for the climbing beans that were planted with it, providing nitrogen for the soil and making a complete, more usable protein when eaten with the corn. The squash plant spread out below, its broad leaves providing shade for the soil and a deterrent to weeds, its bright flowers serving as a distraction for some insects.

Beans and cornbread figure large in the stories of Appalachia, while squash—like many of the multitude of other fresh vegetables grown in mountain gardens—gets less press. But virtually all Appalachian cooks have a version of the summer squash casserole, flavored with minced onion, dotted with butter or bacon grease, seasoned with plenty of salt and pepper, and baked hot and quickly alongside a skillet of cornbread. And in the mountains, affection is keen for winter squash varieties not commonly found elsewhere.

Accounts from early adventurers into the region commonly refer to all winter squash as "pumpkin," but older mountain folks were more inclined to use actual pumpkins as jack-o'-lanterns and to feast on the likes of cushaws and Candy Roasters. Research indicates that the green-and-white-striped cushaw was first domesticated in Mesoamerica and moved up through the Southwest, where it's still a primary domestic food crop, and across the Mississippi into the Appalachian foodshed, much as corn did. Cushaw became a beloved crop across that stretch of the South, most certainly including the southern mountains. Cushaws are close kin to pumpkin in flavor, but are mellower, without that slightly brackish edge. When cooked, the flesh has an earthy quality that makes it a good pairing with meats, especially game.

The Candy Roaster squash is so named for its marvelous sweet taste. It has a creamy-textured flesh more akin to a sweet potato than a pumpkin, and it has a more specific history than the cushaw. Until seeds began to be sold and spread farther afield recently, it had been found only in regions where the Cherokee are known to have lived in western North Carolina, eastern Tennessee, and northern Georgia, suggesting that it might well be an original Appalachian cultivar. The squash was prized because it can withstand winter frost and improves in flavor as it is stored. Like the cushaw, the Candy Roaster has been designated a food worth saving by the Slow Food USA Ark of Taste.

Roasted Candy Roaster or Cushaw Squash

SERVES 2

Both the Candy Roaster and the cushaw squash varieties range from large (10 pounds) to very large (20 to 25 pounds), with some Candy Roasters reaching ginormous (250 pounds!) proportions. Unless you have a very large family, you'll want to select a squash at the smaller end of the spectrum.

Each is delicious as a side dish, simply cut into pieces, roasted, and served with butter and maybe a drizzle of sorghum syrup. You can eat your fill, then puree the rest and freeze it in small portions for baking pies, making soup (use your favorite pumpkin soup recipe), or using in any way you might use a puree of sweet potato, pumpkin, or winter squash.

The Candy Roaster will intensify in flavor and density of flesh the longer you store the fresh squash. It can keep several months in a cool, dry, dark place.

1 pound of squash will serve 2 or make about ½ cup puree

Preheat the oven to 425°F.

Cut the squash in half, or in quarters if it is particularly large, and remove the seeds and stringy fibers from the cavity.

Lay the cut pieces of the squash on a baking sheet, flesh side up so that much of the juice will be caught in the cavity. Roast until the flesh is easily pierced with a fork. This can take 30 to 60 minutes, depending on the age of the squash, the thickness of its flesh, and the size of the pieces. It's okay if the surface browns a little, caramelizing, but if it starts to get too dark before the squash is tender, cover it loosely with aluminum foil.

You can serve these pieces, warm from the oven, with butter and sorghum syrup drizzled over them, and/or you can make a puree.

To make a puree: Allow the squash to cool, reserving any juice. Then scoop the soft flesh from the skin and puree it, in batches if necessary, in a blender, adding the reserved juice if needed.

Freeze the pureed squash in 1- and ½-cup portions in freezer bags with all the air pressed out. These keep well in the freezer up to a year.

Candy Roaster (or Cushaw) Pie

MAKES ONE 10-INCH PIE

The marked tanginess of the buttermilk and sorghum syrup, along with the distinct taste of the Candy Roaster or cushaw squash, take this to a whole new level than that occupied by plain old pumpkin pie. The flavor borders on savory. If you are using the less naturally sweet cushaw, you will want to increase the brown sugar by an additional ⅓ cup.

Because I make this for Thanksgiving, I use a 10-inch pie plate. If you are using a regular 9-inch plate, you may have filling left over. If you have any extra, it can be baked in a buttered ramekin to make a small custard treat.

Single unbaked pie crust (use your favorite recipe or
  ¼ batch of Emily Hilliard's Pie Crust, page 238)
1 cup whole buttermilk
½ cup sorghum syrup
2 large eggs, lightly beaten
⅓ cup (packed) light brown sugar
½ teaspoon ground allspice
½ teaspoon ground cinnamon
¼ teaspoon salt
1½ cups pureed Roasted Candy Roaster or Cushaw
  Squash (opposite)
Whipped cream, for serving (optional)

Preheat the oven to 350°F. Place the crust in a 10-inch pie pan and refrigerate it while you are making the filling.

In a large bowl, whisk together the buttermilk, syrup, and eggs until fully blended.

In a small bowl, combine the brown sugar, allspice, cinnamon, and salt. Whisk the sugar mixture into the buttermilk. Add the squash puree and mix to fully blend.

Pour the filling into the chilled pie crust, leaving about ½ inch of space at the top (do not overfill). Place the pie plate on the center rack in the oven and bake for 1 hour, until the center is no longer liquid but still a little soft.

Transfer the pie plate to a cooling rack and allow the pie to come to room temperature before serving. You can put whipped cream on it if you like, but it's awfully good on its own.

King Daddy's Cracklin Waffles with Candied Candy Roaster

MAKES ABOUT FOUR 7-INCH ROUND BELGIAN "DEEP POCKET" WAFFLES OR ABOUT EIGHT 4-INCH-SQUARE "DEEP POCKET" BELGIAN WAFFLES

John and Julie Stehling opened the Early Girl Eatery in downtown Asheville in 2002 and had an instant hit with their inventive regional cooking and friendly service. Julie became a key supporter of the region's Appalachian Sustainable Agriculture Project, while John combed the back roads for farm stands offering distinctive regional foods that he could put on the menu. Early Girl is where I had my first taste of Candy Roaster squash, and the couple's latest eatery, King Daddy's Chicken & Waffle in West Asheville, is where I enjoyed it most recently in this perfect blend of spicy, bacony, and sweet. The waffles are delicious on their own, as well. You can make the candied Candy Roaster ahead of time.

¾ pound bacon, finely minced

1½ tablespoons Cajun Salt (recipe follows), or to taste

2 cups all-purpose flour

2 tablespoons baking powder

2 tablespoons sugar

¾ teaspoon salt

2 large eggs, separated

8 tablespoons (1 stick) unsalted butter, melted and cooled

1¾ cups plus 2 tablespoons whole milk

¼ teaspoon vanilla extract

Oil or cooking spray, for greasing the waffle iron

Candied Candy Roaster (recipe follows), for serving

Preheat the oven to 250°F.

Divide the minced bacon between two large skillets so that it can spread out in a single layer. (Alternatively, fry it in two batches in one large skillet.) Set the skillets over medium-low heat and cook, stirring occasionally, until the bacon is crisp and the fat has been rendered. Use a slotted spoon to transfer the bacon to a paper-towel-lined plate and let it drain. Then toss the bacon with the 1½ tablespoons of Cajun Salt. You should have about 1 cup of seasoned cracklins.

Mix the flour, baking powder, sugar, and salt together in a large mixing bowl. In a separate bowl, whisk the egg yolks with the butter, milk, and vanilla. Pour the egg yolk mixture into the flour mixture and stir to combine.

Preheat a waffle iron.

Beat the egg whites in a large bowl until medium peaks form. Fold the egg whites into the batter. Stir in the prepared cracklins.

Lightly grease the hot waffle iron. Pour in enough batter to just coat the waffle grid. Close the lid and let the waffle cook until it is golden and crisp, about 3 minutes. Place the cooked waffle on a baking sheet and keep it in the warm oven while you cook the rest. Serve with Candied Candy Roaster.

CAJUN SALT
MAKES ABOUT ⅔ CUP

2¼ teaspoons fennel seed
1 tablespoon ground cumin
2¼ teaspoons ground mustard
3 tablespoons smoked sweet Spanish paprika
2 tablespoons freshly ground black pepper
1 tablespoon salt
1 tablespoon crushed red pepper flakes
1 garlic clove

Heat a skillet over medium heat. Throw the fennel seed into the skillet and toast, shaking the pan, until fragrant, about 2 minutes. Set aside to cool.

Combine the cooled toasted fennel seed with the ground cumin and mustard in the bowl of a food processor fitted with the blade attachment. Let the spices whirl for about 30 seconds, and then add the remaining ingredients. Allow the processor to run for about 1 minute to blend together. Store, tightly covered, in the fridge. This is a great seasoning for grilled fish and meats, and is pretty tasty on popcorn.

CANDIED CANDY ROASTER
MAKES ABOUT 2 CUPS

You can make the Candied Candy Roaster a day or two before you plan to use it; just put the fully cooled pieces in a tightly sealed container with waxed paper between the layers. It's also yummy served as a relish alongside pork, or plopped on top of either of the versions of Old-Style Vanilla Ice Cream (page 96). For information on roasting and using the rest of the Candy Roaster, which can grow quite large, see page 168.

Butter or oil, for greasing the pan
1 cup powdered sugar
1 teaspoon salt
¼ cup maple syrup
3 cups cubed flesh of Candy Roaster or other winter squash (¾-inch cubes)

Preheat the oven to 400°F. Grease a jelly roll pan or rimmed baking sheet.

Use a fork to blend together the powdered sugar, salt, and maple syrup in a large bowl, making a thick glaze. Add the cubed squash and stir to coat the pieces thoroughly. Spread the squash pieces out on the prepared jelly roll pan, leaving a little space between them so they don't clump together. Bake for about 35 minutes, turning the pieces over every 10 minutes, until the squash is tender and just beginning to caramelize a little around the edges.

Use a spatula to remove the squash from the pan and transfer it to a parchment-lined tray to cool. When it is at room temperature, carefully lift it off.

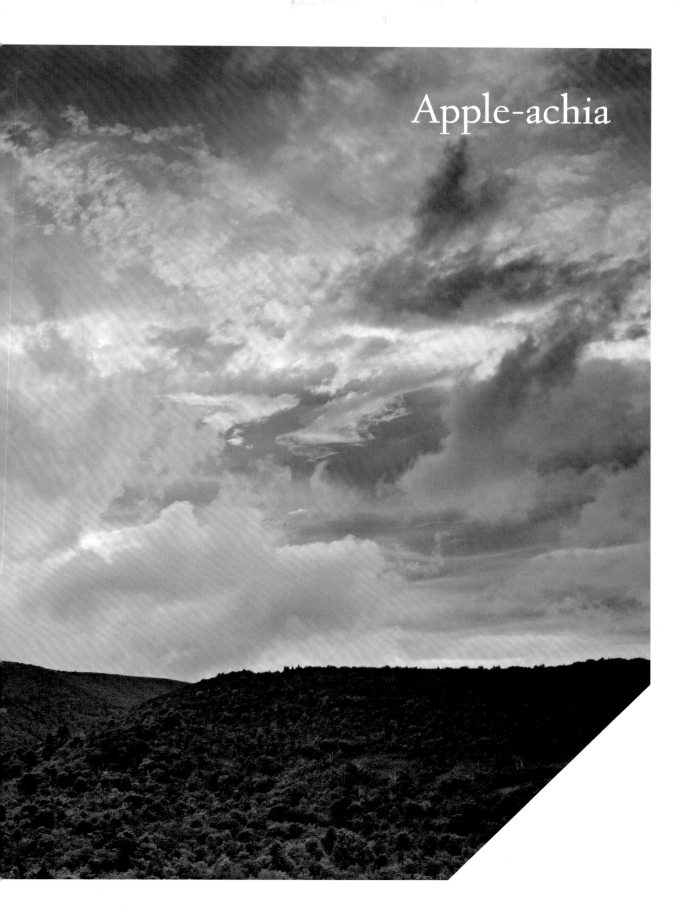

Apple-achia

My friend Barbara Nussdorfer-Eblen is a lyrical artist, so the photo she posts on Facebook in early July has a painterly cast. The apple tree in her side yard bows gracefully low, bearing globes of pale rosy yellow. The gray-columned birdbath nearby is surrounded by a stand of purple-blooming hostas. Between bath and tree are "golden apples in a silver dish like the moon," a friend of Barbara's writes. Barbara responds, "Pristine apples almost ready."

Nine days later, her message is a terse "Overrun by apples . . . !" Barbara has baked two generous pies and bagged six gallon-size freezer bags of applesauce. The photo shows them on a counter with three big dough bowls filled with more fresh apples piled to precarious peaks. "They're still coming," she says.

Now it happens that I have, in my living room, a pair of old wooden screen doors, each measuring six-and-a-half by three feet. I found them at a local resale shop and intended to use them one day to dry apples and green beans in my living room. It occurs to me that that day is here. I write to Barbara and drive down to Hendersonville. Henderson County is the largest apple-producing county in North Carolina, which in turn is the seventh-largest apple-producing state in the U.S. There are two hundred commercial apple growers in Henderson and plenty of U-pick or pick-up orchards, and as I drive into town I notice that Barbara and her husband, Gary, are not the only folks with a tree or three gracing their yard.

We take the screens from the back of my Chevy Astro. Before we even go inside, we fill three grocery bags with apples that have fallen since morning and put them in the van to go home with me. "Are you sure that's all you want?" Barbara asks. I sense a little desperation in her voice.

The sweet warm scent of the apples under the tree brings back a memory of long summer afternoons on the porch swing with my great-aunt Johnnie, her voice tender and curious as she showed me birds landing in the trees, told me their names, made up stories. She asked me if I had a boyfriend yet, and at the age of five, I took my lack of one seriously. She sang songs and made jokes, and even when she was simply talking, there was always a hint of laughter in her voice. I remember also that her hands never stopped

moving. She held a sharp, small paring knife and deftly, in rhythm with the swing, would quarter the small, misshapen yellow-green globes she'd gathered that morning and that sat around us now in bushel baskets. She cut out blemishes and worm holes, throwing the scraps to the yard where the birds convened. She didn't peel the apples. She pared slices from the quarters and let them drop into her ample apron. When the apron was filled, we'd pause and walk to the screen porch where the round oak table had been stretched to oblong with its extra leaves. A sheet covered its top, and as our day progressed, apple slices began to cover the sheet, drying in the breeze. We would walk back to the front porch, maybe stopping in the kitchen to get ourselves a cool glass of iced tea.

The last mess of apples Johnnie pared in the afternoon were "fried" in butter and brown sugar for supper that night. If the day was cool, she made applesauce or apple jelly instead of drying. She worked on those apples until the tree was done bearing, and we counted our luck in the fried pies her older sister Minnie would make, or the apple stack cakes made by her younger, my great-aunt Rae.

Barbara and I carry the screens up the stairs to the light-infused attic where she has her studio. Two sawhorses sit amid the art supplies and we lay one screen across them. We'll lay apple slices on that screen, close but not touching, and then lay the other screen over it to keep out curious cats and flies.

Back down to her cozy kitchen, we make tea and quickly weigh the merits of peeling or not peeling. Not peeling makes the paring time quicker, but the apples take longer to dry and longer to rehydrate when cooking. Plus some peels just don't rehydrate tenderly enough. We decide on peeling, and Barbara gets down a huge soup pot to catch our scraps and boil them to make pectin, a natural gelling substance. Our forebears would have used this for apple and other jellies. Barbara wants to strain hers and add it to her daily fruit juice because pectin is supposed to be healing for arthritis.

We talk and laugh, share stories of our children and our wilder years. We consider the costs and benefits of writing and art. She asks if I've been seeing anyone and I realize that at sixty-five, I take the lack of a boyfriend rather delightedly. Soon we have a pot full of peels and two big bowls full of slices. We merrily spread the slices on the screen upstairs—until we realize we've not covered it by half. Downstairs, there are still a few more mountains of apples. In all, it takes us more than two hours to fill the screen. We peel and slice close to ten pounds. And still there are apples.

"Do you have a Crock-Pot?" I ask. Yes. We keep peeling and paring, this time for apple butter. Soon the pectin is simmering, the spiced butter is bubbling, the kitchen smells like Paradise. After all, Eve did eat that apple.

————

Sheepnose, Limbertwig, Jellyflower Sweet.

Summer Rambo, Winter John, Crow's Egg, Bart.

Flat Head Fallawater, Zesty Z . . . I could go on. And on. And on.

Apples are one of those cultivars that distinguish the southern Appalachians from the rest of the South. Of course apples are grown deeper down in Dixie, but the medium to high humidity, temperate summers, and cold crisp autumns of the mountains provide an ideal environment for growing them, while the cold winter's chill creates natural refrigeration for keeping them. Those long, cold winters also once fostered a need, a longing, for the taste of fresh fruit in the days before supermarkets.

In his encyclopedic *Old Southern Apples*, Creighton Lee Calhoun Jr. tells the story of a backwoods farmer late one winter clearly relishing a Ben Davis, an apple known for making a fine preserve but not much for flavor or zip when eaten out of hand. A "city feller" who was visiting and knowledgeable of apple varieties asked how he mustered up so much gusto over an inferior fruit. "Well, I'll tell ye," the mountain man said, "it sure beats eating snowballs."

Estimates say that at one time between 1,000 and 1,600 different varieties of apples flourished in the southern and central Appalachians, fairly astonishing numbers for a fruit that was not native other than a handful of crabapples. Colonists brought small trees, scions, and seeds from Europe. A scion is a cutting from an existing variety that can be grafted to another in a tricky and labor-intensive process. The tree that grows from the graft will bear apples with identical characteristics to those of the parent fruit, but a tree grown from seed may bear fruit that varies widely from its parent. (Interestingly, seeds even from the same apple will often produce different varieties when planted.) The apple orchards planted from seed in the early years of settlement propagated a remarkable range of varieties.

In 2011 the staff of Renewing America's Food Traditions identified more than six hundred distinct apple varieties still grown in the southern and central Appalachians, inspiring team leader Gary Nabhan to dub the region "Apple-achia." Regional "apple hunters" say there are assuredly even more. Long-abandoned mountain homesteads still often have an extant stand or single tree, and these hunters search for such to identify and bring those apples back into circulation.

Tom Brown, of Clemmons, North Carolina, is such an apple hunter. Tom started looking for heirloom apples—those over one hundred years old—in 1999. He saw his work as a race against time. Development—industrial, commercial, and residential—was destroying the old orchards that once marked rural homesteads. And the older folks, whose memories of apple varieties Tom depended on, were disappearing as well. Even so, on his website, www.applesearch.org, Tom notes that he has personally discovered more than a thousand heritage apple varieties from original trees, and that in the mountains a family might pride itself on having a variety distinctly different from that of the neighbors. His work has taken him all over the country, but Tom told me, "Ninety percent of my apples were found in the states of North Carolina, Tennessee, Virginia, West Virginia, and Kentucky. And that's just my work, not counting the finds of others. There were incredibly more apple varieties here than anyone has ever imagined."

Along the way, Tom has collected some priceless stories as well. An elderly Haywood County, North Carolina, woman told him how her father took the family's apples to South Carolina to sell each year and did well with their Hoover apples . . . until the Great Depression. Suddenly no one would buy those Hoovers, so he started calling them Black Winesaps, and business picked right up again.

Jack Dellinger (see page 110) showed me the apple storage shed his grandfather built, large as a two-car garage, right next to the Dellinger corn mill. "Grandpa Dave was a genius. Could do anything in the world. Around here he was a doctor, dentist, a veterinarian. When he heard the railroad was coming, he bought a sawmill. One day, about 1914, when the mills weren't doing much business, he sawed up a bunch of wood and built an apple storage house. He made two walls, an inside one and an outside one, and poured sawdust between to make insulation. Made all the bins inside out of chestnut. You can't imagine how delicious it smelled in winter inside those insulated walls."

In mountain households, winter smelled like apples.

––––––––

Those early mountain orchards were not entirely about eating, of course. The spread of European apples across the mountain South was primarily aimed at creating cider. Colonists drank cider instead of the New World's water, of which they were initially suspicious. Mountain settlers planted orchards and made cider—fresh and hard—to drink and as a cash crop. As with corn, the liquid product was worth its weight in gold, worth more in the market than the fruit itself. Applejack was the name for the prized apple brandy, made more concentrated by setting it out to freeze in winter, then scooping off and discarding the water that froze on the top, leaving an intense brew underneath. How intense? Joe Dabney tells a story in *Mountain Spirits*: A young man from Sugar Valley in the Georgia mountains told Joe, "My uncle's pickup truck smelled a little like rotten apples and I asked him what he had in there. He had some apple brandy and offered me a drink. I guzzled it down like moonshine," he recalled, "and *damn*, I must have farted fire!" The boy had grown up on corn whiskey.

We have no idea what Thomas Jefferson might have thought of such results, but we do know that Jefferson deemed cider-making a significant art and planted experimental orchards to test new varieties at Monticello. Apples from Jefferson's orchards were propagated all across the mountain South. Cider-making flourished, as did trade in apples for eating and cooking, but with the advent of refrigerated train cars in the early 1900s, the apple market began to shift. Large commercial orchards started to dominate, offering increasingly cheaper and cheaper apples bred for color, shape, tough skins for shipping, and long shelf life. The astonishing variety in taste and texture of fresh apples faded into memory. Cider went flat.

But could it be that the apple worm is ready to turn again?

That certainly seemed a strong possibility to a lively panel on mountain apples at the 2015 Appalachian Food Summit in Abingdon, Virginia. The conference theme was "Revival," and the panel explored how apple orchards might be a part of a culinary economic revival in the region. Moderator Amelia Kirby discussed her work with long-time Appalachian political activist Helen Lewis, trying to convince coal companies to invest reclamation money in reintroducing orchards on strip-mined land. Anthony Slone shared his film on a multigenerational family orchard, underscoring the cultural significance of apples in the region. Foggy Ridge Cider owner Diane Flynt limned the commercial possibilities and difficulties of the contemporary cider industry. And Richmond-based chef Travis Milton, who grew up in Wise County, Virginia, echoed those political, traditional, and economic motivations. But for Travis, apples are also personal.

———————

"You say it 'hur-ruh-kin,' not '-cane,'" Travis Milton advises me one late August afternoon as he takes me on a sharp winding trip up a Wise County mountain two-lane. We're

six-acre North Orchard at Monticello with remarkable historical accuracy, including reintroducing the Hewes Crab Apple, a native Virginia variety beloved by cider-makers. An apple hunter himself, he is credited with finding the Harrison, another prized cider apple, and one that Flynt planted and uses in the mix of varieties she and Chuck selected to create their distinctive blends. Foggy Ridge has been winning awards and accolades for the past decade, and Flynt says she sees her niche among the audience for fine wines. Other recent cideries in the region, such as Asheville's Urban Orchard, are looking for a seat at the bar in the burgeoning craft brewery scene. Urban Orchard maintains a tasting room on the edge of the hip West Asheville neighborhood, with a small rotating selection of their ciders on tap and the pressing room below.

Flynt not only grows heirloom apples, and the two Toms, Brown and Burford, not only find them. All have in a sense become evangelists, actively encouraging others in the region to reclaim old orchards or plant newer ones with heirloom stock. When Tom Brown discovered the Junaluska apple that was said to be the favorite of the legendary Cherokee chief, he grafted and donated trees to the Junaluska memorial and gravesite near Robbinsville, North Carolina, and also donated Junaluska trees to the Western Band of the Cherokee in Oklahoma. And Brown has contributed both knowledge and scions to heritage apple orchards in the region, such as Big Horse Creek Farm in Lansing, North Carolina. Flynt not only encourages other mountain farmers to cultivate orchards of cider stock, she supports them by buying from them for Foggy Ridge. And Tom Burford has traveled the country preaching the pleasures of this heirloom fruit and is the author of the apostolic *Apples of North America: Exceptional Varieties for Gardeners, Growers, and Cooks*. It may be working. Burford, noting that it takes from five to seven years for a new apple tree to mature and bear fruits, says that currently "the demand for heirloom apples is outstripping our ability to supply."

Much of this is on Travis Milton's mind as he shakes his head over the olive-choked strip mine site. Travis notes that the market isn't theoretical; Diane has told him that if he can reestablish the orchards, she can use the cider apples they grow or help find other cider makers to buy them. A viable market for heirloom apples strengthens the case that Amelia Kirby and Helen Lewis have been making to the coal industry. Helen, a leader in the field of Appalachian studies and a longtime activist in the region's coal country, began working to revive Wise County's apple economy as far back as 1955. Now in her nineties, Helen sees this moment as a potent one. "This is a time with a lot of potential," she says. "We might even be able to get some of the mining companies to give back

the land now that they've exhausted it for what they can use. Maybe even put up some money to reestablish old orchards. It would be good press, and they sure could use some of that," she says, her eyes twinkling.

There's more to it than just getting the property back and planting trees, of course. The soil itself would have to be reestablished after the ravages of stripping. And an heirloom orchard requires a lot of workers. Travis and the others have talked about the idea of involving a college in the reclamation of The Hurricane, of making it a laboratory for students who would then provide the hard-to-find manpower needed to keep an orchard healthy and thriving. It's not unprecedented. In 2011 the Browning family of Wallingford, in eastern Kentucky—whose century-old orchard was celebrated in third-generation heir Frank Browning's elegant 1998 book, *Apples*—gave the property to nearby Morehead State University, which uses it now as a hands-on classroom for budding orchardists.

"It's a lot of pieces that would have to come together. It's not quite a miracle that's needed, but it's close," Travis says as he shakes his head again and turns. I'm walking behind him as we pick our way back to the car, the sun beating hot on this land that was once covered in fruit-bearing trees. Suddenly his arm shoots out to stop me—the left one, with the Hewes Crab Apple tattooed near his shoulder. "I can't believe it," he whispers, and I peek around him. I see only more scrub and a scraggly thicket of nondescript trees. And then I make out, in their midst, the familiar gnarly trunk and limbs, dotted with a handful of hiding apples.

Travis scruffs through the underbrush, pushes aside branches, reaches up, plucks a fruit, brings it to his nose, sniffs, and grins. He displays it to me proudly. A Ralls Janet. Or Rawle's Genet. Or Royal Janette or Rock Remain or any of some two dozen other names for this apple, tender and aromatic, one-half the parentage of the modern Fuji. Most likely originating in the orchard of Caleb Ralls of Amherst County, Virginia, in the mid-century, but also rumored to be an immigrant from France, the Ralls Janet has a history as multilayered as its greenish, then goldish, then pink and russet–striped skin.

But Travis is thinking of none of this as his eyes shine and he says, "Holy . . . I can't believe . . . I mean . . . this is my great-granddad's apple. Right here."

The Art of Apple Butter

The secret to making rich apple butter—dark as sable, thick as pudding, and deeply fragrant—is to cook the apples very low and very slow. In pioneer days, this was done outside in a large cast-iron pot over an open fire, the apples stirred with a wooden "spoon" that could have stood duty as a small boat's oar. Children took turns stirring as the pot cooked all day, and sometimes until the stars came out. Sometimes communities would have an apple stir-off, where everyone came together for the process, now replicated at apple festivals around the mountains come fall.

When the butter was finished, the cook would dip it into crocks to be covered and kept in a springhouse or other cool place, although it wouldn't last long. Those same helpful children would eagerly eat their reward, spread on biscuits and cornbread, sandwiched between the layers of stack cakes, or used to ice a quick single-layer cake for supper.

The advent of gas stoves moved the process inside, although this necessitated the cooking of apple butter in batches, so it didn't really make the process any easier. Then along came the Crock-Pot, modern apple butter's very best friend. With a 6-quart slow cooker you can now cook down 5 to 6 pounds of apples to make 3 to 4 pints of apple butter while you're sleeping. It takes 10 to 12 hours, so you have time to read or play a little music before bed and then wake up to the smell of warm apple butter for brunch.

Start by peeling, coring, and chunking the apples into 1-inch pieces. Place them in the slow cooker, set it on high uncovered, and cook for an hour. Then turn the temperature to low, cover the pot, and come back a whole lot later to see how things are going—8 to 10 hours later is about right. They'll lose at least a third of their volume in the process. So when they have, and when they break and crumble when you poke them with a fork, taste and add sweetening and spice (see opposite), and give it all a good stir. Then turn the heat back up to high and cook, covered, for 1 hour more. Taste and adjust the spices, then mash the apples with a hand potato masher, or puree them with an immersion blender right in the pot, or run the mixture through a food processor or blender to make a velvety butter.

You can put the butter up in hot sterilized jars, following the jar manufacturer's directions. Or if you go through apple butter quickly, you can simply put it up in clean jars and store them in the fridge, where they should keep for 6 to 8 weeks.

There seem to be as many ways to sweeten and spice apple butter as there are varieties of apples. Some apples are spicy, some are tart, some are sugary, and most are a mix and then some. Cooking will intensify the flavors, but also sometimes change them. Some cooks prefer to put the spices and sugar in up front to let them mingle and marry through the whole cooking process—my pal Sheri Castle does, and she makes one fine apple butter—but I like to wait and see, to taste the pureed apples and consider what a particular season's butter might call for. Here are some themes and variations for you to consider. Use them as is, or as a starting point to wing out on your own.

SHERI CASTLE'S VINEGAR KISS: For 5½ pounds of peeled and cored apples, use 3 cups sugar, 3 teaspoons ground cinnamon, ½ teaspoon ground mace, ½ teaspoon ground cardamom, ¼ teaspoon ground cloves, ½ teaspoon ground allspice, and ½ teaspoon kosher salt. Cook as described opposite, but just before mashing or blending, add 2 to 3 tablespoons unfiltered organic apple cider vinegar. Trust Sheri. The vinegar rocks it.

IMLADRIS FARMS APPLE BUTTER: Walter Harrill's proprietary blend sells like hotcakes every fall. For about every 5½ pounds of apple chunks, Walter adds 2 cups of sugar, and just before the final hour adds a generous teaspoon of cinnamon and ½ teaspoon each of ground nutmeg and cloves—more to taste if desired. Walter believes that variety is key in choosing the apples, and that will have more impact on the final flavor than any blend of spices. He recommends you use at least 3 different apples in each batch and select them to get a balance of sweet, tart, and aromatic. Galas, Granny Smiths, and Golden Delicious from the grocery will do for base apples, but he urges you to seek out local growers and add an heirloom or three to the mix. "And tell folks to not be afraid of Red Delicious," he adds. "If they come across a good price for a bushel, snatch it up. It makes great compost, and then you can go find a real apple to make real apple butter."

LUNDY'S SPLASH: I like to put a bit of Kentucky twist on at least one jar out of the slow cooker, adding a splash of good bourbon. You know, for the grown-ups' biscuits. (You can take out most of the finished apple butter from the cooker and just spike the last jar's worth.) One year I cooked up an especially floral-tasting batch of butter that seemed to call for cardamom, ginger, and coriander rather than cinnamon. I hit it with a shot of Southern Comfort and that went down just fine.

Fried Apples SERVES 4 AS A SIDE DISH

Apples were so plentiful in the mountain South that it's fair to say there was not a single table that wasn't graced with this delicious dish on a regular basis. Apples were so diverse in variety in the region, and in taste from orchard to orchard, that most cooks tasted first and then added and adjusted the sweetening to harmonize with the apple's flavor. I suggest you taste and then imagine if the particular apple you have would dance better with the dusky umami of sorghum syrup, the lighter tones of brown sugar, or the pure sweet notes of maple syrup.

4 medium apples
1 tablespoon bacon grease or butter
2 tablespoons sorghum or maple syrup, or
   ¼ cup light (packed) brown sugar

Quarter the apples, remove the cores, and slice the apple quarters ⅛ inch thick, slicing them the long way.

In a skillet or sauté pan with a lid, melt the bacon grease over medium heat. Add the apples and toss lightly to coat. Cover and let sweat for 3 minutes. Then remove the lid and add your chosen sweetening, tossing lightly again to coat.

Continue cooking uncovered for a few more minutes, until the apples are tender and the juice has been absorbed to make a light glaze. Set the pan aside to let the apples rest for a few minutes before serving.

Fried Pies MAKES 1 DOZEN HAND PIES

I once shared my great-aunt Minnie's recipe for fried apple pies with a very wonderful food magazine whose editorial department fretted that they were just too plain. Could we add spices? they asked. Or glaze them? I maintained those were things no mountain cook would do. How about confectioners' sugar, then? Nope. Raisins? I said I'd never known anyone to put raisins in a fried pie, and bless their hearts, they asked me if I knew for *certain* that no one ever had. To which I answered honestly, no, and they sighed with relief and made raisins "optional." But people, they're not.

It occurred to me as I wrote about mountain apples that the problem may have been with the apples the magazine folks were using. Commercially dried apples from commercially grown fruit would have a lot less zip than those tart but sweet small green apples my great-aunt Johnnie dried each year and Minnie used for her fried pies. And mountain cooks will tell you not to bother with drying apples from the grocery store, which are still bred more for cosmetics and staying power than flavor. Short of drying my own, I have good luck with unsulfured organic apples from the health food store. I look for apples that are rosy brown and still have some flex in them. Brittle dehydrated apples don't cook up as nicely. The same is true for dried peaches. But with the right fruit, sweetened with sorghum and fried in lard, well, you just don't need anything more.

2¼ cups all-purpose flour, plus more for dusting
1 teaspoon kosher salt
½ teaspoon baking powder
¾ cup skim milk, warmed until steaming
½ cup lard or solid vegetable shortening, chilled and
   diced
2 cups unsulfured dried apples or peaches
⅓ to ½ cup sorghum syrup
Lard or an oil with a high smoke point, such as
   peanut, for frying

(recipe continues)

In a medium bowl, mix the flour with the salt and baking powder. In a large bowl, combine the milk with the lard and stir until most of the lard is melted but there are a few pea-sized pieces left. Add the flour mixture and use a fork to blend until a dough forms. Gather the dough and knead it on a lightly floured surface until smooth. Roll the dough into a 6-inch-long log, wrap it in plastic wrap, and refrigerate until chilled, at least 2 hours.

Meanwhile, combine the dried fruit with 2 cups of water in a medium saucepan and bring to a boil. Cover, and cook over low heat, stirring occasionally and adding water as needed, until the fruit is very soft and the liquid has been absorbed, about 45 minutes.

Remove the pan from the heat. Mash the fruit a bit with a potato masher, and then add ⅓ cup of the sorghum and mash together until fully blended. Taste, and add more sorghum if desired, stirring to incorporate it fully. Allow the filling to cool to room temperature. (This can be refrigerated until you are ready to fry the pies, but bring it back to room temperature before you do.)

Remove the dough from the refrigerator. Remove the plastic wrap, cut the log into 12 equal pieces, and roll each piece into a ball. Working with half of the balls at a time (store the others in the fridge), roll out each ball on a very lightly floured surface to form a 6-inch round. Brush the edges with water. Mound

2 tablespoons of the apple filling on the lower half of each round. Fold the dough over the filling to make a half-moon, leaving a ½-inch border, and press the edges together to seal. Using a lightly floured fork, crimp the edges. Transfer the pies to a large, lightly floured baking sheet and repeat with the remaining balls of dough and filling. Note that you want to be sure to seal the pies well so no filling slips into the hot grease, which would cause it to pop and splatter. I use a bit of cold water on my fingers to secure the seal, making sure it dries before frying.

In a wide, heavy skillet over medium-high heat, heat enough lard to make a pool about ½ inch deep. When it's hot enough that a tiny pinch of dough dropped in dances and turns golden, about 375°F, very carefully lay a few pies in the skillet (I use a metal spatula), making sure not to crowd the skillet. Fry the pies until the bottom turns golden, about 1 to 1½ minutes, and then turn them over and fry the other side. Remove, and drain on a wire rack set on top of some paper towels. Repeat until all the pies are fried.

Allow the pies to cool a bit before biting into one. These are so delicious as soon as they are cool enough to eat, but they are also good the next day. If you plan to keep some, allow them to cool completely and then store them in a tightly lidded container at room temperature.

Pork & Kraut in Cider Gravy with Noodles SERVES 4

This is another dish where braising for several hours turns an unheralded cut of meat into a rich, flavorful meat-studded sauce, this one with a sweet/sour tangy twist. Make this with a homemade or good-quality deli-style kraut for the fullest flavor. Drain, and if it's a long-strand kraut, chop it lightly. Pork butt steaks are thin chops, a little fatty with connective tissue and bone, which gives flavor. They are sometimes called "breakfast pork chops."

I use a slow cooker to make this, but if you prefer, you can cook the browned pork in a covered heavy Dutch oven at 275°F; just be sure to increase the water to ¾ cup. This is perfect accompanied by Fried Apples (page 189).

Salt and freshly ground black pepper
1 tablespoon bacon grease
4 pork butt steaks with bone, each about ½ inch thick (about 1 pound total)
1 teaspoon Dijon mustard
1 cup apple cider
½ tablespoon all-purpose flour
⅓ cup finely chopped sauerkraut
2 cups curly egg noodles

Salt and pepper the steaks on both sides.

Melt the bacon grease in a heavy skillet over medium-high heat. Add the meat, in batches if necessary, and brown it on both sides (this takes about 3 minutes per side). When the steaks are browned, lay them in a slow cooker set on high. Deglaze the skillet with ¼ cup of water and add this to the slow cooker. In a small bowl, stir the mustard into the cider until dissolved, and add this to the pot as well. Cover, and cook on high for about 3 hours, until the meat can be pulled apart easily with a fork. Taste, and add more salt if necessary, remembering that sauerkraut is also salty.

Remove the meat from the slow cooker. Transfer the juices to a separate bowl and place it in the refrigerator. When the meat is cool enough to handle, shred it into small pieces. Discard any gristle, pieces of fat, and bones. Set aside the shredded meat.

When the juices have chilled enough that the fat has risen and solidified on top, scrape it off, reserving a tablespoon to make a gravy-like broth. Reserve the defatted juices.

Melt the reserved tablespoon of fat in a large saucepan over medium-low heat. Sprinkle in the flour and stir steadily to make a light roux. Slowly add the reserved pan juices, still stirring so the flour doesn't lump. When the sauce begins to thicken, stir in the meat and add the sauerkraut. Cover and simmer over low heat for 8 to 10 minutes.

While you are heating the meat, cook the noodles according to the package directions.

Combine the noodles with the meat and sauce, and serve immediately.

Apple Stack Cake

MAKES ONE 5-LAYER CAKE

No dish is so emblematic of the mountain South as apple stack cake. Its ingredients are modest, but when its parts are assembled, it stands tall and proud. It requires patience, but it rewards with a subtle sweetness that is both complex and addicting.

Sorghum-scented stack cakes filled with layers of cooked apples show up only in Appalachia and the Ozarks and some scattered pockets of the west where Appalachians migrated. It appears to be a cake based on the Eastern European tradition of tortes with many thin layers glued together by a sweetened filling, and so it likely came to the region with the earliest immigrants from Germany. It reflects the pioneer spirit of converting something old into something totally new with the ingredients at hand. While European tortes were the purview of the rich and royalty—saturated with sugar, filled with egg, cream, fresh fruit, and expensive chocolate—the Appalachian stack cake is almost austere, embellished only with cooked dried apples and whatever sweetener was easily at hand.

Apples dried from tart but tasty heirlooms are superb, and that is what is used in the unsulfured dried apples I buy now from my local farm store in western North Carolina. You can also find good dried apples at a natural foods market. Commercial dried apples found in the grocery are often sugared or treated with preservatives, so I avoid them. Look for dried apple pieces that still have some tenderness and bend to them, and that are tan in color.

The recipe I offer here is based on that of my great-aunt Rae, who would make the cake for my father. I bake the layers one at a time in a cast-iron skillet because I like the ritual and don't own that many cake pans.

1 pound (about 5 cups) dried unsulfured apples
5 cups all-purpose flour, plus extra for dusting
1 teaspoon baking soda
½ teaspoon salt
⅔ cup butter, at room temperature
1 cup granulated sugar
1 cup sorghum syrup
2 large eggs, beaten
1 cup whole buttermilk
1 cup (packed) light brown sugar
½ teaspoon ground mace
Vegetable shortening or butter, for greasing the skillet

Start the filling first: Put the apples in a large, heavy saucepan or Dutch oven and add enough water to cover. Bring to a boil over high heat; then turn the heat down and simmer, stirring occasionally, until the apples are tender enough to mash with a potato masher. You may need to add a little more water to keep the apples from sticking, but you don't want the final mixture to be soupy. It will take about an hour for the apples to become tender, and during that time, you should make the dough and set it to chill.

To make the dough: In a large bowl, sift the 5 cups of flour with the baking soda and salt. In another large mixing bowl, cream the butter and granulated sugar enough to blend; then add the sorghum syrup and beat to blend. In a small bowl, blend the eggs and buttermilk. (Note that this recipe does not use baking powder, so buttermilk is necessary to activate the baking soda.)

Alternate adding the flour and egg mixtures to the butter mixture, stirring well to incorporate each addition. I find it's best to do this with a large wooden spoon so as not to overwork the dough. You want a soft ball that holds together. Cover the bowl and place it in the refrigerator to chill until it's time to bake.

When the apples are cooked, mash them and stir in the brown sugar and mace. The end result should be a thick puree with some little lumps no larger than a pea. If it is too runny, continue to cook it a bit, stirring until any liquid evaporates and it's the consistency of apple butter. Remove from the heat.

Preheat the oven to 350°F.

Prepare the pan: Liberally grease the inside of a 9-inch cast-iron skillet with shortening and sprinkle it with a tablespoon of flour, shaking and turning to coat the bottom of the skillet and about ⅛ inch up the sides.

Flour a flat surface for rolling and place the chilled dough ball on it. Using floured hands, roll the dough into a log about 10 inches long. Use a floured sharp knife to cut the log into five 2-inch-long pieces. Roll each piece lightly in the flour to make a ball. Pat one ball into a disk and put the others back in the refrigerator.

Place the disk in the greased and floured skillet, and pressing lightly with floured palm and fingers, flatten it evenly so it spreads out to just touch the edges of the pan all around. Don't pat too hard and don't press it up against the side of the pan, or it will stick. Prick the dough lightly with a fork.

Bake until the top is golden and the cake has pulled slightly away from the edges of the pan, about 15 minutes. The layer will not rise like a normal cake layer—it will look like a big cookie, only much more tender. Run a butter knife around the inside edge of the pan and gently nudge underneath the layer to loosen it. Turn the layer out onto a rack and allow it to cool for about 5 minutes. Then transfer the layer to a cake plate and spread some of the warm apple mixture over the top, right up to the edges. The apples should be about ¼ inch deep and you should use no more than a fourth of the mixture, perhaps less.

Allow the skillet to cool sufficiently to pat in the next layer of dough as before. Proceed, stacking each successive layer while warm and spreading it with the apple mixture. Leave the top layer bare, however.

Allow the cake to cool completely. Then wrap it very well in plastic wrap (use several layers) and allow it to "ripen" at room temperature for 2 to 3 days before slicing and serving.

Colin Perry's Sorghum & Apple Sticky Pudding SERVES 8 TO 10

Eastern Kentucky–born and –raised chef Colin Perry plies his art now in Montreal at Dinette Triple Crown. The food there taps into traditions of both the far North and the high country South, as in this delectably oh-so-sticky pudding. "I tend to use a lot of maple syrup in my cooking up here, because it's so delicious and so accessible. But sometimes the taste of sorghum is the only taste that will do," he says.

Really fresh leaf lard has become more available in recent years from artisan butchers and specialty stores. If you can't get real lard, then use butter. Shortening and grocery-store lard aren't worth it.

Colin serves this with vanilla ice cream and fried apples. I thought the pudding was divine on its own, but if you would like to go for broke, you can find the recipes here: Old-Style Vanilla Ice Cream on page 96 and Fried Apples on page 189.

¼ pound leaf lard, cut into large cubes, at room temperature, plus a little to grease the pan
1 cup (packed) light brown sugar
¾ cup plus 2 tablespoons all-purpose flour
¾ cup plus 1 tablespoon stone-ground white cornmeal
1 teaspoon baking powder
1 teaspoon baking soda
1 teaspoon salt
1½ tablespoons ground ginger
1½ teaspoons ground cinnamon
½ teaspoon freshly grated nutmeg
⅛ teaspoon ground cloves
1 cup apple butter (page 186)
1 cup whole buttermilk
2 tablespoons bourbon
2 large eggs
1 large egg yolk
1 cup sorghum syrup
½ cup heavy cream

Preheat the oven to 350°F. Grease a 10-inch round cake pan.

Place the lard and brown sugar in the bowl of a stand mixer fitted with the paddle attachment. Mix on low speed to combine, and then increase the speed to high to cream them together. Mix until the mixture becomes smooth and a very light brown, scraping down the sides of the bowl as needed; this takes about 20 minutes.

Meanwhile, whisk together the flour, cornmeal, baking powder, baking soda, salt, ginger, cinnamon, nutmeg, and cloves in a large bowl. In a separate large bowl, whisk together the apple butter, buttermilk, and bourbon.

Once the lard-sugar mixture is ready, reduce the speed to medium and add the eggs and egg yolk, one at a time, until incorporated. Add the flour mixture in thirds, alternating with the apple butter mixture, mixing only until the batter is smooth each time.

Pour the batter into the prepared cake pan and bake for 40 to 45 minutes, until a toothpick inserted in the center comes out dry. Turn out of the pan onto a rack to cool while you make the syrup.

Combine the sorghum and cream in a heavy-bottomed saucepan, and bring to a boil. Then reduce the heat to low and simmer for 10 minutes. Whisk until well blended.

Transfer the cake to a serving plate. Poke holes throughout the top of the cake with a fork, and slowly pour the syrup all over the cake until it has been absorbed. Serve slightly warm.

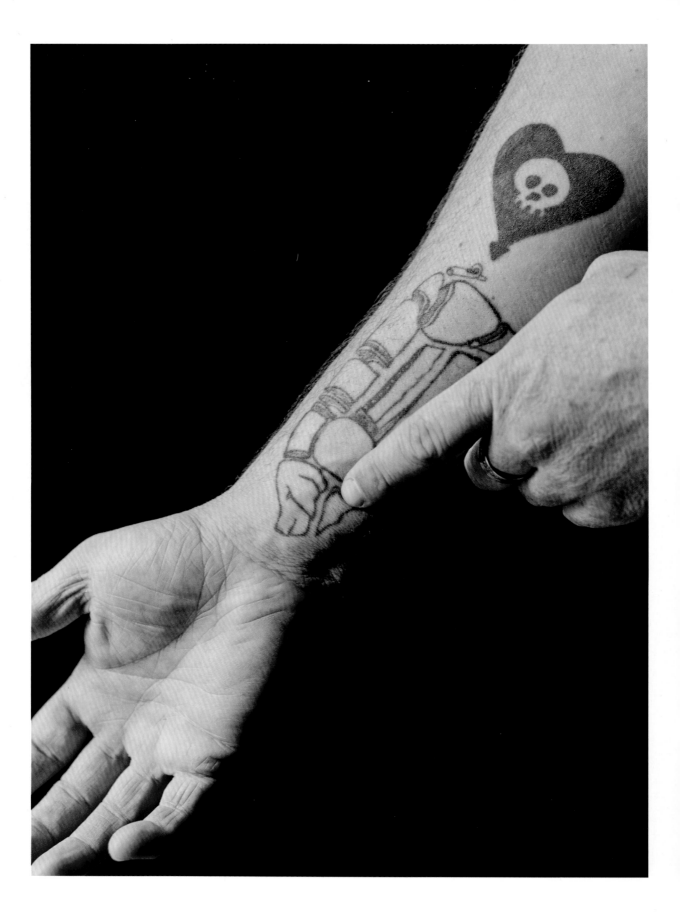

Travis's Tattoos

When I ask chef Travis Milton to parse for me the differences between fatback, white bacon, salt pork, and streak-of-lean, he rolls up his right sleeve. On the inside of his arm is a dark blue tattoo of a hog, its portions marked. Pointing his finger to the critter's chin, Travis begins: "Now right here is where you find your hog jowl."

Travis isn't the only kitchen professional with a pig up his sleeve. Once the mark of a short-order hash slinger with either a muddy or a military past, a tat or twelve these days is nearly as necessary for a top chef as is a keen knife.

Many chefs opt for a favorite ingredient, and Sean Brock—whose tats are immortalized on the cover of his best-selling cookbook, *Heritage*—sports an Appalachian garden on his left arm. He'll walk you through it pointing out an 18th-century pumpkin called the Winter Luxury, golden Cherokee Wax beans, his favorite radish, and six varieties of varicolored carrots.

Fruits and vegetables twine up Travis Milton's left arm as well, but there are other images, and if you ask, he will share the whole interwoven story.

At the base, around his wrist, a ring of faces, inked completely in black except for their piercing white eyes and the carbide lamps on their heads: "This is based on a Wes Freed illustration for the documentary Coal Country. I wanted miners here because everything that comes after is built on their backs. I wanted coal at the bottom of the story because this is my dream about what can rise from the ashes of coal. How a world after coal can be sustained by the land and by the food."

Above the miners, just inside the wrist, is a golden, plum-shaped tomato. "That's the Powers tomato, hybridized by my relatives on my dad's side from Scott County, Virginia, over a century ago. You can buy the seed now from Seed Savers Exchange.

"On the other side is where my greasy beans start topping out. And here's this beautiful watermelon radish. There was always a plate with fresh radishes, turnips, tomatoes, fresh green onions in the kitchen as long as they were in the garden. There'd be a plate on the table for the meal, a pitcher or glass with green onions sticking out.

"And then, on the back of my elbow, my great-grandfather Wheatley's favorite tomato, the German Johnson. One of the first things I realized when I started cooking in Richmond was that, to most people ten years ago, there was a tomato and that was it. For me, tomatoes had names and seasons and different colors and tastes, and back when I first got to Richmond, nobody knew what I was talking about when I'd ask for a German

Johnson. The world's changed a ton since then, but that was the moment when I knew my life, my culinary world, had not been like most of my peers."

Travis looks at that tomato for a moment before moving his finger up to where there are broad, rippling leaves and deep purple-red stalks. "Rhubarb," he says, almost sighing. "That was my favorite thing in the world. We'd go into the garden when I was a kid and I'd grab a stalk and chomp on it, all the while picking beans, weeding, planting. That's what I wanted. It was like candy to me. Still is.

"And then I have this tattoo of the patch from my great-grandfather, who I called Poppy, taken directly from his farm hat. Even when I came to Richmond, I would still go home every summer and work on the farm with him. I just wanted to hang out with him. If that meant running the cattle and shelling beans on the porch, I was in."

The tattoo patch reads "R&J Farms: Whole Hereford" and the actual hat now hangs by the door at Travis's house. Next is the seal of Wise County, where Travis was born. There's a shovel and a pick in the seal, and Shovel and Pick is the name he's chosen for his Appalachian restaurant in Richmond. "The men on both sides of my family, some of them were miners and a lot of them were farmers, so the shovel and pick are mine, too."

Near his shoulder is a cluster of Hewes Crab Apples in yellow-red so tart it makes your mouth water to look at it.

"That crab apple I love to death because my great-granddaddy Wheatley grew them. He was a master tree grafter. He quartered the tree in his yard so that four different apples would grow and there would always be one ripe and in season. He would use it for a lot of things, including wine, which he kept in little jars hidden around the house. We found them after he passed away—tucked in a drawer or hidden in a notch in a tree in the yard. I've got a vinegar mother from my grandmother that probably came from apple cider vinegar from there, this eighty-five-, ninety-year-old living thing.

"So this is my dream," he says, pointing to one last image. "There's this wonderful harvest moon shining down from the top," Travis says. "And that's what I hope. That this great big beautiful light shines down on a harvest that grew from the ashes of coal."

Travis Milton's Strawberry Rhubarb Relish MAKES 1½ CUPS

Chef Travis Milton loves rhubarb so much, he had an image of it tattooed on his arm. He also created this dynamite side dish that he serves with fried chicken. Its sweet-tart flavor is terrific with any pork dish, too, and it can be used as a condiment on a meaty sandwich.

1¼ pounds (about 5) rhubarb stalks, cut into 2-inch pieces
½ pound strawberries, halved
½ cup fresh mint leaves
2½ tablespoons sugar
½ teaspoon salt
¼ cup crushed walnuts, toasted, for garnish (optional)

Place the rhubarb in the bowl of a food processor fitted with the blade attachment. Pulse until the rhubarb is finely chopped or shredded. Transfer it to a mixing bowl.

Place the strawberries and mint in the food processor and pulse to make a coarse sauce. Stir the strawberry mixture into the rhubarb, and add the sugar and salt. You can chill it, covered, until you are ready to serve, but it's best if brought to room temperature before you do. Top with the crushed walnuts, if desired.

Preserving

Little Pisgah Mountain, in the Blue Ridge range near Fairview, North Carolina, has three peaks. One is largely empty, save for the usual communications tower clutter. On the second stands the imposing house of a former Florida governor. The third and last is graced with a weathered gray trailer shaped like a canned ham. About twenty yards away sits a second crumbling minitrailer, not as charmingly formed but shaded by the same tall trees.

"My grandfather brought that Shasta up here sometime in the 1940s or '50s, when he married his second wife," Walter Harrill says. "He moved it to the top of this mountain and the two of them lived there happily for several years."

Walter pauses for a beat while I contemplate the joys of a perfect union and a simple life.

"Then she bought that other trailer and moved into it and they lived unhappily together for several more." Chuckling, he nods his head in the direction of a tiny red-painted wooden shed that stands a few feet beyond the trailers, on the other side of a narrow dirt road. "When they finally got divorced, he built himself that little house and that's where he lived out the rest of his life."

Even in an era that has gone mad for the concept of the "tiny house," the minuscule living space C. B. Harrill called home taxes the imagination. Walter shows me the three-foot-long shelf where he put his two-burner gas camp stove, and eventually a tiny microwave above. Abutting this "kitchen" was a sleeping pallet set on a stack of plywood his grandfather cannibalized from time to time for repairs. The small woodstove sat across from the bed on the opposite wall, with space enough for his grandfather's chair between them. The chair faced a chest freezer where he kept his food, and on top of that a small television. ("We all thought it was a black-and-white set, but when he died, my aunt cleaned the screen and we discovered it had been a color TV all along. He smoked two cartons a week.")

It's possible C. B. Harrill didn't much care if the TV was color or not, because Walter says it wasn't his favorite thing to watch anyway. His grandfather's chair faced the door and he preferred to "watch the mountain."

I can see his point. From the threshold the land stretches through a grove of widely spaced scrub crab apples, locusts, poplars, chinquapins, and one giant gnarled and wind-twisted white pine. It then begins a quick descent rippling down through thick brush into a narrow, verdant valley. In the distance, it rises and ripples again into dark blue-green ridges. The door frames this vista like a mural.

We step through that door into a soft late-April breeze. It's a crisp and sun-dappled day with a bright blue sky and feathery clouds. There are tiny yellow blooms in the pale green grass, birds flitting from limb to limb, and in the blueberry bushes that speckle the slope just beyond and below the tiny house, a handful of Orchard Mason bees are hard at work, nuzzling the ivory bell-shaped buds.

"Glad to see 'em," Walter says. "An Orchard Mason is a native bee, thirty times more efficient than a honeybee."

Walter knows his bees and his berries. He and his wife, Wendy, are the owners of Imladris Farm, which in the decade and a half of its operation has become the Asheville area's premium supplier of locally crafted jams and preserves. Imladris blueberry, black-berry, raspberry, and "berry best" jams, apple butter, and smoked tomato ketchup grace the tables at some dozens of fine restaurants across North Carolina. They're sold in gift shops and gourmet markets around town, and online. Walter sets up shop from the back of his truck outside the Early Girl Eatery on sunny Saturday mornings, and locals know to take the "early" seriously if they don't want to find he's sold out. Their preserving business hasn't made them rich, Walter says, grinning, "but it's enabled us to raise our son as the seventh generation on a mountain family farm. I would call that 'rich' in an even better sense."

The roots of those riches are here, in his grandfather's berry patch.

————

Preserving foods by means of drying, burying, curing, and fermenting was essential to the settlement of the mountain regions and a part of the foodways of both native peoples and the Europeans who began moving in during the 18th century. Fermented pickles, potted meats, and sweetened jams and conserves were made and stored in crocks and earthenware containers or in jars sealed with wax. Canning came much later. Packing food in wide-mouthed jars that could be vacuum-sealed with screw-on lids—patented by John Mason of New Jersey in 1858—ensured the food's safety, extended the time for keeping food, and broadened the scope of what could be "put by." Mountain women embraced this concept of canning food so enthusiastically that the mason jar became a symbol of mountain life, and a useful container for potables as well.

Appalachian food historian Joe Dabney notes that by the start of the 20th century, a young mountain bride's merit would often be judged by her peers—and her in-laws—based on how many cans of food she put by in the first year of her marriage. Cellars were filled with shelves along the walls, or canning rooms or sheds were built to accommodate colorful armies of glass jars filled with beans, tomatoes, and corn from the garden; venison and squirrel from the woods; chicken and dumplings, vegetable soup, and beef stew ready to plop into a pot come wintertime. And then there were the pickles and condiments: bread-and-butter, sweet-and-sour, and dill pickles; ketchup of both green and red; chowchow; piccalilli; and relish. Translucent jellies sparkled like jewels; jams and preserves held berries suspended in thick syrup; butters of apple, grape, pumpkin, and squash were flavored with spices, but also with the time it took to cook them.

Canning was often communal work, with the women of a family or neighborhood gathering at one person's house to share equipment and harvest for a few days, moving to another the next. The hot, hard work that began in July was tempered by breaks to sit on the porch and string beans and drink iced tea, share laughter, and gossip. During the Depression and the war years that followed, community canning facilities were built in some areas through the Appalachian South. These kitchens, outfitted with large pressure canners and other equipment that an individual family might not have, allowed home gardeners to process more volume and a wider range of produce. They also were a gathering place for women and children who would share in the day's work. About a dozen survive in southwest and central Virginia, and they have seen an upswing in interest and use in recent years. Additionally, commercial-grade kitchens have opened in recent years in eastern Kentucky, northern Georgia, and western North Carolina. Kentucky State University literally rolled out a mobile canning unit in the spring of 2015 that can travel to rural communities and allow small-scale farmers to process food for resale.

Most of these facilities can be rented for personal use, but the additional intention is to provide small farmers with a means to create value-added products for resale. Blue Ridge Food Ventures, outside of Asheville, provides not only a state-of-the-art commercial kitchen but also information and support in negotiating regulations, product development, and marketing for western North Carolina entrepreneurs. This contemporary focus on canning for cash is itself a continuation of tradition. Mountain women traded canned goods for services from the doctor or midwife, and for goods from peddlers and the merchants in town. In *The Edible South,* Marcie Cohen Ferris notes that in the 1920s female agricultural extension agents began encouraging their clients in the rural South to sell eggs, butter, produce, baked goods, pickles, and preserves not only to local merchants and peddlers but also in farmers markets that the agents organized. The money provided the women with some financial independence, was often used to pay for further schooling for the children, or simply allowed the family to stay on the farm during lean economic times that might otherwise have lured them to factory work elsewhere.

C. B. Harrill wasn't thinking about preserves when he planted his two hundred acres on Little Pisgah with blueberry bushes, but his grandson says he was thinking about a way to keep himself on this piece of land.

"The original road up here was a sled road, steeper than sin," Walter says. "Way back, way before my grandfather's time, they planted corn up here. See the little Methodist church over there?" Walter points to a white steeple down the mountain and in the distance. "The Marlowes, my mother's people, had a sawmill and a gristmill there. And to get the corn from here to there, they would have brought a sled up and three oxen. When the sled was loaded, they'd have hitched one ox to the front, to lead it down the mountain, and two to the back, to slow it down so it didn't run away over the first ox or away from them. It seems like a strange place to grow a crop." And indeed, the mountainside had not been cultivated for some time when his grandfather bought his acreage mid-century. It was 1955 when he decided to cover it with blueberry bushes.

"Everybody knew you couldn't grow blueberries up here, everybody except my granddad."

Blueberries were prolific in the North Carolina coastal region, but about the only place they grew in the mountains was Graveyard Fields, a popular hiking destination from milepost 418 on the Blue Ridge Parkway, where the bushes produced a type of wild blues with very small berries. The Cherokee gathered the tiny tart berries in a time-consuming process that yielded valuable nutrition for a lot of labor, an equation that doesn't balance out in the modern fruit market.

"But my granddad knew of a domesticated version of those same berries, the highbush," Walter says.

Highbush berries belong to the same family of plants that includes the rhododendrons and azaleas that blanket the southern Appalachians. Like the wild berries, highbush blueberries thrive in the mountains' mineral soil, but they produce plumper, tastier fruit. Walter's grandfather planted the former cornfields in highbush and when the berries came in, usually about July 4th time, he opened his fields to U-pick customers. It became an annual destination for families in the area and for regular tourists.

"U-pick was a wonderful thing for Granddaddy because he wanted to live here. People want to come to pick in the cool of the morning and evening, so you've got to be around, and that suited him fine. But U-pick fields are not a particularly lucrative agricultural proposition. Most farms that do it now use it to bring people out to a farm store where they sell other products. My granddad would go get spent shuttles from the textile mills over in Shelby and he'd make things from them. Candlesticks, lamps. He did handcrafting to sell to the pickers, and that brought in a little more cash, though not much. He didn't need much."

Walter points to a water pump with a pipe running underground to a spring farther down the mountain. "My dad and I put that in a few years back. Granddaddy didn't have water up here for over fifty years. He'd drive twenty-five minutes down this mountain and then another fifteen over to where there was a pipe down by Hickory Nut Gap. People still go to get their water there, comes out of a spring and they say it tastes really good. He'd have a truck full of empty Pepsi bottles that he filled up."

The berries paid for gas for the truck, the Pepsis, and a few other essentials. "It's not a lucrative thing to do. And people think it's a deal for the farmer because the pickers are doing the 'hard work,' but the hard work is what happens all the months leading up to when the berries set. The planting, the cultivating."

As Walter's grandfather aged (he died in 2000 at the age of eighty-six) "the fields got away from him." Walter gestures beyond the clearing, where the bees are humming in bushes that stand in open sun, to an army of scrub trees inching in, like enemy soldiers in camouflage. "Those trees and the scrub will about choke the berries out if you don't stay right on it. For the last years of my granddaddy's life, my dad and I would come up in the spring and have an annual blitzkrieg, hacking the scrub that had grown out of the blueberry patch, but that would hardly do it at all."

———

Home canning was not confined to the southern Appalachians, of course. Farm wives across the country embraced this new kitchen technology in the mid-19th century, and putting food by for the winter is how a rural family survived. In towns, anyone who had a garden, fruit trees, or berry bushes planned to spend several days in the heat of summer sweating through the aptly named "hot water bath" or "pressure" rituals. Commercially canned products were available as well, but they didn't really begin to compete with home canning until after World War II, when the canning industry that had produced rations for the war turned to developing a domestic market in peacetime. Tins and jars with colorful, tempting labels spread across the land as groceries carrying multiple brands and options replaced simple general stores. Boom times made the price of food go down and the ability to buy go up.

Canning is hot and hard work, but as Walter pointed out, that's only the end of the story. Home canning to stock a family larder and to create some extra income begins with planning for a big garden, tilling the soil, planting seed, cultivating, backbreaking weeding. It involves harvesting day after day after day as the weather allows but doesn't necessarily bless. And when crops fail, winters can become lean to desperate. It's no wonder then that by the second half of the 20th century, through much of the country, canning was on the wane. It's actually a wonder that, in the southern mountains, it still held on.

In the summer, my great-aunts, aunts, and cousins who had gardens—that was nearly all of them—canned. My mother was a willing helper, stringing beans and breaking them, scraping corn off the cob, cutting bad spots out of tomatoes, picking grapes from my aunt Rae's vines. Her rewards were small diamond-sided glass pints of jam, paraffin-topped glasses of apple jelly, quart jars filled with full beans and sweet corn. We carried these back to the pantry in our kitchen in the city, not to get us through the lean winter but to remind us of home with their distinctive flavors and the memories they evoked. But aside from the occasional windfall from a neighbor's pear tree put up as pear honey some summers, my mother did not can. She cooked fresh vegetables for us in season, and for the winter, she cultivated a discriminating taste for what was pretty good and what was "not fit to eat" from the cans at the grocery. She doctored them in the pot with ham, bacon and butter, plenty of black pepper, onions, and sometimes a little salt.

My Aunt Lib, who lived in Corbin, didn't can either, that I remember. She worked a full-time job at Belks department store downtown. But her cupboards contained jars put up by her mother, Granny Tart, and her sister Caroline and Caroline's husband, Loren, who also provided all of us with shuck beans. Women with gardens and time at home canned; women without them did not.

I didn't realize it then, but that was a period of transition in foodways, and it was evidenced in the hot, tiny kitchen my mother presided over in the city. There she might try a 10¢ box of Jiffy cornbread mix for supper one night, throwing out half the chalky sweetened pone and declaring it "not fit to eat." She found the cake mixes "acceptable," though, especially for making fruit cocktail pudding, a quick go-to that mimicked the cobblers of home-canned fruit with a cakelike crust she'd had as a child. She fell in love with tiny Le Sueur peas in a can, somehow still sweet and if not crisp, at least not mushy. She never had a can of carrots or potatoes in the cupboard in her life, for you could always find them fresh at the grocery. She was thankful for frozen broccoli, but scornful of frozen corn. She had no use for commercially canned green beans that had no actual beans in the limp pods, and those that did she altered alchemically with white bacon and onion before she would set them before us. Whatever "quick" or processed food she bought, she measured against a palate honed on freshness and flavor and memory, and those that made the cut were worthy.

"Did your mother can her own vegetables or did she buy them at the grocery? Did she use box mixes or bake from scratch?" a young college student doing an oral history asked me a couple of years ago. I responded much as I did above. "Was her choice 'aspirational'?" she followed up, and I must have looked confused. "Do you think she was choosing foods she saw in advertisements because, as an Appalachian, she wanted to be more like the rest of America?"

I thought it was one of the oddest questions I'd heard so far, but then I was asked variations of the same thing by a young folklorist, and then by a graduate student working on her thesis not long after.

"Aspirational eating" is a term used in the study of foodways that, in its most simplified explanation, means that we eat the foods of those we aspire to be. The theory suggests that the movement that began in the region in the mid-20th century toward convenience foods and commercial products, toward Pop-Tarts for breakfast instead of homemade biscuits and Mamaw's jelly, is not simply about availability, convenience, inexpensive price, or taste preference, but is also largely fueled because people from this part of the country, who so often are portrayed as "other," aspire to be instead "the same." Like those they've seen selling foods on billboards and TV.

It was a hard premise for me to wrap my head around in that first conversation,

although not long after, in the Southern Foodways Alliance's magazine, *Gravy*, Kentucky novelist Silas House wrote a fine explication in an essay on his aunt's small country store and its jar of pickled baloney: "Pickled baloney was a delicacy in the rural stores of Appalachia, showcased right on the counter, where no one could miss it. Most people headed straight for that jar when they were setting for a spell at Dot's. Others eyed the jar with desire, knowing they couldn't afford to add it to their bill." For people raised in hard times like his parents, House concluded, "pickled baloney was a symbol of attainment."

My father, who was an orphan at age nine and spent some years as a boarder in a mountain school, once told me bitterly about the minuscule portion of tapioca they would be served of an evening. "My dream was one day to have all the tapioca I could eat," he confessed, laughing. I made him a mixing-bowl-full once, but, a moderate eater, he was satisfied after only a dessert-dish-full and the knowledge that the rest was there for him, if needed.

Was that aspirational eating?

I thought about my mother, who I remember working tirelessly most days of her life, cooking, cleaning, washing clothes and hanging them on the line, washing pots and pans in an old porcelain sink. What did grocery canned goods mean to her? She relished the home-canned goods that we were gifted, adjusted the store-bought ones to suit her rigorous standards of taste. I thought that she loved her aunt's jams as much for the memory of place and people they evoked. But what meaning might those commercial jams and vegetables have also held? Did those grocery jars and tins represent a different life? Perhaps an easier one; perhaps one she desired?

Was that aspirational eating?

————

"I spent a lot of time in my formative years up here on the mountain and at my other grandparents' place," Walter says. Nevertheless, a farm life was not in his plans. "I thought, 'How can I make a bunch of money?'" So he got a degree in medical technology, but it wasn't work he much cared for. "It's how I met Wendy and she's the light of my life. But she was in med tech, too, and neither one of us was happy."

When the opportunity came to move rent-free into an old house on his mother's parents' land, six miles away, as the crow flies, from where we stood, Walter and Wendy took it, thinking the change of scene might make things more interesting.

"I called it Imladris because I'm a Tolkien geek. I wasn't thinking about branding or if people would know how to spell it, or anything like that, I just wanted it to be a name with a good feeling and I was just doing a little farming on the side as a hobby." But with the birth of their son, Andy, and Walter's desire to spend much more time with his son, that hobby became a vocation.

"I was coming up here helping Granddaddy with his berries when I could. I saw right away that he wasn't making much on the U-pick, so I said, 'Let's get you a better price.' I took twenty pounds to the tailgate market one weekend and sold out in twenty minutes. Forty pounds in about forty minutes the next weekend. It was exciting, but we realized right away we had a couple of more weeks and the blueberries would be gone. So Wendy and I started picking raspberries and blackberries as fast as we could."

It was Wendy who suggested they turn those berries into jam and sell it for a higher return. Walter laughs. "I infamously said, 'That's a foolish idea.' See, in my family we didn't buy jam. We went to my grandma's or to my aunt's and said, 'Do you have any of that great strawberry preserve left?' And she'd go down in the root cellar and come back with a jar or two."

But Walter quickly discovered that there were plenty of people who did buy jam, and who were especially eager to buy the jam that he and Wendy were making. It was local. It was organic. It was simple but incredibly tasty. It was everything the locavore, artisanal, and natural aspirational food scene bubbling up in Asheville wanted a jam to be. Soon he had left his job and was selling at an outdoor kiosk at the newly opened Grove Arcade in downtown Asheville. That's where John Stehling, chef and then new owner with his wife, Julie, of the Early Girl Eatery, found him in 2002.

John says, "When we started Early Girl I made my own jams. I thought they were great. I was going to sell them one day and be wildly successful. Then I had Walter's and Wendy's and I was like, 'Shit, this is good! No, *really* good!' Like if you made your own jam this is how you would dream it would turn out. At this point I was having an inkling my jam dream was in jeopardy. As I got to know the good folks at Imladris I realized they had the same value system as myself. It was a no-brainer to start serving it in the restaurant."

The Stehlings not only served the jam (in jam pots made by then-local potter LeAnne Ash), they printed table tents telling the Imladris story, and the jam's popularity spread. "A lot of this story comes down to John Stehling," Walter says. "At one point, another restaurant that seemed to me to be their competitor wanted to buy jams from us and I said no because I wanted to honor that connection. John heard about it through the restaurant grapevine and called me up and said, 'Hey, Walter, that's not how I want you to do business. I want you to be as successful as you can and want to be.'"

So how successful is that? I ask.

He answers me by talking about his son, Andy, the seventh generation to live in the same lovely cove in the Blue Ridge Mountains. They raise rabbits now at Imladris, and Andy, who is twelve, helps with the raising and the slaughtering, keeps hens and sells the eggs, works the fields and the jam pots with both Wendy and Walter.

"It's a life that's a good life to grow up in, I think," the father says. "And it's a life that he may grow up and decide he wants no part of, or only a little of, or go away from and come back to," says the man whose literary hero famously wrote, "Not all who wander are lost."

And as we joke for a moment about the dreams that fathers have for sons, mothers for their daughters, the word "aspirational" comes up. I tell him about the concept of Appalachian aspirational eating. He raises a shaggy black eyebrow and looks off to the peaks in the distance for a moment, thinking. Then he says, "See, I think assuming 'aspirational' for a motivation assumes that those of us living here, in the mountains, are desiring to be a part of the world 'out there.'

"But the truth of it is, we look 'out there,' at the rest of the world, and then we kind of shake our heads and say, 'Well. I just hate it for them.'"

Old-School Tomato Gravy

MAKES ABOUT 1⅓ CUPS

Ketchup delivers sweet-tart-spicy complexity to the table. But Tomato Gravy is a quick winter fix intended to remind you of the sharp tang of the summer garden. As such it's a pretty simple affair, mingling the smoky fat of bacon (or olive oil, if you prefer) with the robust burst of brightness in a can of homegrown tomatoes.

I confess, I don't can tomatoes. I like to use Muir Glen Organic Fire Roasted Tomatoes in this and other recipes for the extra dimension that the roasting seems to give them, although any good-quality canned tomato will do. If you are using your own beautiful bounty put up in a mason jar, you will want to drain them before chopping, reserving the juice. Home-canned tomatoes are often more watery, so you will add the juice as you cook the gravy to maintain a saucy consistency without it becoming too thin. You can add herbs like basil and thyme to the recipe, but remember that you are not making a spaghetti sauce, but a simple thickened gravy.

As an accompaniment to Kale Potato Cakes (page 64), Tomato Gravy often appears at breakfast. It's also great with Perfect One-Eyed Jack (page 134) or with hot biscuits (page 269). Try it with main events like Salmon Cakes (page 228).

2 tablespoons bacon grease or olive oil
½ medium yellow onion, finely diced
1 tablespoon all-purpose flour
1 (14.5-ounce) can (2 cups) diced tomatoes,
    with their juices
½ tablespoon sorghum syrup
Salt and freshly cracked black pepper
2 slices bacon, fried crisp and crumbled (optional)

In a heavy skillet or saucepan, melt the bacon grease over medium-high heat. Add the onions and sauté until they are just starting to turn translucent, about 2 minutes. Sprinkle the flour over them and cook for 1 to 2 minutes, stirring constantly, until flecks of flour are beginning to turn golden.

Add the tomatoes and stir in the sorghum syrup until it dissolves. Reduce the heat to a low simmer and cook for 20 to 30 minutes or so, stirring frequently to keep the tomatoes from sticking. Add a little water or tomato juice, if needed, but you are aiming for the consistency of a thick gravy, so not much.

When the tomatoes have largely disintegrated, remove the pan from the heat and add salt and cracked black pepper to taste. Both commercial and home-canned tomatoes can vary in the amount of salt already added, so it's important to taste and season accordingly. Traditionally, lots of cracked black pepper was used.

Serve hot, with the crumbled bacon sprinkled over the top if you desire.

Extra can be stored in the refrigerator for up to 2 days and reheated in the microwave or in the top of a double boiler.

Icebox Green Strawberry Pickles

MAKES ABOUT 2 CUPS

I'd not heard of "green strawberry pickles" before in my life, then suddenly encountered them on the menus of three cool contemporary Appalachian restaurants in a matter of weeks. And while they didn't originate in the region, their super tang fits the flavor profile perfectly, pairing with any number of classic dishes.

The pickling brine is based on a recipe my pal Sheri Castle uses for pickling ramps. It works really well with the bite of the berries. You will likely need to go strawberry picking to get the unripe strawberries that are white or pale green and with just a tinge of pink at the top. If the berry is any riper, the pickle will end up mushy, not crisp.

2 cups green strawberries, hulled
1-inch piece of cinnamon stick
1 cup apple cider vinegar
1 bay leaf
3 tablespoons sugar
1 teaspoon pickling salt
1 teaspoon coriander seeds
1 teaspoon mustard seeds
¼ teaspoon whole black peppercorns

Sterilize a 1-quart jar and lid and ring. Pack the green strawberries and cinnamon stick into the jar, leaving 1 inch of headspace.

Pour ½ cup of water into a medium saucepan and add all the remaining ingredients. Bring to a boil over medium heat, stirring to dissolve the sugar. After it boils for about 5 minutes, remove the pan from the heat and let the mixture cool completely.

Once it is cool, pour the brine over the berries to cover, leaving ½ inch headspace. Seal the jar and refrigerate it. Let it sit overnight before serving. Stored in the refrigerator, the pickles will keep for up to a month, if you can keep from eating them.

Spiced Pickled Peaches

MAKES ABOUT 2 QUARTS

This recipe produces a delightful pickle that is not too sweet or spicy but more floral. It's the perfect accompaniment to fried chicken and summer sandwiches and belongs on any table laden with vegetables from the garden.

The recipe comes from my Asheville friend Chris Bryant. The recipe here is for 2 quarts, which can be kept in the refrigerator for several weeks, but of course you can use the water-bath method to process and seal the fruit according to your jar manufacturer's instructions.

Here are a few of Chris's helpful tips: "Use firm but ripe peaches, as overripe ones may fall apart and underripe ones are impossible to peel. Whole peaches hold up best to pickling, so look for the smallest fruit available. Larger peaches may need to be halved, so you'll have to remove the pit. Look for a loose-pit variety labeled 'freestone.'"

4 pounds small ripe peaches
2 cups distilled white vinegar
1 cup apple cider vinegar
4½ cups sugar
¾ cup sliced fresh ginger
1 bay leaf
2-inch piece of cinnamon stick
1 teaspoon whole allspice berries
½ teaspoon whole cloves
½ teaspoon whole black peppercorns
¼ teaspoon whole Szechuan or pink peppercorns
  (optional)
¼ teaspoon coriander seed
¼ teaspoon mustard seed
⅛ teaspoon crushed red pepper flakes

Sterilize two 1-quart canning jars with lids and rings.

Fill a large bowl three-quarters full with ice water and set it next to the stove. Fill a large pot three-quarters full with water, set it over high heat, and heat until nearly boiling. When the hot water is ready, use a sharp paring knife to cut a shallow × in the bottom of each peach and drop the peaches into the water. Cook for about 30 seconds, or until the skin is loose and "shrugs" when touched. Use a slotted spoon to transfer the peaches to the ice bath. (You might have to do this in batches, adding more ice as you go.)

Grab another large bowl, fill it halfway with water, and add 1 cup of the white vinegar. Remove a peach from the ice bath, and working from the × end, pull the skin from the peach. Continue, dropping the peeled peaches into the vinegared water as you go.

Let the peaches sit in the vinegar water while you prepare the syrup. Combine the remaining 1 cup white vinegar, the apple cider vinegar, and all the remaining ingredients in a 4- or 5-quart nonreactive pot. Set the pot over medium-high heat and bring to a boil. Then cover the pot, reduce the heat to a gentle simmer, and let simmer for 7 minutes.

Uncover the pot, increase the heat to medium-high, and bring to a low boil. Use a slotted spoon to transfer the peaches to the syrup. Let the peaches simmer until warmed through, 4 to 7 minutes depending on size and ripeness. You want them just pliable enough to nestle together in the jars but not so soft they break apart.

Transfer the cooked peaches and syrup to the prepared jars, being sure the peaches are submerged, and leaving ½-inch headspace. Lid the jars and let them cool to room temperature before storing in the refrigerator. The refrigerated pickled peaches will keep for a month.

Will Dissen's Pickled Ramps

MAKES 1½ QUARTS

Eating ramps with potatoes and in eggs was a custom I was fully familiar with, but when I saw a jar of pickled ramps for the first time at a store in West Virginia about 1990, it struck me as a novelty—perhaps not arch, like the tins of "possum meat" meant to be put on a shelf as a souvenir, but not something to be taken seriously. I was quite wrong.

As the popularity of sweet-garlicky ramps soared nationally in the 21st century, with-it chefs began pickling their own as a way to extend the short season for fresh ramps. These, by chef William Dissen of The Market Place in Asheville, North Carolina, are like a tangy, garlicky sweet pickle.

1 tablespoon whole black peppercorns
1 teaspoon mustard seeds
½ teaspoon caraway seeds
½ teaspoon fennel seeds
½ teaspoon cumin seeds
2 tablespoons kosher salt, plus more for the boil
2 pounds ramp bulbs, cleaned, green leaves
   cut off 1 inch above the red stems
2 cups sugar
2 cups white wine vinegar
2 bay leaves

Sterilize a 1-quart glass jar with lid and ring.

In a heavy skillet set over medium heat, toast the peppercorns, mustard seeds, caraway seeds, fennel seeds, and cumin seeds until fragrant, about 2 minutes. Set aside the spice mixture.

Fill a large bowl three-quarters full with ice water and set it next to the stove.

Fill a medium pot with water and bring it to a boil over high heat. Once it is boiling, add enough kosher salt to the pot to taste like the ocean. When the water returns to the boil, add the ramps. Cook for 30 to 45 seconds or to the point where they are tenderized but still crisp. Use a slotted spoon to remove the ramps from the pot and plunge them into the ice water to stop the cooking. Drain, and place the ramps in the sterilized glass jar.

In a separate pot, combine the toasted spices, sugar, vinegar, kosher salt, and bay leaves and bring to a boil over high heat. Once the salt and sugar are dissolved (this takes about 2 minutes), pour the mixture over the ramps. If canning, seal the jar and proceed to the canning process. If not canning, allow the ramp mixture to cool to room temperature and then cover and refrigerate the jar, waiting for 3 days before eating. It will keep for a month in the refrigerator.

Kentucky Kimchi MAKES 2 QUARTS

The Korean food I've savored has always seemed both exotic and extremely familiar to me. The presence of pork, the heartiness, the salty umami themes, and the sharp, sour, hot pickles all have resonance with the Appalachian table. No wonder then that Louisville chef Edward Lee's *Smoke and Pickles* is one of my favorite contemporary cookbooks. His recipe for Red Cabbage–Bacon Kimchi seems just a step or two away from a hot, tart mountain kraut. I've adapted it here, substituting smoked Spanish paprika for the pork, banana peppers for the classic Korean ones, and bringing the apple and turnip a little more to the fore. My son-in-law makes this now as well, and we are hard-pressed to keep it in stock (see photograph on page 209).

1 medium-sized red cabbage (about 2 pounds)
¼ cup kosher salt
¼ cup brown rice flour
2 tablespoons sugar
3 small carrots
1 small red onion
1 medium green apple
1 medium turnip
1 banana pepper
2 garlic cloves
1 ounce fresh ginger
¼ cup fish sauce (see Note)
2 teaspoons smoked Spanish sweet paprika
2 tablespoons crushed red pepper flakes

Shred the cabbage and place it in a large colander. Sprinkle the salt over the cabbage, toss well, and let it sit for 40 minutes.

While the cabbage is sitting in the salt, make a paste by combining 1½ cups of water with the rice flour and sugar in a small saucepan. Bring the mixture to a simmer, stirring, over medium-low heat and cook until the mixture thickens to a runny paste. This takes a minute or two. Remove from the heat and allow to cool.

Rinse the cabbage, shake off the excess water, and transfer it to a large bowl.

Peel and shred the carrots. Quarter the onion and then slice it crosswise into thin, short strips. Repeat the procedure with both the apple and the turnip. Remove the stem and seeds from the banana pepper and slice it into thin strips. Add all this to the cabbage and toss to mix well.

Use a Microplane to grate the garlic and ginger into a small bowl. Add the fish sauce, along with the paprika and red pepper flakes. Pour this over the cabbage mixture, and using clean latex gloves to protect your hands, mix thoroughly. Pour the cooled flour paste over the cabbage mixture and mix thoroughly.

Pack the mixture tightly into a half-gallon glass jar with a lid and ring (or two 1-quart jars). Make sure there is an inch of headspace for air between the mixture and the top of the jar. Cover the jar with cheesecloth, hold it in place with a rubber band, and allow the jar to stand at room temperature for 24 hours. After 24 hours, secure the lid and refrigerate the jar for 4 to 5 days, checking occasionally to release pressure if needed by loosening the lid and letting the gas out. The kimchi will keep for several weeks in a covered jar in the refrigerator.

NOTE: Fish sauce can be found in the Asian foods section of most groceries, near the soy and oyster sauces. If your supermarket doesn't carry it, look for an Asian grocery.

Preserved Lemons MAKES 6 LEMONS

Citrus fruit was one of the prized exotic ingredients mountain homesteaders could trade for or buy by the end of the 19th century. My mother always put an orange or tangerine in the toe of my Christmas stocking, as her mother, Iva, had always done for her and as Iva's mother had done. It was considered a present worthy of marvel and delight.

Oranges, and later grapefruit, would be sectioned and mixed with shredded fresh coconut—another exotic product that arrived around Christmastime—to make Ambrosia for the holiday table. To extend the season, the peel could be candied, or lemons sliced and put up in a salt brine. This delicious, more elaborate version of preserved lemons comes from chef Shelley Cooper and is an essential part of her Jonas Ridge Grilled Trout (page 282).

6 whole lemons
1 cup salt
1 cup sugar
1 cup pickling spice
4 cups distilled white vinegar

Sterilize a 1-quart jar with lid and ring.

Bring 6 cups of water to a boil in a medium pot over high heat. Add the lemons and cook for 5 minutes. Drain. When the lemons are cool enough to handle, cut off and discard the ends. Cut the lemons into thin slices and layer the slices into the jar, leaving 1 inch headspace.

Combine the salt, sugar, pickling spice, and vinegar in a small saucepan, bring to a boil over high heat, and boil for 10 minutes. Pour this brine over the lemons to cover them and fill the jar, leaving ½ inch headspace. (You may have extra brine, which you can discard.) Cover with the lid and ring, and refrigerate for 10 days before using. These will keep for a month, refrigerated.

Pickled Baloney with Peppers

MAKES 2 QUARTS

When I was growing up, pickled baloney in a giant jar was ubiquitous in country stores throughout Appalachia, a treat that required the shopkeeper to pull the meat from the brine, lay it out on a cutting board, and chop off a slice to be handed to the customer along with some crackers and a paper plate. Eventually suppliers started packing the baloney in smaller jars to be taken home, or toted in lunch pails, and not long after that, little hot dogs joined them.

It's impossible to say who first thought of pickling baloney at home, but whoever did was a genius. This allowed the inclusion of home-grown peppers, sweet and hot, and the option to choose all-beef hot dogs or a fine deli baloney for the meat. Pretty to look at in the jar, yet still totally wicked, this is pedigreed enough to put on a charcuterie plate or serve as antipasto, but I'll still take mine with crackers, and maybe a swipe of mustard.

1 pound mixed banana peppers and sweet baby
   bell peppers
1 pound good deli baloney, in one big piece
1 teaspoon whole allspice berries
1 teaspoon mustard seeds
½ teaspoon celery seeds
2½ cups apple cider vinegar
½ cup sugar
1½ tablespoons vegetable oil
1 teaspoon kosher or pickling salt

Sterilize two 1-quart canning jars with lids and rings.

Slice the peppers into ½-inch-thick rings, pushing out the cores as you go. Dice the baloney into ½-inch cubes.

Arrange the peppers and meat in the canning jars. Mix the allspice, mustard, and celery seeds in a small bowl and scatter about half of the mixture into the jars. Leave 1 inch of headspace.

Combine the vinegar, 1 cup of water, and the sugar, oil, salt, and remaining spice mixture in a small saucepan and bring to a boil, stirring to dissolve the sugar. Pour this brine slowly into the jars to submerge the peppers. Let stand for 2 minutes so that any air bubbles can rise to the surface. Top off the jars with brine to ensure that the peppers remain submerged, leaving ½ inch of headspace.

Close the jars with the sterilized lids and rings. Refrigerate for at least 1 day before serving. It will keep for 3 weeks, refrigerated.

Salmon Cakes SERVES 4

From our present-day perspective, the arrival of commercially produced canned foods in the mountains may seem like a negative influence on the foodways, one that leads in a direct line to Big Macs and buckets of faux fried chicken. But we forget that some of those cans from the grocery brought variety, as well as vitamins and minerals, to households that largely grew their own foods. And that's how Salmon Cakes, made from tinned fish, became one of the most beloved suppers of the mountain South.

My mother always wanted her salmon cakes to be full of flavor. The result was a patty that was enticingly crispy on the outside and chunkily full with celery, pickle, and onion in addition to the salmon. Almost like a fried salmon salad. These are great for either a simple supper or a protein and calcium—rich breakfast. Serve them with Old-School Tomato Gravy (page 218) or Kentucky Kimchi (page 224) on the side if you'd like.

1 (14.75-ounce) can salmon, drained
⅓ cup diced white onion
⅓ cup diced celery
⅓ cup diced kosher dill pickle
1 tablespoon Dijon mustard
1 cup finely crushed saltines (from about 2 dozen crackers)
½ teaspoon lemon pepper, plus more to taste
Salt, if needed
1 large egg, beaten
Olive oil, for pan-frying

In a large bowl, break the salmon apart with a fork, leaving in the softened bones and skin, which are highly nutritious. Use the fork to stir in the onion, celery, and pickle, then the mustard. Mix in the crushed saltines and add the lemon pepper. You may want to taste here and decide if you need salt or more lemon pepper.

Stir in the beaten egg and mix well with a spoon, using the back of the spoon to lightly compress the mixture together. Refrigerate, covered, for 10 minutes.

When you are ready to fry the salmon cakes, remove the mixture from the refrigerator and use your hands to form it into flat patties, about ⅓ inch thick and 3 inches wide.

Heat enough olive oil to cover the bottom of a large heavy skillet set over medium heat until a fleck of salmon mix dances in the oil. Do not allow the oil to smoke.

Add the patties to the skillet, being sure not to crowd them. Fry until the first side is crispy golden brown, about 1½ minutes, then flip and fry the other side, also until golden. Use a spatula to move the cooked patties to a rack or onto paper towels to drain for a moment, and serve hot.

Persimmon Custard Pie

MAKES ONE 9-INCH PIE

Wild persimmons ripen in abundance and need to be eaten or processed at that very moment. Persimmon butter, pudding, and pies are made in the early fall when the fruits turn delectable after the first cold days. Nowadays we can freeze persimmon pulp, meaning this lighter-textured autumn delight can substitute for the traditional pumpkin on the Thanksgiving table. If you can't find wild persimmons, use very soft Hachiyas, but not Fuyus.

To prepare the pulp, remove the stems from the persimmons. Cut the fruit in half and force it through a food mill to remove the seeds and skins, collecting the strained pulp in a bowl. (Alternatively, use your fingers or a sturdy spatula to push the fruit through a fine-mesh sieve into a bowl.) Discard the seeds and skins.

Single unbaked pie crust (use your favorite recipe or ¼ batch of Emily Hilliard's Pie Crust on page 238)
½ cup (packed) light brown sugar
½ teaspoon ground cinnamon
¼ teaspoon salt
2 large eggs
1½ cups half-and-half
1 cup persimmon pulp, thawed if frozen
2 tablespoons butter, melted
1 teaspoon apple cider vinegar

Preheat the oven to 350°F. Line a 9-inch pie pan with the crust and place it in the refrigerator to chill while you prepare the filling.

Combine the brown sugar, cinnamon, and salt in a bowl and set it aside.

In a large bowl, whisk the eggs until the whites and yolks are fully blended. Whisk in the dry ingredients. Blend in the half-and-half and the persimmon pulp, stirring until combined. Whisk in the butter and vinegar.

Pour the filling into the crust and bake for 45 minutes, or until the center is set. Remove and allow it to cool completely before slicing and serving.

A Sweet Squeeze

A connection to the land he grew up on is what brought Doug Harrell back to the Blue Ridge mountain farm near Bakersville, North Carolina, that has been in his family since 1796. That's a half century before some enterprising agriculturist entrepreneurs introduced sorghum cane—a variety of sorghum grain that produces a sugary juice in its stalk, much like sugarcane—to the United States and thereby gave the mountain South its most distinctive sweetener.

Squeezing sorghum (putting it through a horse- or mule-drawn mill to extract the juice) and boiling it down to create a thick amber syrup that is not only sugary but also tangy and buttery became a means of providing sweetness across the country as the Civil War shut down the sugar industry of the South. But sorghum syrup doesn't produce dry crystals the way sugarcane does, and when an inexpensive process for extracting sugar from beets was discovered, most folks gave up the tedious—and exacting—work of making sorghum syrup.

Not in the mountain South, however, where sorghum squeezings were often community events. One farmer with a mill could grind the cane of several farms in a day, the families gathering for potluck, games, tale telling, and courtship. Moving on into the modern era, a taste for sorghum's rich umami and the way it seems to convey subtle tones of mineral and grassy flavor kept it the preferred sweetener in the Appalachian region. And in very recent years, it's those qualities that have caused a resurgence in interest, especially among southern chefs such as John Fleer and Edward Lee.

And this is where Doug and his wife, Barbara, come back into the story. Retiring from a longtime printing business in the Piedmont, they were looking for a way to finance a return to the beautiful, hill-sheltered farm Doug was raised on. His parents were dairy farmers, but gave that up with the rise of huge commercial dairies. The farm and the old house sat idle, and Doug and Barbara decided that if they could generate some income from it, they could move back.

"We tried growing Christmas trees," Doug tells me one morning over strong coffee, hot biscuits Barbara has made, and plenty of sorghum butter. But since tree farms don't require a lot of capital up front, there was an oversupply in the market and it was hardly worth the effort. "We started looking for something that was not quite so accessible," Barbara explains. Sorghum normally requires a substantial investment in equipment that keeps the field more limited, but Doug and Barbara were ahead on that count because a lot of old dairy equipment from the family business could be repurposed.

Even so, it has not been easy. Doug, who is in his early seventies, says that when it's time to boil, he is in the barn "at two in the morning. We go until nine at night, and most of that time, I'm skimming." Raking the foam from the boiling syrup is a hot and painfully repetitive job. And he notes that sorghum-making is as much art as science. He says he still feels like a novice, even though he's been at it for half a dozen years. But his sorghum is sold in a regional supermarket chain and is in stores and restaurants in Asheville.

Doug's syrup tends to be dark and have a distinct mineral tang. And his labels identify it as "Sorghum Molasses." That's what my family called it when I was indoctrinated into its sweet mystery as a child, but the term can be confusing since molasses is actually a syrup that is the by-product of any sugar production. It is not as flavorful, subtle, or enticing as sorghum syrup, so the National Sweet Sorghum Producers & Processors Association, of which Doug is a board member, discourages labeling it as molasses.

He laughs. "You've got to call it molasses up here in the mountains, or you can't sell it. Old-timers, that's what they call it and some of them will even tell you their granddaddy grew sugarcane. Of course you can't grow sugarcane this far north, at this altitude, so you know what they are talking about is sorghum cane. But you sure can't tell them it wasn't sugarcane Granddad was growing and molasses he was making."

Kentucky and Tennessee are currently the two largest commercial sorghum syrup–producing states, but there are folks through the whole Appalachian region who continue the tradition, supplying sorghum to family and friends. (Following a lead from a friend, I call an older farmer in the Toe River Valley at one point and ask if I can come buy a jar from him. "No, honey," he tells me on the phone. "I don't make enough to sell. But if you need some, just come on up and go into the barn. They's some jars in a big box I leave out so anybody who runs out can come get it.")

I asked Doug if the sorghum business was lucrative, and he shook his head no.

"But it's enough to keep us here," and his hand takes in the hill that vaults up steeply behind the old dairy barn, the mules grazing on it, the gnarled apple trees. "And being here is what counts."

Sorghum Butter

ENOUGH TO GRACE 18 BIGGER ISN'T
BETTER BUTTERMILK BISCUITS (PAGE 269)

I can't tell you why sorghum syrup blended at the table with soft butter tastes better on a hot biscuit than putting the two on separately, I can just tell you that it does, unequivocally. And that's why generations of mountain mamas have taught their babies how to do this. Sorghum Butter is also good spooned into a hot baked sweet potato.

3 tablespoons butter
6 tablespoons sorghum syrup

Put the butter in a small bowl and let it come to room temperature. When the biscuits go in the oven, pour the sorghum over the butter and use the tines of a fork to first mash and then mix the two together until blended. When the biscuits come out and one is cool enough to open, spread sorghum butter in the center and eat.

Orange Sorghum Vinegar

MAKES 3/4 CUP

Ever since I came up with this concoction, it's been one of the most useful ingredients in my kitchen. As you might expect with both vinegar and orange juice, it's tart and citrusy, but the sorghum syrup's buttery sweetness takes it to a level of pure satisfaction. I use it on fresh salads—both greens and fruit—and to brighten soups and roasted vegetables, such as the Roasted Root Vegetable Salad with Bacon & Orange Sorghum Vinegar (page 47). I even take a little tot when I'm feeling a cold coming on.

Make it in a small quantity to keep it tasting fresh. I put leftovers in a small covered jar in the refrigerator, but I can't tell you how long it will last since I always use it up within a matter of days.

½ cup white wine vinegar
2 tablespoons sorghum syrup
2 tablespoons freshly squeezed orange juice

Pour the vinegar into a small glass jar with a lid. Add the sorghum and shake or stir until dissolved. Add the orange juice and shake or stir to combine. Use as directed in recipes, and store any that's left over, covered, in the refrigerator.

Black Is the New Jam Cake

MAKES ONE 9-INCH LAYER CAKE

Jam Cake was so common at reunions and celebrations in my childhood that I was astonished when I grew up and discovered not everyone knew about this dense, slightly spicy cake that gets its moistness and mysterious flavor from the addition of a couple of cups of jam.

As a child, I would take a piece largely to consume the icing, leaving most of the cake on my plate. I was never reprimanded, because there was inevitably an adult at the table who totally "got" the complicated flavor profile that had a deep, subtle sweetness and a hint of the exotic.

I grew into Jam Cake, though, and as an adult have looked for elements (cocoa, black walnuts, thick buttermilk, allspice) to deepen and darken its impact. Not long ago I noticed I'd eaten a piece, consuming all the cake and leaving the thick end wedge of traditional caramel icing untouched.

This version is rick and dark, and an icing made of Sorghum Sea Foam (page 236) seems to provide both the caramel taste and a balanced contrast.

12 tablespoons (1½ sticks) butter, at room
   temperature, plus more for greasing the pans
3 cups all-purpose flour
2 tablespoons unsweetened cocoa powder
2 teaspoons ground allspice
2 teaspoons baking powder
1 teaspoon baking soda
¼ teaspoon salt
1 cup (packed) light brown sugar
4 large eggs
⅓ cup whole buttermilk
2 cups seedless blackberry jam
1 cup broken black walnuts, toasted
Sorghum Sea Foam, for icing

Preheat the oven to 350°F, and place a rack in the center of the oven. Grease two 9-inch round cake pans with butter, and line them with rounds of parchment paper.

In a large bowl, sift together the flour, cocoa powder, allspice, baking powder, baking soda, and salt. Set aside.

In the bowl of an electric mixer fitted with the paddle attachment, cream the butter and sugar until all graininess disappears and the mixture begins to lighten, about 10 minutes, scraping down the sides as needed.

Add the eggs, one at a time, beating to fully incorporate after each egg.

Add a third of the flour mixture and beat to incorporate, scraping down the sides of the bowl to be sure all is included. Add half of the buttermilk and beat to blend. Repeat the process, ending with the final third of the flour mixture.

Add the jam and beat to incorporate. Remove the bowl from the mixer and fold in the black walnuts. Pour the batter into the prepared cake pans, filling them only two-thirds full. (Extra batter can be baked as cupcakes or used for pancakes.)

Bake for 30 minutes or until a toothpick inserted in the center comes out clean. Remove the cakes from the oven and allow them to cool in their pans on a wire rack for 20 minutes. Then gently run a knife around the inner edge of each pan to loosen the cake, invert them onto a flat surface, and remove the pans. Remove the parchment paper, and gently turn the cakes over. When the cake layers are fully cooled, place one layer on a plate and prepare the Sorghum Sea Foam. To ice the cake, spread about ⅓ of the Sea Foam on the top of the layer on the plate, then gently place the other layer on that, top side up. Use a rubber spatula to spread another ⅓ or less of the Sea Foam to cover the sides of the layers, and then spread the remaining Sea Foam on top.

Sorghum Sea Foam

MAKES 48 CANDIES OR ENOUGH ICING
FOR TWO 9-INCH CAKE LAYERS

This brown sugar version of Divinity is a favorite in the mountains—a sweet that can be quickly made from ingredients almost certain to be on hand. It was the first candy my mother taught me to make, letting me beat the egg whites while she carefully poured the syrup in. A helper was good in those days as we had no electric beaters, and my mother's instructions for knowing when the candy was ready to dip out always began "Just when you think your arm is about to fall off . . . " I use an electric hand beater today as that eases things. I also substitute sweet sorghum syrup for the white Karo syrup my mother used because it gives this intense sweet another dimension of flavor.

This recipe also makes the terrific icing for Black Is the New Jam Cake (page 235) or your favorite chocolate layer cake. Make sure the cake layers are cool before spreading the icing.

4 egg whites
½ teaspoon cream of tartar
2 cups granulated sugar
2 cups (packed) light brown sugar
½ cup sorghum syrup
⅓ cup hot water
½ teaspoon vanilla extract

Lay out a piece of waxed paper about 36 inches long.

In a large mixing bowl, beat the egg whites with the cream of tartar until they form stiff peaks. Set aside.

In a saucepan with a long handle that you can easily pour from, mix the sugars, sorghum syrup, and hot water until just blended. Stir gently so you don't splash the mixture up the sides of the pan. Place the pan on medium-high heat and bring to a boil, gently stirring as you do.

When the mixture begins to boil, stop stirring, insert a candy thermometer, and continue to boil until it reaches the hard ball stage. This happens pretty quickly, so don't let your attention wander.

Immediately pour the hot syrup in a thin, steady stream into the egg whites, beating the whites vigorously as you do. Don't plop it in all at once, but keep the stream coming. Drain as much syrup as possible from the pan, but don't worry about scraping out the dregs. Just set the pot aside and keep on beating. (You can soak the pan later in hot water to dissolve any syrup that hardens while you finish the candy.)

Add the vanilla. Beat the candy, moving the beaters around the bowl to make sure all is being incorporated, until it begins to lose some of its gloss and hold its shape. You can judge the latter by stopping the beaters and lifting them. If the candy on them streams back into the bowl and disappears, keep beating. If it holds its shape on the beaters and stands in ridges in the bowl, it should be ready. You can test by dropping a teaspoonful onto the waxed paper or a plate. If it stays in a nice mound or forms a peak, it's ready. If it flattens and spreads, keep beating. (If you're making this as an icing for cake, you are looking for the same consistency, but you will want to have the cooled cake layers ready to ice as soon as the Sea Foam is ready, and work quickly to get it on the cake.)

When it's ready, use two teaspoons to drop generous mounds on the waxed paper, scooping up the Sea Foam with one spoon and using the second to scrape it off the first and onto the paper. Allow the candy to sit for several hours, until the outer shell hardens and the inside is firm enough that you can gently lift it from the waxed paper without leaving a glop behind. If you can resist, it's even better if you store the candy in a covered tin, with waxed paper between layers, for 24 hours.

Sweet Potato Sonker with Milk Dip SERVES 8 TO 10

Mount Airy was Andy Griffith's hometown and said to be the inspiration for television's Mayberry. Surry County, North Carolina, where it sits, is famous for something else, though: the sonker.

Some sonkers are made with a cakelike batter while others come with a pie crust. Among the crusters there are schisms as to whether a sonker has a top crust, a bottom crust, or both. And then there are a few devoted outliers who make their sonkers with no crust at all, but with delectable dumplings floating on top of a sauce of hot sweetened fruit. All sonkers seem to have in common a sweetened milk "dip" that is poured on top and baked to a glaze, although at least one sonker-maker makes the dip with moonshine.

Fillings can be made with any fruit or berry, but the two overwhelmingly preferred are peach and sweet potato. In her delightful cookbook *Sweet Potatoes*, April McGreger, founder-chef of the Farmer's Daughter line of jams and condiments, offers a superb recipe for the latter. In keeping with the spirit of sonker riffing, however, Emily Hilliard, blogger at *Nothing in the House*, came up with a few change-ups for this version, including increasing the sorghum syrup for a deeper mountain note.

You should know that the Surry County Annual Sonker Festival is the first Saturday of every October in Lowgap, west of Mount Airy, to benefit the historic Edwards-Franklin House. It's a day of sonkers and mountain music.

8 tablespoons (1 stick) unsalted butter, at room temperature, plus more for greasing the baking dish
⅓ cup all-purpose flour, plus more for dusting
1 recipe Emily Hilliard's Pie Crust (recipe follows)
6 medium (about 3 pounds) sweet potatoes, peeled
2 teaspoons salt
1½ cups sugar
1 cup sorghum syrup
3 cups whole milk
2 tablespoons cornstarch
1 teaspoon vanilla extract

Butter and lightly flour a 13 × 9-inch baking dish (see Note).

On a floured surface, roll out one chilled dough ball into a large rectangle that will fit into the baking dish. Transfer the rolled-out dough to the prepared baking dish, and press it down gently to line the dish and form the bottom crust. Place the dish in the refrigerator to chill.

Put the whole peeled sweet potatoes in a large pot, add cold water to cover, and add the salt. Place the pot over medium heat, cover, and bring to a boil. Then reduce the heat to a simmer and cook until the potatoes are fork-tender, about 25 minutes.

Use a large slotted spoon to transfer the cooked potatoes to a cutting board to cool. Measure out and reserve 1½ cups of the cooking liquid to use later. Slice the cooled sweet potatoes into rounds, making them as thin as possible without breaking them.

Preheat the oven to 375°F.

Remove the dough-lined pan from the refrigerator and layer the sliced sweet potatoes on top of the crust. In a medium bowl, combine 1 cup of the sugar, the sorghum, the ⅓ cup flour, the butter, and the 1½ cups reserved cooking liquid. Mix well and pour over the sweet potatoes.

(recipe continues)

Roll out the remaining dough ball into a rectangle a little smaller than the first. Cut it into strips that are about ½ inch wide, and form a lattice crust on top of the sweet potatoes.

Bake for about 40 minutes, until the crust is golden brown (the sonker will not be fully baked at this point).

While the sonker is baking, prepare the milk dip: Whisk ½ cup of the milk with the cornstarch in a medium saucepan, making sure all the cornstarch is dissolved. Add the remaining 2½ cups milk and the remaining ½ cup sugar. Set the pan over medium-high heat and let it come to a boil. Let boil for 1 minute to thicken. Then remove from the heat and stir in the vanilla.

When the sonker has cooked for 40 minutes, pour 2 cups of the prepared milk dip over the entire surface. Return the sonker to the oven and bake for 15 minutes more or until it is caramelized around the edges and brown on top. Remove the dish from the oven and let it cool for at least 20 minutes before serving; the milk will continue to be absorbed and thicken.

Serve the sonker just warm, with the remaining milk dip on the side for drizzling.

NOTE: Feel free to use a different shaped baking dish, just as long as it has roughly the same capacity as a 13 × 9 and is about 2 inches deep.

EMILY HILLIARD'S PIE CRUST
MAKES ENOUGH FOR 1 SONKER OR FOR 4 PIE CRUSTS (SEE NOTE)

4 cups all-purpose flour, plus more for dusting
1 tablespoon sugar
2 teaspoons fine sea salt
1½ cups (3 sticks) unsalted butter, cold, cut into slices
1 large egg
½ cup ice-cold water
1 tablespoon apple cider vinegar

Whisk the flour, sugar, and salt together in a large mixing bowl. Using a pastry blender or fork and knife, cut in the butter. Make sure pea-sized butter chunks remain to help keep the crust flaky.

Lightly beat the egg in a medium-sized bowl. Whisk in the ice-cold water and the vinegar.

Pour the liquid mixture into the flour-butter mixture, and combine using a wooden spoon. Mix until the dough comes together in a shaggy mass. Be careful not to overmix. Use floured hands to divide the dough in half and then form into 2 balls. Wrap each ball tightly in plastic wrap. Let them chill in the refrigerator for at least 1 hour before rolling out and beginning the sonker recipe.

NOTE: If you cut this recipe in half, it will work for a two-crust pie.

Country Pie 4.0 MAKES 1 PIE

Country Pie originated in my kitchen twenty-five-plus years ago, when I decided to riff on a Louisville version of pecan pie with walnuts and chocolate chips. I added oatmeal to the mix, and a rich rendition was born. I named it in honor of the Bob Dylan song of the same name, and like Dylan's best work, it's been covered and embellished since. This latest iteration owes much to a young cook and musician friend, Joel Swaggert O'Brien, who, among his many skills, does a mean hambone, both the onstage kind and the one you put in the bean pot. Joel opted for dried fruit instead of chocolate chips in his Country Pie 3.0. I upped the sorghum syrup and added coriander. You are welcome to play it as it lays, or take a break with an improv of your own.

Note that the viscosity of sorghum syrup can vary, and that can affect the moistness of this pie's filling. Use a syrup that is almost, but not quite, as thin as maple syrup. If yours is thicker, add a splash of warm water when you mix it with the melted butter.

Single unbaked pie crust (use your favorite recipe,
   or ¼ batch of Emily Hilliard's Pie Crust on
   page 238)
8 tablespoons (1 stick) unsalted butter
¾ cup sorghum syrup
½ cup sugar
1 teaspoon ground coriander
½ teaspoon salt
3 large eggs
¾ cup English walnut pieces
½ cup rolled oats
½ cup chopped dried dates
½ cup chopped dried figs

Position one oven rack in the center and another in the bottom position. Preheat the oven to 350°F.

Line a 9-inch pie pan with the crust and place it in the refrigerator to chill while you are making the filling.

Melt the butter in a small saucepan over medium-low heat. Add the sorghum, then the sugar, coriander, and salt, stirring until dissolved. Pour this into a large mixing bowl, using a spatula to be sure you get it all. Allow to cool to lukewarm.

In a separate bowl, beat the eggs with a whisk until well blended and foamy. Slowly stir the eggs into the butter-sorghum mixture. Stir in the nuts, oats, dates, and figs.

Pour the filling into the chilled pie crust and bake on the bottom rack of the oven for 15 minutes. Then move the pie pan to the middle rack and bake for an additional 40 to 45 minutes, until the center is a little jiggly but not liquid or sloshy.

Allow the pie to cool completely before slicing.

Honeyed Applesauce MAKES 2¾ CUPS

The early settlers who brought European honeybees to the Appalachian region regarded the small seasonal honey crop as a treasure to be savored sparingly. Although beekeeping grew and swarms spread, making it possible to harvest wild honey, it was still hard to come by and scarce enough in my childhood that it was most often served like jam, as a topping for biscuits from the oven, and only used rarely in recipes. Still, some dishes simply call for its delicate, flowery presence. When making apple butter, sorghum syrup is the perfect element to intensify the apples' taste over long, slow cooking with plenty of spices. For applesauce, though, you want a lighter hand with the spices and a dose of honey. Not only does that create a sweet, floral undercurrent, it will let the natural flavor of your apples shine. Choose heirlooms if you can get them and don't worry about blemishes or bruises; you can cut them out when you're peeling, coring, and cooking. Raw unfiltered honey from a local beekeeper is best.

3 tablespoons honey
2-inch cinnamon stick
5 whole cloves
4 whole, unbroken cardamom pods
2½ pounds apples

Bring ¼ cup water to a boil in a large, heavy saucepan. Add the honey and stir to dissolve it. Then add the cinnamon, cloves, and cardamom pods, and remove the pan from the heat.

Peel, core, and slice the apples into eighths. Add the apples to the saucepan, stir to combine, and bring to a boil over medium-high heat. Cook, stirring to keep the mixture from scorching, until the apples are softened enough to be pierced by a fork, about 12 minutes.

Remove from the heat and remove the whole spices. If you leave a clove behind, not to worry, but make sure to get all the cardamom pods. Puree the apples in a blender or food processor until smooth to your preference. I like mine with little lumps of apple about the size of rice, but if you prefer smoother, go for it.

This is delicious served warm immediately, and delicious if cooled in the refrigerator. It's just delicious.

Husbandry

It's a fall day with air so crisp that all the buskers in downtown Asheville are wearing shoes. I cross the street amid a flurry of tourists in fleeces, then break away to cross again to Pack Square. There a little boy in a hoodie is petting a small statue of a piglet while his toddler sister holds up her arms, asking to be lifted onto the back of the mama sow. Their mother laughs as she complies, then points to the bronze turkeys that follow the pigs, to the trotter and bird prints embedded in the concrete that surrounds this downtown artwork. She turns to her friend quizzically and says, "I don't get it. What's this all about?"

It's about a part of Asheville's and Appalachia's history that has largely gone unnoted: the drovers' roads, and the livestock commerce in the early 19th century that linked the region to the rest of the country.

Traditional narratives of Appalachian life have commonly held that the region was "isolated" to such an extent that the people became, as writer William Goodell Frost proclaimed in the *Atlantic Monthly* in 1899, "our contemporary ancestors." That was a trope so widely in circulation that Jack Weller's controversial 1965 look at "contemporary" Appalachia was called *Yesterday's People*—a concept that still has great traction with drive-by journalists today. But the fact is that while individual homesteads in the deepest hollers might well take some getting to and from, the region at large was well connected to the rest of the country from fairly early on.

After all, Appalachia was itself a passage, a throughway from the coastal and Piedmont regions of the United States to the fertile plains of the Midwest and the frontier beyond. And the abundance of resources in the mountains, discovered early and exploited quickly, required the use of the many rivers as highways in the 1700s. It meant there were well-traveled trails for hauling salt, timber, and ultimately coal, leading both in and out of the territory by the start of the 19th century, and it sparked the development of those trails into improved roads. Some of the earliest commerce along those rivers, trails, and turnpikes was the transport of mountain-raised livestock to be sold in the plantation South.

We are not talking about an occasional small herd of cows, or a couple of pigs being

walked to a nearby market. This was a highway of meat, and depending on the season, it might be packed bumper-to-bumper with four-footed critters, or even great flocks of turkeys, ducks, or geese. Accounts from the era likened the pig drives to a great river—a muddy, mouthy, rowdy one—stretching seemingly unbroken from Kentucky and Tennessee into North Carolina and then the Deep South.

Deep South landowners/slave-owners planted cash crops—cotton, tobacco—finding it more profitable to buy meat raised elsewhere than to turn their land to grazing. Mountain settlers discovered that the wilderness they were carving into was a cheap place to raise pigs, cows, and sheep that could be turned loose to find fodder on the steep slopes or high ridges. Those animals were a valuable commodity to be sold farther south. The balds in the region had been grazed for millennia, first by large woolly mammoths, later by bison and elk, and ultimately by the cattle of the settlers, their pigs foraging on fall mast up and down the steep hills. Fences were built around homesteads to keep roaming livestock out, not in, and these animals provided a small economy in cash or trade for the "isolated" homesteaders.

Deep South barons used slavery to turn their land into cash generators, but slavery also implicated larger landowners raising livestock in the mountain South. In *Slavery in the American Mountain South*, Wilma Dunaway's study of the limited plantation culture in southern Appalachia, the author notes that slaves were often used as drovers, shepherds, and "cowboys," a term that predated the Revolutionary War in the region. Slaves and free blacks often filled the more skilled positions, such as blacksmith, as well, and soon there was a self-sustaining industry of hostels for the drovers moving livestock.

Livestock stands sprang up every ten miles (the distance a cow or pig could reasonably be driven in a day) along the roadsides. Cooks and servants were needed for the hostels, and again, those positions were often filled by leased slaves.

The Buncombe Turnpike, completed in 1827, connected Tennessee and Kentucky stock owners, as well as North Carolinians, to southern markets. Livestock moving along the road included turkeys, geese, cows, and oxen. In October, November, and December the narrow road was packed with porkers in a continuous wave from Tennessee through Asheville to the South Carolina state line. Their pointed porcine hooves churned up the dirt, turning the crisp autumn blue skies into a cloud of red-brown dust, and what is now Biltmore Avenue in downtown Asheville into a river of mud.

And then the Civil War largely wiped out the industry (and the argument from some Ashevillians against turning their lovely, touristic city into a seasonal pigpen). Emancipation meant the elimination of free labor in the mountain livestock industry, and the stock itself was pillaged and decimated by both sides looking to cut off supplies to the enemy. The Appalachians sent as many soldiers to the Union as to the Confederacy, and so its resources were fair game for destruction from either. Large livestock operations became a thing of the past.

But the tradition of the small farmer allowing his extra cows and pigs to fatten on mast, then sending them to more local markets, continued well into modern times.

————

Ossabaws were the pigs brought into the South by Spanish explorers in the 1500s, and are prized for their ability to store fat. At Chuck Talbott's Woodlands Pork farm in West Virginia, they've been bred with hybrid sows to produce a hog that has a long snout and long thin legs "that can really get them around the mountains. You should see them going up and down those steep slopes. They're like watching a bunch of dirt bikes run around," Chuck's partner Jay Denham says.

The pigs start out on pasture planted in corn, beans, and squash—a feast the wild marauding pigs of early Appalachia might have scavenged from an unprotected pioneer garden. Then they are turned loose in the woodlands to fill up on acorns, hickory nuts, and walnuts, pawpaws, and persimmons, which is why before Chuck, Jay, and their third partner, Nic Heckett, put a pig on this land, they established a forestry program, culling all the non-mast-producing trees and cataloging nut drop and fruit production. They started with a dozen or so Ossabaw boars, and now raise and slaughter about a hundred hogs every season.

The temperate climate that allows for the slow salt cure that layers flavor over flavor in meat is found in what cure aficionados call "the ham belt," a path girding the world that runs through the notable meat-curing regions of Spain, Italy, Eastern Europe, China, and smack through the Appalachian South and the Ozarks.

I tell Jay I like to say that the mountain South is "the buckle on the ham belt," and he laughs and says, "Exactly. But it's not just about the climate and the method; it all comes down to the meat.

"Commodity pigs are slaughtered at six to eight months," Jay says, "but that's actually when the 'money fat' starts to come in. You can tell a pig's age by the fat rings, kind of like you can do with a tree, you know. So there's a third fat layer that comes in at about eight to twelve months. We raise our pigs for the fat, because that's where the flavor is."

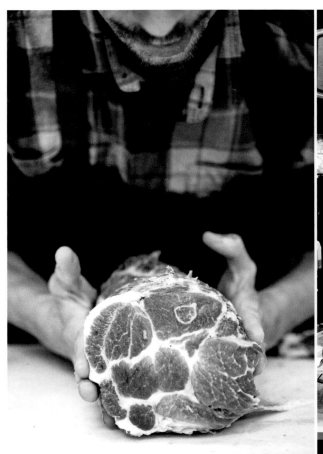

Fat was also the goal for mountain farmers back when working the land and keeping the homestead going could require as much as 3,000 calories a day. Fatback fried in a skillet and served alongside greens or beans was not only tasty but also a way to build up energy reserves. More fat on the hog meant more lard for frying and baking. And fat could be ground into sausage to give it that wonderful unctuous quality. Jay says it takes about a year and a half for one of their premium hogs to reach their target weight of 325 pounds.

The hogs are slaughtered in the mountains of eastern Kentucky at The Chop Shop, a stockyard and processing facility in Hazel Green owned by Jonathan Whitt and established with help from a grant from the state. Cattle production has been on the rise in the region in recent years, and the facility allows farmers to realize more profit from their livestock by processing and selling the meat instead of selling animals to the stockyard. The University of Kentucky has been training local workers at The Chop Shop in butchery and processing skills, but Jay takes his own crew to the facility to cut the meat for maximum use.

The hams made from Woodlands Pork cure for several years and are sold largely to restaurants, bringing a premium price. But Jay has been working with mountain farmers to raise Mulefoot hogs, a breed he says was traditionally raised in Kentucky specifically for curing.

In Louisville, I get to see Jay's passion for curing at his Curehouse warehouse. It sits off a thoroughfare cluttered with fast food and cheap goods, and it's easy to wonder if you can possibly be at the home of a fine charcuterie. But when you open the metal door, there is no mistaking. The intoxicating smell of salted pork permeates everything. I look to my left, where row after row of mahogany- and russet-colored hams are hanging from tiered racks, like fat-crusted mandolins. I know that when I get home, my dog is going to love me.

Jay hands me a small, fragrant stuffed cloth bag that smells of pork and sage and sour, and says, "That's old-school sock sausage. You'd stuff it in a clean old sock and hang it to cure. We put it in cotton bags now; socks don't exactly fly with the USDA. You're gonna love that." He is right. Fried up at home, the taste is both meaty and cheesy, sharp yet humming in the mouth. (The dog doesn't get any.)

————

It was the covenant of my childhood, a promise offered on every other freshly painted barn along U.S. 25 when we went up home to Corbin in the summers: "See 7 States Atop Lookout Mountain. See Rock City, Chattanooga, Tennessee." It was, the signs said, the 8th Wonder of the World.

So in the summer of 1968, I was filled with thrilled anticipation when a boyfriend drove me down to meet his family in the fabled city. But instead of a world of vistas and marvels, we rode at a perilous pitch into a smoky, gloomy jungle of industrial buildings, endless freight trains, clanking metal machinery, and sad-eyed, worn-down-seeming people going about the business of producing iron, running freight on trains and trucks, bottling Coca-Cola, and churning out Moon Pies. Once actually atop Lookout Mountain, I peered through a telescope aimed presumably at the convergence of seven sovereign entities, but all I could make out was the vague outline of drooping trees beneath a shifting miasma of red-tinged smog. The next year Chattanooga would be dubbed "The Dirtiest City in America" by CBS News anchor Walter Cronkite on national television.

I think about that first disappointing trip as I am driving into Chattanooga in early spring 2015. On this new day, the sky is a brilliant blue above a city that seems intent on imagining itself into a brand-new story. A young chef/restaurateur, Erik Neil, meets me at his flagship, Easy Bistro & Bar, in a soaring downtown space that would not be out of place in Manhattan. This building was the first Coca-Cola bottling plant in the country, Erik tells me, the sweep of his hand taking in the black walls with steel accents, the high plaster ceilings, the tall bar tables and low lime-green couches that flank the dining area. "This building was empty for twenty-eight years before we took it over in 2005. There were people who thought we were crazy." But Erik saw a coming together of interesting pieces, and what they suggested was a terrific possibility.

"My mom married a guy who lived here, so I started coming to Chattanooga when I was in college. Growing up in Louisiana, my relationship with food was strong. I knew that's what I wanted to do, but for most, that meant going to the Northeast or San Francisco, and that Bedouin chef route didn't appeal to me." Wanting to be closer to his family, he moved to Chattanooga in 2000 and began working in restaurants, where he met his wife, Amanda, who'd been born in Soddy-Daisy just up the road. She was working front of the house but had experience helping to run a small business with her family. The couple worked out a business plan and found interested investors.

"The city leaders really do have a progressive vision and they created a food infrastructure that is very sophisticated for a city this size," Erik says. "We have a luxury in farms, produce, people dedicated to that sustainable scene. Civic leaders put money into establishing a farmers market, but the foundations here also put money into establishing distribution channels to groceries, restaurants, and also to a food bank so the farmers get that support."

In 2014 Erik and Amanda took over the operations of Main Street Meats, a new "old-fashioned" butcher shop and eatery. The concept behind Main Street Meats is simple: to use as much locally raised meat as possible, and to use the whole animal.

Part of creating a sustainable butcher shop is weaving a web of connections, from the farm to the rancher, to the cutting table, to the customer, a problem that not only intrigues Erik's business sense but also appeals strongly to the intellect of Main Street Meats' head butcher, thirty-something Milton White.

Milton—tall, soft-spoken, bespectacled, and perpetually wearing a wool British flat cap—has a way of backing into his vocations. He grew up nearby. His grandparents had a big garden and he grew up conscious of the canning and cooking that went on around it, but his early interests were math and science and he thought he'd end up with a degree in engineering. In his teens, he decided to become a vegetarian, and because his mother wasn't into making suppers with no meat, he taught himself how to cook and thereby discovered a passion.

"Vegetarian cooking naturally led to Asian food and especially Japanese, and I got a job as a sushi chef. I was drawn to the simplicity and the subtleness. I started reading everything I could and discovered that what we were doing wasn't really authentic, but I picked up knife skills there and that intrigued me." He got a job working at Easy Bistro and eventually took over the head pastry chef position, for the opportunity to learn the science of baking. Having returned to eating meat, he became intrigued with charcuterie, attended a workshop in Asheville, and then did a six-month apprenticeship with the butcher at Link 41, the meat shop back in Chattanooga, which would eventually become Main Street Meats.

"What attracted me to Link 41 was they worked directly with the farmers in the area, and they worked with the whole animal." It was also a suddenly useful skill set, as Milton developed an allergic reaction to working with flour, scotching his promising pastry career. So he left Easy and became the head butcher at Main Street Meats. Eventually

Erik and Amanda Neil became the new owners. "I pretty much just wanted to work with Milton," Erik says, laughing. "He's the soul of the shop, and so much of making connections to the community, making what we do vital, depends on him."

"I take a lot of pride in knowing how to take things apart and put them back together," Milton says. "I like science, solving problems. Making salami, it was all chemistry. Butchery was all about anatomy, like a 3-D puzzle. In America, we cut a pig to get the most pork chops as possible, but in Italy, they want the *coppa*, the back of the neck. If you butcher with a preference for certain cuts, you eliminate or get others. You have to think about all of that before you make that first cut.

"So a lot of what I do is to try to educate people. And when a customer comes in with a recipe and we don't have the specific cut it asks for, I have to know what else it might be called, or what they can substitute. Those are some of my most interesting conversations. We have cooks and chefs from the restaurants come in and hang out. And I do classes here. When you take something you know and talk it through to someone who doesn't understand, and they walk away knowing so much more, that's really something to me. What I love is that I really wanted to make this something for the community."

That connection is important for Erik as well. The website for Main Street Meats contains photos and a brief description of the eight nearby farms from which they source their meat and cheese. There's a link inviting interested consumers to set up a visit with any of the partner farms. I ask both Erik and Milton about Cloudcrest Farm, just over the line in Rossville, Georgia, owned by Diane and Jim Johnson, a founding partner in Link 41 and Main Street Meats. I would swear the lenses in Milton's wire-rims light up. "I can't exactly explain it," he says, "but I could tell you if a cut of meat came from one of their animals. It's richer, deeper, just beautiful meat."

Erik says, "They have the best pork I've ever had. Their pigs are happy and you can taste it."

————

Pulling up to a farmstead, it is not uncommon to be met by a barking dog, guarding the homeplace for its owners. Arriving at Cloudcrest Farm, though, is the first time I have ever been met by a guard turkey. From my van, the tom looks tall, as high as my waist, feathers glossy and red wattle wagging like a warning as he tells me in no uncertain terms to wait until I get clearance. Reinforcements hover in the background, a second

turkey who keeps his peace but casts a sharp, wary eye. Jim Johnson walks up grinning, shoos away his sentries, and holds out a hand in welcome.

I alight and even though my shoe plops into mud made by melt of an unusual spring snow, I feel like I'm standing in heaven. The 283 acres roll softly down to the valley on one side, reach up to the trees of Missionary Ridge on the other. This piece of northwest Georgia land, once remote, now only twenty minutes away from downtown Chattanooga, has been in Diane Johnson's family for five generations, reaching back to the early 1800s.

Jim and Diane live in a white frame farmhouse on the property, the one with the wide, easeful porch and an addition or two on the back. The sort of old farmhouse that has grown along with the families that occupied it.

The kitchen is both loved and lovely, with a large family table, wooden counters scarred from cutting, handmade baskets and pottery put to use holding vegetables and fruit. Jim makes espresso in a Moka stove-top pot and Diane passes me a small rounded cup with the familiar gray glaze and blue design of Louisville's Hadley Pottery—the Farm Boy pattern. Both seem pleased that I recognize my cup's origins, and Jim begins to recount the many paths they took to land back here, a place where it seems they should have always been.

Both Jim and Diane grew up in New Orleans, but Jim's grandparents had farms in Kentucky, where he spent summers, and Diane's family, too, came back every summer to the homeplace where her dad grew up, Cloudcrest. "It was very different then," she says, remembering the area in the early 1970s. "All the mills and factories filled the air with pollution, and I would think, why would anyone want to live in Chattanooga? But when we got to the farm, it was sort of an oasis. I watched my grandmother make applesauce from the apple trees right here. My dad would pick blackberries and he made the best jam and pies. From those experiences, Jim and I both learned to really appreciate real food, and the life on the farm. We wanted to keep that connection."

The road back to the homeplace was anything but straight, however. Jim served in the navy and merchant marines, earning a degree in law as he did. "When I got out, I went back to New Orleans and looked up Diane." I ask if they had dated in high school and Jim says no, she was five years younger. "But I remembered her," he says with a tender smile in her direction.

By the time they married in 1977, Jim says, "I had bought an old beat-up farm in Nelson County, Virginia, outside of Charlottesville. It had a two-story chestnut log cabin from 1821, one of the oldest buildings in the county. We *really* were going back to the land then, to what we remembered of our grandparents."

But it was harder to make a living from a working farm than in his grandparents' day. Eventually, Jim explains, they ended up raising food for themselves, including the hogs they'd once hoped to sell. "We had a kill day just for family and friends the first of every December. But I wanted to stop spending so much time on the phone, trying to find a home for my meat."

They tried a second farm in Louisa, Virginia, with a focus on beef. "I was trying to figure out how to make it viable, like my grandparents did. You've got to work with the existing system, but make it work for the farmer."

The way to do that, Jim decided, was to create a cattlemen's association that allowed the farmer to "own" the animal all the way to the grocery. The prevailing model, where the calf is sold to a middleman who then processes the beef and takes the profit, leaves the farmer with the short end. The association Jim started in Virginia would have allowed the farmer to share in that final profit, but before it got underway, the beef market took one of its periodic dives in price and the project was scotched.

"I've never been able to farm full-time. I've always worked off the farm," Jim says a little ruefully, although he owns that he loves the work of his Chattanooga law practice, which largely represents whistle-blowers and anti-discrimination cases. For a while in Virginia, it looked as if law would be his life. The family moved off the farm and to a suburban development.

"What I missed were the animals," Diane says. "I missed the connection to the earth. And to animals. I mean, there were deer, coyotes, owls, birds everywhere, but I missed the stewardship, the relationship with animals you raise."

By the time we get to this part of the conversation, we've returned outside to walk the barnyard and fields. I am struck by the fact that I've never seen more beautiful farm animals in my life. Even the hogs have presence and personality.

"Our animals have an unstressed life; they live in environments suited to them genetically," Jim explains. "And we appreciate them, so they enjoy human contact. I think that's how farming once was and is meant to be. That's the relationship of the shepherd to his sheep. There needs to be that direct connection."

Making that direct connection to their market, as well, Jim says, is what seems to be making the farm at Cloudcrest viable. "I thought about my grandparents' place outside Jefferson County, and I don't know that any of the animals they raised ever went farther than Louisville to market." That didn't work when they were in Virginia, he said, but by the time Diane and Jim came to Cloudcrest in 2005, to live with and help her aging parents, who have since both passed away, "the food scene had changed. You could sell directly to the consumer, to restaurants. You could sell just to people."

It's less than ten miles from the rural peace of Diane and Jim's place to Main Street Meats, where they now sell what they raise at Cloudcrest. As I drive back into the city under a clear blue winter sky, I consider that Chattanooga was once one of the destinations for that long-ago river of meat flowing down from the mountain balds and valleys. Large land and livestock owners could make good money when the distant markets for their animals held. The small mountain farmer less, but enough maybe to fix up the barn, replace an old plow. But when those faraway markets failed, so did the larger farms dependent on the livestock industry. Small farmers, though, were still able to find "markets" for that new calf or sow's litter among their neighbors—sometimes a cash sale, sometimes a trade for something truly needed.

I park in front of Main Street Meats and see that a line is already forming to order the nightly dinner special (Pork Bouillon, Farro, and Winter Kale Soup; Meatloaf with Colcannon) or the juicy burger with house pickles. While I wait, I admire the deep red brisket, the unassuming bavette steak, the spicy merguez and no-nonsense liverwurst in the wide butcher's case. I suddenly find myself thinking about the subtly sour sock sausage I bought from a young local farmer back home who said to me, "I do what I do because of my granddaddy. He taught me everything." It dawns on me that in the small North Carolina mountain town where I live today, I can still come by all the meat I need—beef, pork, bacon, sausage, chicken, an heirloom Thanksgiving turkey, and the occasional package of venison—from people who live within twenty miles of me. Some from the farmers markets, some from the small meat processor up the street, some from my neighbors' freezers. And while it can sound romantic to preach eating locally, to open a neighborhood butchery, to celebrate sustainable husbandry, it is, in the mountain South, also a reality that has stood the test of time.

Skillet Fried Chicken &
Milk Gravy SERVES 4

Not every mountain farm had a cow or a pig, but virtually every household had a flock of chickens and they most often graced the Sunday table. Those that mountain farm wives cut up and fried were not only smaller, leaner, and keener-flavored than commercially bred birds today, they were sectioned into smaller pieces that fried in the skillet to a perfect crust while leaving the meat juicy and sweet. I recommend you halve the breasts for frying. What's important is to have the pieces of chicken in the skillet roughly the same size.

Additionally, skillet-frying is a different beast than deep-frying. Deep-frying is quicker and in a restaurant or fast-food joint, more economical, so that most of the fried chicken you encounter "out" is deep-fried. Restaurants that actually skillet-fry will tell you up front that your order will take about 30 minutes to be ready. That's because skillet-frying, in the mountains, is actually a form of braising in oil that tenderizes and keeps the chicken juicy while producing a delicious crust.

To do this, you need a skillet with a tight-fitting lid. Chicken fryers in mountain kitchens are often wide (a 10- to 12-inch skillet or Dutch oven–style pan) and have a lid that is dappled on its inside surface with raised metal nipples that collect steam and oil as the chicken sizzles. When enough liquid gathers, it will release and "rain" back into the pan, producing a noise that sounds like a little waterfall. Traditional cooks often said that's when you knew your chicken was done and it was time to take the lid off and crisp it.

One final word: Lard is really what chicken should be fried in. Good leaf lard is becoming more readily available and that's what you should look for. Mountain cooks of my mother's generation often fried in vegetable shortening as it became more readily available because fewer people slaughtered their own meat. It can make a good fried chicken, as does peanut oil, but lard is best. Make sure whatever oil you fry in is fresh, and have some Bigger Isn't Better Buttermilk Biscuits (page 269) ready for serving.

1 cup all-purpose flour
1 teaspoon salt, plus more to taste
¼ teaspoon freshly ground black pepper,
    plus more to taste
1 whole chicken (2 pounds), cut into 10 pieces
    (wings, drumsticks, thighs, breasts halved)
1 cup whole milk
Lard or peanut oil, enough to fill the pan
    ½ inch deep

Place the flour, salt, and pepper in a gallon-sized plastic bag, close it, and shake to mix. (You can also use a similarly sized clean paper sack.) Add the chicken, a couple of pieces at a time, and shake to coat each piece well. (The chicken skin should be fresh and damp enough that the flour sticks to it well. If it doesn't, dredge the pieces in milk or buttermilk before breading.) Put the breaded pieces aside to let the breading dry slightly and set. Save 1 tablespoon of the remaining seasoned flour for making the gravy.

In a large, heavy, lidded skillet, heat the lard on high heat until a fleck of the breading dropped in the pan dances and sizzles invitingly. Carefully lay the chicken pieces in the hot grease, skin side down. They can be nestled close together, but they should not touch. If the skillet is going to be crowded, fry in batches or use more than one skillet.

When the skillet is full, turn the heat down to medium and let the pieces fry until the first side is just turning golden, about 2 minutes. Then turn the pieces over and allow them to fry until just light golden on that side. Cover the skillet, turn the heat to low, and braise the chicken for about 25 minutes. The heat should be high enough that you hear the chicken sizzling, but not so high that it browns the chicken too quickly. You can check occasionally, turning the heat lower if needed.

When the pan side of the chicken is a deep golden brown, gently turn the pieces over, turn the heat up just a bit, and cook uncovered for a couple of minutes to

(recipe continues)

brown the first side and crisp the crust (this takes about 4 minutes). Place the chicken pieces on a rack set over paper towels, and let them drain for a moment before transferring them to a warm serving plate. Keep the chicken warm while you make the gravy.

Drain off all but 2 tablespoons of the fat in the frying skillet, and use a metal spatula to loosen the flecks of breading that may be sticking to the bottom or sides. Set the skillet over low heat and sprinkle the reserved tablespoon of seasoned flour into the drippings, stirring constantly until the flour is lightly browned. It will take a minute or two.

Slowly add the milk to the skillet, stirring constantly to keep the mixture from lumping. When all the milk has been added and there are no lumps, increase the heat to medium-high, still stirring. Cook until the mixture begins to bubble and thicken, just a minute or two. Remove from the heat, taste, and add salt or pepper if needed. Serve immediately.

Delicious Pork Chops SERVES 4

After chickens, pigs were the most common critter raised for food in the mountains. Families without a hog of their own might participate in a neighbor's slaughter day and come away with fresh pork to cook or cure for the winter, or enough chops to feed a family. Unlike modern, plastic-wrapped pretenders-to-be-white-meat, those chops were not pale, thick, lean, or boneless. They were, however, delicious.

Yours can be, too, and there is little you need do to make them so if you start with the right meat to begin with. That would be a chop from the rib, and it will have the classic pork chop shape: a chubby club with a short handle. There will be bone in the handle and running along one edge. There will be very visible fat. Such chops go by different names but all have the word "rib" in them.

Fried Apples (page 189) make a fine accessory here, as do Kentucky Kimchi (page 224), and of course Mama's Mashed Potatoes (page 50) or Bigger Isn't Better Buttermilk Biscuits (page 269).

4 pork bone-in rib chops, ½ inch thick (about 2½ pounds total)
Salt to taste
Lemon pepper to taste
Bacon grease, for cooking
1 tablespoon all-purpose flour (optional, for gravy)
1 cup whole milk (optional, for gravy)

Season the chops on both sides with salt and lemon pepper, rubbing lightly so the seasoning adheres. In a wide, heavy skillet (of course cast-iron is best) on medium-high heat, melt enough bacon grease to just coat the bottom of the pan. You don't want a puddle—just a sheen.

Lay the chops in the skillet with a little space between them. If your skillet size demands, fry them in two batches rather than nestling them together.

Turn the heat up a bit to brown the first side quickly, about 3 minutes. Flip the chops over and when they just start to turn brown, turn the heat down to low and cover the skillet. Let sizzle on low for 5 minutes. Then remove the lid, and if the chops need to brown a little more, turn up the heat and do it quickly. Transfer the chops to warm plates.

If you'd like to make a gravy, brown the flour in the skillet drippings over medium heat, and then slowly pour in the milk, stirring. Bring to a boil, stirring, and continue to stir until it just begins to thicken. Season with salt to taste, and serve immediately.

Doorbell Pork, Hominy & Wilted Greens SERVES 4 (OR 6)

Chef Travis Milton told me a story about going with his mother and brother to see his ailing great-grandmother. She was thrilled to have her family visit, but also anxious. A prolific cook who fed her family well all of her life, in her solitary older days she kept only a few essentials in the house. As soon as her kin arrived, she began to apologize and fret that she had nothing to feed them.

"Then right in the middle of a conversation she suddenly perked up and said, 'Wait a minute! I know!' and took off to the kitchen," Travis said. They heard her bustling about for a bit, and when she returned, it was with a bowl of Spam Salad. "It was a recipe she'd read in a magazine and cut out, and she'd remembered she had the Spam. My brother was pretty wary, but I was so tickled I kept eating until it was all gone. And she was so tickled at that, she gave me the recipe. I've got it framed above my desk at work. Someday I'm going to tattoo it on my arm."

The need to feed anyone who crosses her doorstep is a deeply ingrained characteristic of virtually every mountain woman I've ever known. I've watched my own mother put a plate of four perfect pork chops—one for each of us—on the table just as the front doorbell rang. As my father made his way slowly down the hall to the door, my mom took the chops straight back to the kitchen, chopped them up, and mixed them with something close at hand so that as an unexpected guest or two made it back to the dining room, she was greeting them with an ample "casserole" and saying, "You timed it just right! Pull up a chair."

It's in this spirit that I came up with a recipe using canned hominy. If you are making supper for four, you can serve the chops as is and the hominy as a side, but should the doorbell ring at that crucial moment, you know what to do.

1 recipe Delicious Pork Chops (page 265)
1 (25-ounce) can Mexican-style hominy
1 teaspoon sorghum syrup or (packed) light brown sugar
2 teaspoons apple cider vinegar
1 cup chiffonade of mustard, turnip, or kale greens
¼ cup minced green onions, white and green parts
Salt and freshly ground black pepper
Hot sauce, for serving

Prepare the Delicious Pork Chops, and while the chops are cooking, drain the hominy, reserving ¼ cup of the liquid from the can. Dissolve the sorghum syrup in the reserved hominy liquid and stir in the vinegar.

When you remove the chops from the skillet, turn the heat down to low and scrape the bottom of the pan lightly with a metal spatula to loosen any crust. Add the drained hominy to the drippings and stir to coat it. When the hominy is warm, add the greens and stir to coat. Pour the hominy liquid over the mixture and turn the heat up until the liquid is lightly bubbling. Continue to stir and toss the hominy and greens until the greens are wilted and the liquid is almost all evaporated. Remove from the heat.

Toss the green onions into the mixture. Taste, and add salt and pepper as needed. If you are serving four people, serve immediately with the pork chops on the side. If unexpected company has arrived, chop the chops into bite-sized pieces, toss the pieces with the hominy mixture, and serve immediately. It's a nice idea to pass hot sauce on the side.

Bigger Isn't Better
Buttermilk Biscuits

MAKES 12 TO 16 2-INCH BISCUITS

The soft red winter wheat that grows well in the southern Appalachians is perfectly suited for oven-rising biscuits. Mountain mamas, keen to get everyone fed and the chores of the day begun, often made the biscuits small so that everyone got a hot one from the first batch while the second (and sometimes the third) was baking.

This basic recipe is especially fine with fried chicken, country ham, or pork chops. It came to me twenty-five years ago from chef Louis Osteen, who made his name cooking in the style of the Low Country in Charleston and Pawleys Island, South Carolina, but hails from the upstate, Anderson, in the foothills of the Blue Ridge. That and his passion for bluegrass music—not to mention his impeccable biscuits—make him pretty much an honorary mountain man to me. Incidentally, country singer Dwight Yoakam's grandmother, Earlene Tibbs of Betsy Layne, Kentucky, used bacon grease for the fat in her biscuits, and then daubed a spot of it on top of each one before baking. You can substitute ¼ cup bacon grease for an equal amount of butter in this recipe.

Although it is no longer milled in Knoxville, Tennessee, White Lily is still the preferred soft wheat flour for most Southern biscuit makers. Soft wheat has less protein and less gluten, making it a good choice for light biscuits. If you have a local mill, ask your miller if they do a soft wheat flour and try that.

The important thing to remember with biscuits is to use "light hands" when mixing them, as you would for pie dough. I am in favor of using fingers to blend the flour, fat, and liquid, and learning a feel for the dough by making them often—because depending on your flour, the humidity, maybe even the phase of the moon, you may need a little extra of one of the ingredients. But don't stress too much.

8 tablespoons (1 stick) butter, cold, diced, plus extra for the cookie sheet
2½ cups soft flour, plus extra for rolling
1½ teaspoons baking powder
½ teaspoon baking soda
1 teaspoon salt
1 cup whole buttermilk

Preheat the oven to 350°F. Lightly butter a cookie sheet.

In a large bowl, sift the flour, baking powder, baking soda, and salt together twice. Cut the butter into the flour mixture and use your fingers to lightly mix the flour and butter together until they form pea-sized clumps. Add the buttermilk all at once. Quickly and lightly mix it in until the dough just holds together.

Turn the dough out on a well-floured surface and gently pat it down; then fold it over and gently pat it down again. (Gently. Really.) Lightly roll the dough out to a thickness of about ¾ inch and cut out biscuits with a straight-sided 2- or 2½-inch biscuit cutter. Cut straight down, without twisting. Place the biscuits on the prepared cookie sheet with space between them and bake for 15 to 20 minutes, until the tops are just turning golden. Serve immediately.

VARIATIONS

To make a classic "cathead" biscuit, don't roll out but take a piece of dough about the size of a large egg and lightly round it into a dome, then place it onto the prepared cookie sheet.

To bake in a cast-iron skillet, butter the interior lightly (or use bacon grease), then nest the biscuits starting from one in the center and circling out until the pan is filled. The biscuits can touch one another.

Slow Cooker — Roasted Pork Shoulder SERVES 4

Thrifty homesteaders knew how to cook all cuts of the hogs that were slaughtered in the winter. The shoulder, slow-roasted with fat and bone, produced a richly textured, deeply flavored meat worth smacking your lips for. Modern mountain cooks use the slow cooker to create the same effect that roasting in a woodstove, kept going all day for heat as well as cooking, once provided.

I buy pork from one of several producers in my neck of the Blue Ridge who pasture their pigs and process them humanely. They also tend to raise heritage pigs that naturally come with more fat, and the cuts I favor reflect that. The last roast I cooked like this weighed about 3½ pounds at the market with a top fat layer about an inch deep. I trimmed that fat to ½ inch and the roast was then about 3 pounds.

½ tablespoon salt
½ teaspoon freshly ground black pepper
1 3-pound pork shoulder or butt, bone-in
2 tablespoons apple cider vinegar
1 tablespoon sorghum syrup
1 small yellow onion
1 tablespoon cornstarch

Rub the salt and pepper into all sides of the roast, including the top fat. Place a heavy skillet over high heat and as it is warming up, place the roast in the skillet, fat side down. The heat will render enough fat for browning the rest of the roast without sticking. When there is enough fat to coat the bottom of the pan well and the fat on the roast is turning golden brown, flip the roast over and brown the next side.

Brown all sides of the roast. This may entail using tongs to hold the roast to brown the short edges, but it only takes a minute or so and is worth it since it will intensify the flavor. You may also need to spoon some of the rendered fat out of the skillet as you are browning—the point is to sear the meat, not deep-fry it.

When the roast is browned all over, place it in a slow cooker. Carefully pour off the grease from the skillet. Add ½ cup of water to the skillet and deglaze it. Remove the skillet from the heat and add the vinegar and sorghum, stirring to dissolve the syrup. Pour this mixture into the slow cooker.

Peel the onion, quarter it, and break apart the sections. Scatter the pieces around the edge of the roast in the pot. Cover, and cook on the high setting for 30 minutes. Then turn to low and cook for 4 hours.

The pork roast will be well done but meltingly tender when the inner temperature is 165°F. Remove it from the pot and allow it to rest under a tent of foil while you make the sauce.

Strain the pan juices to remove the onion pieces. Degrease the juices and pour them into a small pot set over medium-high heat. In a small bowl, whisk the cornstarch with ½ cup of water to form a slurry. When the juices in the pot begin to bubble, whisk in the cornstarch slurry. Continue to whisk as the mixture bubbles for about a minute and thickens. Remove from the heat.

To carve the roast, begin on the side away from the bone to yield larger, uniform pieces. Pass the sauce on the side.

This makes a wonderful winter meal served with individual baked sweet potatoes.

Chipped Country Ham & Gravy

SERVES 4

My mother's Chipped Beef and Gravy was one of the most delicious foods to come out of her kitchen. That may be hard to believe for anyone who has eaten only the gelatinous mess served up in institutional cafeterias and deserving of the moniker S.O.S. But my mom made her gravy with both patience and bacon grease, and that made all the difference. For many years, I did, too.

Then, I don't know if the companies that made dried beef and sold it in those little glass jars changed their methods, or if something in my palate shifted, but while the gravy remained delicious, the beef suddenly seemed tasteless and papery, barely there at all. I flirted briefly with bresaola, but the slightly musty sweetness of the Italian dried beef didn't jibe with the gravy. The meat needed to be the very essence of salt.

"I make mine with country ham," Travis Milton said. Eureka!

You can serve this over toast made with June Hill's Salt-Rising Bread (page 298) or with Bigger Isn't Better Buttermilk Biscuits (page 269). Make the biscuit dough first, and start them baking while you make the gravy.

2 tablespoons bacon grease
¼ pound country ham
2 tablespoons all-purpose flour
2 cups whole milk
Salt and freshly ground black pepper
4 Bigger Isn't Better Buttermilk Biscuits or pieces of toast

If there is visible fat on the ham that can be easily removed, do so and set it to the side. Cut or tear the ham into pieces about the size of a 50¢ piece and about ¼ inch thick.

In a heavy skillet over medium heat, render the removed fat by pressing the pieces with the back of a spatula as they are frying. After about a minute, remove and discard any bits that did not render. Leave the melted fat in the pan. If you have no fat to render, you can use a little of the bacon grease, just to slick the skillet.

Add the ham pieces to the skillet and sauté briefly, until they just start to turn a little golden, 1 or 2 minutes. Remove the ham and set it to the side.

Add the bacon grease and let it melt. Turn the heat to low and sprinkle the flour over the grease, stirring steadily as you do. I like to use the back of the spoon, so it doesn't lump. Continue to cook and stir until the mixture begins to turn the color of brass (this takes 8 to 10 minutes). Then slowly add the milk, stirring steadily to incorporate it. When all the milk has been added, continue to stir until all is warmed through and the mixture is the thickness of heavy cream, about 6 minutes. Add the sautéed ham and stir to coat. Taste, and season as necessary with salt and pepper—and I mean it when I say "taste," because often the ham and bacon grease are salty enough with no addition needed. Remove from the heat and serve over toast or biscuits.

Winter Vegetable Stew with Ham Seasoning SERVES 4

The Joy of Cooking notes that someone once defined "eternity" as a ham and two people. In mountain kitchens, however, a holiday ham spelled "opportunity." We ate our fill at the table, and once the meal was finished, our hospitable hostess would return the remains of the beast to the kitchen and begin taking them apart with the skill of a surgeon.

Solid pieces the size of a palm would be sliced for sandwiches later. Smaller slabs might fill the morning biscuits or be chopped into ham salad. The meaty bone and shank ends that held tempting meat riddled with fat and tendon were set aside to serve as "seasoning meat." That meat might flavor any manner of beans, greens, or field peas, but in the winter, this hearty ham-laced vegetable stew was just the ticket, especially when served with Real Cornbread (page 120).

Up in my neck of the woods these days, the mountains of western North Carolina, the supermarket sells those choice fatty, bony pieces as "ham seasoning meat," so I don't have to cook a whole ham first. But who's calling that a hardship?

1 pound ham seasoning meat
½ head cabbage (about ¾ pound)
1 to 2 russet potatoes (about ½ pound total)
2 to 4 turnips (about ¾ pound total)
2 to 4 carrots (about ½ pound total)
1 large yellow onion
Salt and freshly ground black pepper
1 teaspoon sorghum syrup

Separate as much meat as possible from the fat, skin, and bones and set the meat aside. Put the rest in a wide soup pot or Dutch oven, add 4 cups water, and bring to a boil over high heat. Turn the heat down to a steady simmer, cover, and cook for 30 minutes.

While the broth is cooking, prepare the vegetables: Trim the bottom from the cabbage but leave the core. Cut the cabbage from crown to base in 4 wedges.

Peel the potatoes, and quarter or halve them lengthwise to make 4 pieces. Trim and peel the turnips and carrots, and if needed, halve them to make 4 pieces of each. Peel and quarter the onion.

When the broth is ready, remove the pot from the heat and spoon the solid matter into a strainer set over the pot. Press down gently to return the juices to the pot, and then set the strained matter aside to cool. Taste the broth and add salt as needed. (Hams vary in their saltiness, so the broth will also.) Stir in the sorghum until dissolved.

Layer the vegetables in the pot, with the cabbage and potatoes on the bottom. Don't worry if they are not fully covered by broth; just try to tuck them in as best you can. Bring the broth to a boil, then cover the pot and turn the heat down to a lively simmer. Cook for 30 minutes.

While the vegetables are cooking, use your fingers to pull the meat you initially reserved into small pieces, discarding any hard gristle. Separate any meat from the cooled bones, fat, and skin. Reserve the meat and discard the remaining bits.

When the 30 minutes are up, gently incorporate the meat into the vegetables and broth, trying not to break up the vegetables too much as you do. Cover the pot and allow it to sit off the heat for at least 15 minutes before serving. Pass black pepper at the table to season to taste.

Root & Sausage Pie SERVES 6

Shepherd's Pie is a classic rural winter supper with hearty meat and vegetables simmered in the oven, topped with a "crust" of mashed potatoes, lightly browned. This hills and holler variation substitutes cornbread for the potato crust and ups the savor with sausage for the meat.

This recipe is very forgiving when it comes to pans. I used a 10-inch skillet and my recipe tester used an 8-inch. Both worked fine. You can also prep the sausage and vegetables in a skillet on the stovetop and then transfer them to a baking pan. If you'd like a creamier crust, increase the milk in the cornbread topping by ¼ to ½ cup. You can also choose a coarse or fine cornmeal, yellow or white, to suit your taste.

FILLING

1 pound bulk breakfast sausage
½ medium yellow onion, chopped
1 cup chicken, vegetable, or beef broth
1 teaspoon Hungarian sweet paprika
½ teaspoon salt
2 cups chopped parsnips
1 cup chopped carrots
1 cup chopped turnips

TOPPING

1 cup stone-ground cornmeal
1 teaspoon salt
½ teaspoon baking powder
½ teaspoon baking soda
1¼ cups whole buttermilk

Preheat the oven to 425°F.

Prepare the filling: Heat a large ovenproof skillet over high heat and add the sausage, breaking it into ½-inch pieces with a spoon as it cooks. When the meat begins to release its juices, add the onion and stir. Fry until the meat has begun to brown and the onion has softened and started to turn translucent, about 5 minutes. Transfer the meat-and-onion mixture to a bowl.

Return the skillet to medium-high heat and deglaze it with the broth, stirring to dissolve the brown bits. Stir in the paprika and salt, and add the parsnips, carrots, and turnips. Allow to come to a simmer, and then cover. Cook for 7 minutes, or until the vegetables are just tender.

Remove the skillet from the heat, and stir the sausage and onions into the vegetables. Set aside.

Make the topping batter: In a bowl, blend the cornmeal, salt, baking powder, and baking soda. Add the buttermilk, stirring well. The mixture should be thick but pourable.

Starting at the outside rim of the skillet and moving inward, pour the cornbread batter evenly over the sausage and vegetables. Use a spatula to smooth over any empty places and cover the top completely with batter.

Bake the pie: Place the skillet in the oven and bake for 15 minutes, or until the batter is set. If the top is not invitingly flecked with browned spots, put the skillet under the broiler for 1 minute. Watch carefully, as it can quickly go from brown to burned.

Serve hot, directly from the skillet.

Shredded Beef Shank &
Buttermilk Dumplings

SERVES 4 WITH SIDE DISHES, 2 WITHOUT

A cow was rarely butchered for consumption at home. Its meat was less amenable to curing and sausage than that of a hog, and a cow taken to commercial slaughter could often provide some much-needed cash and sometimes a piece of the less choice cuts of beef. When the grocery or butcher shop became a source of fresh meat, mountain cooks like my mother often preferred cheaper cuts with plenty of fat, bone, and connective tissue. That's because she had mastered those magical alchemies in which time and low heat transform a tough, scrappy piece of meat into intensely rich bits of flavor. The airy, buttery dumplings in this dish add another layer of richness to what is really a simple soup.

I use a slow cooker to make this, but if you prefer, you can brown the steaks in a skillet, increase the water from 1 to 4 cups, and then braise the meat in a heavy Dutch oven at 325°F for about 2½ hours.

2 beef shank steaks, about ¾ inch thick, with
    marrow bones (about 2 pounds total)
Salt and freshly ground black pepper
1 tablespoon bacon grease
1 teaspoon apple cider vinegar
½ tablespoon all-purpose flour
Buttermilk Dumplings (recipe follows)

Salt and pepper the steaks on both sides. (Go a little light on the salt as it intensifies during the slow cooking.)

In a heavy skillet, melt the bacon grease on medium-high heat, and brown the steaks on both sides. Transfer the browned steaks to a large slow cooker turned to the high setting. Use 1 cup of water to deglaze the skillet, add the cider vinegar to the water, and pour this into the slow cooker. Cover and cook for about 4 hours on high, until the meat can be pulled away easily with a fork.

Transfer the meat to a bowl, and place it in the refrigerator to chill. Pour the juices into a separate bowl and refrigerate them, too.

When the meat is cool enough to handle, shred it into small pieces, discarding any hard gristle. Use a spoon to scoop the marrow from the bones, and crumble it into the meat. Discard the bones. Set aside the shredded meat.

When the fat has risen and solidified on top of the meat juices, scrape it off, reserve 1 tablespoon, and discard the rest. You should have 1¾ to 2 cups of juices remaining.

Start making the Buttermilk Dumplings. When the first batch of dumplings is simmering in the boiling water, prepare the meat and broth:

Melt the reserved tablespoon of fat in a large saucepan over medium-high heat. Sprinkle in the flour and stir for about 1 minute, making a light brown roux. Whisk in the reserved juices slowly, so the flour doesn't lump. Bring the liquid to a simmer and when it begins to thicken, stir in the shredded meat, cover, and heat through. Taste the stew, and season with salt and pepper as desired. Add dumplings as they are finished, spooning the broth over them and covering the pot to keep the stew warm. When all the dumplings are cooked and added, serve immediately.

BUTTERMILK DUMPLINGS

MAKES 20 SMALL DUMPLINGS

These are small, soft drop dumplings and although there are few ingredients, good buttermilk gives them a burst of flavor. If you want to jazz things up, you can add a tablespoon of minced chives to the dry flour for savory dishes.

Appalachian cooks often made dessert by simmering a pot of sugared fresh or dried fruit in cider, water, or juice and then dropping dumplings into it. Sort of a cobbler, inside out. These dumplings are delicious used in that way, or you can add a tablespoon or two of sugar and a dash of mace, ginger, nutmeg, or cinnamon to the flour for a little extra flavor.

This recipe makes enough for the Shredded Beef Shank recipe (opposite) but can be doubled or tripled, if needed.

1 large egg
¼ cup whole buttermilk
¾ cup all-purpose flour
½ teaspoon salt
Oil, for greasing the spoon

Fill a wide pot with water to reach 6 inches deep. Bring the water to a boil.

While the water is coming to a boil, beat the egg and buttermilk in a large bowl until blended. Use a fork to stir in the flour, about ¼ cup at a time. Add the salt and mix until blended. The dough should be soft and sticky, but not runny. Use a greased teaspoon to scoop out the dough in little balls, about as big as the end of your thumb, and drop them into the boiling water.

The dumplings will sink, and then in a minute or so, rise to the surface and float. Use a spatula to nudge any that seem to be sticking to the bottom of the pan. Don't crowd the pan, and cook in batches if needed. Let the dumplings cook for 10 minutes. Then remove them with a slotted spoon, shaking it gently to drain them. Transfer the dumplings to the pot of hot sauce or stew, spooning some sauce over each dumpling, and cover to keep warm while you cook the rest. When all are ready, serve immediately.

(Leftover dumplings and sauce can be reheated and eaten the next day, but the texture of the dumplings will be markedly thicker and chewier.)

Shelley Cooper

Chef Shelley Cooper has lived a mobile, high-flying life: after culinary school at Johnson & Wales, she cooked for chef Louis Osteen in Charleston, had a rise and fall in the Los Angeles food scene, a gig in New Zealand, a sojourn working at lodges in Alaska ("You work 24/7. You have to think ahead."), and another in Hawaii.

But when the owners of Chattanooga's StoneFort Inn told her they wanted her to take the helm at TerraMáe, she knew she had landed a fine dining restaurant with Appalachian Bistro roots. And when they sold that property and asked her to take over the Dancing Bear Appalachian Bistro in the Smokies, she knew she had come home.

Growing up in the late 1970s and '80s, Shelley spent three-quarters of the year in Memphis with her Mississippi Delta–born mother and grandmother. But in the summer, her father (her parents divorced when she was very young) would take Shelley and her brother to their old homeplace in the Blue Ridge Mountains. "Memphis was so hot, so humid, so flat when he would get us in the car. We would drive and drive and then suddenly it would be cooler, and we'd be winding into high greenness. Then up a gravel road, and I'd open the door and kick off my shoes and run through that soft, soft, soft, soft green grass. My grandmother and aunt would come out the screen door, to the front porch and we would just hug and hug. And I was home for the summer."

Her mountain grandmother's house was full of cousins and relatives all summer long. "There could be twenty people in the house sometimes. My uncle Bill ran moonshine and smelled like Old Milwaukee. He was skinny as a pen. My aunt Marie would make these cinnamon rolls. No one was supposed to come in the kitchen when she made them because that was her domain, her time. But she would let me go in to watch, to learn. To me, it was a big deal. I was fascinated by it and that farmhouse is where I learned to cook. I loved the whole peeling, and boiling, and frying and mashing, and how everything had a season and a different way to cook.

"Most of the cooking was done on the coal-burning stove. My grandmother had a newer stove, but the old one is what she preferred to cook on. You would wake up and smell the coal and the damp mountains in the air. You'd not want to get out of the bed with its feather pillows, the handmade quilts. But then you'd smell the country ham, the biscuits, and the hot cast iron. And you'd get right out of that bed and to the table where

you'd find five or six varieties of homemade jam and applesauce, fried potatoes, sausage, bacon.

"There was an orchard and one of the chores was to fill buckets with whatever apples were in season. We would dig potatoes and beets, pick whatever needed picking. And we'd eat whatever we were picking, dirty fingers and all. There were potatoes in the ground sprouting for the next year. And water—like silk, like velvet—was drawn from the well.

"Marguerite, my father's mother, and my papaw worked so hard and they didn't complain. Their whole generosity came from what they put in the earth and it gave back, and to me that's the purest way of giving."

Shelley stands and walks back to the kitchen to get a fresh pot of coffee and I look out the window where a late winter snow is starting to fall. I'm imagining winter on that mountain farm; imagining her grandmother crocheting afghans in a rocker by the fire. Shelley comes back, fills my cup, and throws me a curveball.

"My grandparents didn't live there full-time. My uncle had a cabin and other family members were there and helped with the property, but when it wasn't summer, my grandmother was a chemistry professor at Christian Brothers University. She was the first woman to receive a doctorate in chemistry from the University of Memphis. She was fifty-seven then."

Marguerite Cooper, a single mother from the mountains, got her bachelor's degree in North Carolina in 1937, then married, raised a family, and after that went back to school and became a professor whose students called her "Dr. Mom."

At Dancing Bear, trout and rabbit and squash casserole and butter beans show up in artful, but honest, preparations. "I am so proud of where I come from, of who raised me, and ultimately, all of this is an homage to my mountain grandmother, her strength and her love."

Shelley Cooper's Jonas Ridge Grilled Trout SERVES 4

The southern Appalachians I knew as a child were literally flowing with food in the abundant rivers and lakes that jeweled the region. When we were serious about supper, we ran a trotline across a channel and once or twice a day the fisher would pull the string to see what might have been lured.

Chef Shelley Cooper vividly remembers summer trout suppers at her grandmother's place. Pulled fresh from the river, the trout were cooked outside in cast-iron skillets over an open fire. "I like to serve this the way I remember it as a child on Jonas Ridge, family-style on a picnic table with the sounds of crickets and ice-cold running water from the mountain stream in the background. It's best if you eat it barefoot," she says.

4 whole fresh trout (8 to 10 ounces each), dressed, rinsed, and patted dry
4 tablespoons butter, at room temperature, plus more for the skillet
Kosher salt and ground white pepper
16 slices Preserved Lemons (page 225)
½ cup combined fresh tarragon and fresh basil leaves, torn

Prepare a fire pit or a large grill with charcoal and several water-soaked sticks of an aromatic grilling wood, such as maple or pecan wood.

While the charcoal and wood is heating, prepare the trout by rubbing each one inside and out with 1 tablespoon of the butter. Season the fish on both sides with salt and white pepper. Go a little light on the salt, as the preserved lemons are intensely salty.

Stuff the cavity of each trout with 4 slices of preserved lemon and 2 tablespoons of the tarragon-basil mixture.

Rub butter on a lidded cast-iron griddle or skillet, greasing it well. When the coals are glowing and the soaked wood is smoking, place the trout on the griddle, cooking in batches if necessary to maintain some room between the fish. Center the griddle over the coals, and cover with a lid. It should take approximately 15 minutes for the trout to be done (the fish will flake easily when a fork is inserted near the center). Check for doneness at 10 minutes, since the cooking time can vary with the heat of the fire.

Appalachian Spring

I recall the drives we made regularly in my childhood, on old U.S. 25, on our way to Corbin. Somewhere south of Mount Vernon, the narrow two-lane would suddenly be flanked by jagged, silvery rock stretching to shutter the sky. In the summer, kudzu and scrub blanketed those walls in a green so dark it was almost black. But in the spring, on our first trip "up home" after the cold post-Christmas winter, the green was pale and sparser, dappled sometimes with white and yellow, purple and pink.

"Well," my father would say, and swallow hard at the stark and fragile beauty.

My mother would spy a tree, gray barked and leaning, seeming ready to tumble from the weight of its years yet bearing shoots of impossible pale green. "Would you look at that good old tree?" she'd say. "Isn't that something? Isn't that a miracle?"

My first trip on this book's journey was also in the spring. I went to Staunton to visit the Frontier Culture Museum before the weather got too hot, the crowds too bustling. Spring in the Shenandoah Valley is spread out, expansive, welcoming. It's impossible not to believe in possibility. One of my first visits in Staunton is—really—to a store called Nu-Beginning.

John Matheny makes sure I've had enough to eat and my coffee cup is full before he pulls up a mix-and-match chair at my table. John, with his wife, Stella, are the owners of what is officially called The Store for Nu-Beginning Farm. A small man with gray hair and beard, glasses, and the look of a playful professor, he tells me instead that he spent most of his life "in one part of the corporate world or another. Then right after the 9/11 attacks, Stella and I realized it was time to move back home."

Stella wanted to be closer to her mother, then in her nineties, so the couple bought her house in Greenville, about twenty minutes south of Staunton. "It had a root cellar and three acres. We built a greenhouse and got a flock of Nubian goats. That's where we got the name Nu-Beginning Farm, and we thought we'd start a goat-related business but found out we were in violation of local zoning."

So they began raising and selling produce instead at Staunton's farmers market. And jam. And Stella's pound cake. And they started buying from other farmers. "And I thought it would be great to have a place where you could buy those things all during the week, and maybe a little breakfast/lunch place where we'd feature those products and

use that food on the menu and serve locally roasted coffee." Like the old general store, I say. But with better coffee, he adds with a laugh.

So he found a partner, a coffee roaster, and it seemed like a dream until his partner abruptly pulled out, taking the mechanical roaster, along with the chairs, tables, and dishware, with him.

"I thought that was it," John says, shaking his head but still grinning. "See these tables and chairs? People loaned them. Just started bringing in a chair here and there sometimes. Another local coffee roaster stepped up and did forty bags of coffee for us and gave me an old grinder. Cups. Glasses. Everything on loan or a gift from the community because they wanted us to be a part. I've got twenty years of restaurant management in my career, and that's unheard of. Unheard of in corporate America, but here in this mountain town, that's just how it is. They want to support us." He reflects for a moment, then waves his hand to take in the store, "So we support them back."

The tables and chairs sit cozily but haphazardly at the front of the store while the middle of the room is filled with open shelves stocked with products from the region, such as handmade soaps and creams, maple and shagbark hickory syrup, bags of locally roasted coffee, and locally made cookies, crackers, bread, and jams. ("If we run out of jam in the kitchen, we wait for the next order and ask what kind of jam that person wants, and that's the jar we open," John says.)

Beyond the shelving there's an open cooler filled with local produce, serving as a display case for customer sales but also as the walk-in for the kitchen, as that's what the cooks use for each day's changing menu.

The Store itself is in a tiny older strip mall that sits sideways to the street a good ways away from Staunton's cool little downtown. I would not have found it on my own, but a friend in Staunton has told me that the scones there are spectacular. He is right, except these are the real deal, British scones, and spectacular is too spectacular a word. These are *proper*. "That's Sam," John says, referring to Samantha Iles, the restaurant's primary cook and scone baker. "We were buying 'scones' from another source. She came on with us and immediately asked, 'What's that?' Then she went back in the kitchen for about thirty minutes, came out with these, and said, '*This* is a scone,' and that's what it's been since."

Samantha tells me the company's name, Nu-Beginning, suits her. A native of Surrey, England, she was the cook on a yacht, worked in the film industry, was married, divorced, "all in a jumble," she says. She landed in Staunton between film catering gigs and found work at The Store. While we're talking, a tall, grizzled cabdriver comes in, sees immediately that I'm not from around there, and asks me if I've had any of Samantha's mushroom gravy yet. I shake my head "no," and he heads straight to the kitchen, and while John looks on smiling, the cabbie grabs a cup from the shelf, a ladle from a rack, and dips out a taste for the "stranger." It's lovely. Velvety and with a hint of spring from subtle herbs. The three of them watch as I taste, let it linger, smile and shake my head "yes." They all smile and nod in return.

Samantha. John and Stella. Ian Boden. Right down the road from the Frontier Culture Museum, it's hard for me not to paint these newly arrived Staunton folk as modern-day versions of the immigrants, the pioneers memorialized there. Each of them has landed in a contemporary Appalachia that, like the one of the past, holds both promise and risk. They are carving out new stories for themselves, intertwining both land and community. It's the story I've seen here, and in Asheville, and Chattanooga and Knoxville. But I am also mindful of what Ian Boden told me up front: he looked at the farmers market and knew the food was here, but he looked at the surrounding cars and their license plates to see if he could stake his economic claim with a restaurant.

South of the Alleghenies, along the swath of the Blue Ridge and Smokies, there has been an economy based on tourism and second homes of the gentry for more than two centuries. But not far north of Staunton and other towns, like Asheville, with farmers market parking lots filled with license plates from D.C. and New York and Florida, there has been coal: eastern Kentucky and West Virginia, East Tennessee and southwest Virginia. That's a generalization, but it's a fairly apt and really useful one. In areas with vibrant tourism or, like Chattanooga, towns where younger artists and entrepreneurs can now put down roots while connected to the world outside via the Internet, there is a food-savvy market that can potentially sustain the sustainable—but expensive—food movement. In coal country, things are more complicated.

————

I meet Wendy Johnston by chance. One of the perils or pleasures of riding shotgun with me is the frequent detour into parts unknown also called "Oops, we're lost." Luckily, my companion one August morning in Princeton, West Virginia, is chef Edward Lee, who, like me, thinks "lost" is a synonym for adventure, an adjunct of opportunity. He is fairly dancing in his seat when my meandering to get us back to the interstate after a breakfast of brown beans, cornbread, and slaw dogs takes us instead down a street that is near deserted except for a parking lot farmers market.

Ed is out of the van, to the first stand. "Isn't this okra gorgeous," he says, eyes sparkling. And indeed, it is! Perfectly striated plump cylinders of pale khaki are streaked with rose to deep reddish purple stripes. Just looking makes my mouth tingle. But, okra?

I turn to the woman at the stand. There's a red-haired daughter and a dark-mustachioed husband standing farther behind her. She gets the question in my eyes immediately and laughs. "I know. Not supposed to grow around here. But these are actually an okra I got from folks in the Alabama mountain region. Hill Country Red, they're called." Then her brow wrinkles. "Even so, they're not really supposed to grow this far north and high up. Some people might say they're a sign of global warming." I get the sense from the curious expression on her face that she is waiting to see if we are "some people," and when Ed and I nod, she nods back. As we talk more, I learn that conversations with Wendy Johnston often contain a good measure of mountain pride counterbalanced by a concern about what is happening ecologically in the region.

Perhaps that comes with the territory of being Sid Moye's daughter. Sidney Floyd Moye Jr. was born in 1945 on a farm near the edge of the New River Gorge canyon. His father and grandfather were both underground coal miners, but Sid worked for forty-three years as a printer and when he retired, there was nothing he wanted more than to go fishing in the rivers and streams he'd loved as a boy. He got in touch with the proper West Virginia officials to see about getting a fishing license and was tickled to discover that at sixty-five his driver's license could be used for that. His fishing was free. But the pleasure was short-lived. On the Earthjustice website, where Sid is honored as a "Mountain Hero," Sid wrote: "Then I get a letter from the West Virginia Department of Health and Human Resources. They were telling me that the streams in southern West Virginia had been polluted with mercury and PCBs and all sorts of heavy metals, and that sort of thing. They said: 'You can go ahead and go fishing and catch a small amount of bass. But you shouldn't eat more than four portions each year of the fish.' That really hit me. We can't even eat the fish here now."

So instead of becoming a fisherman in retirement he became an activist in the movement to stop mountaintop removal. Wendy became his partner in protest, and her parents turned their twenty-five-acre homestead, Mountain Valley Farm, into a nature preserve and educational center where young people from around the country came to learn sustainable farming methods and Appalachian traditions of making do and figuring out. When Sid died in January 2014, he left the property, where his wife, Dana, still lives, in a perpetual land trust.

Wendy and Steve Johnston's 230-acre farm is forty minutes away from Sid and Dana's place, north of Athens, West Virginia. Steve, who is also a farm equipment repairman and auctioneer, grew up on this piece of land. There's a small grove of bearing chestnut trees that he planted when he was fifteen, and he became the farm manager at the age of twenty-five. Now in his mid-fifties, Steve and Wendy have been married for a little over ten years, and her children from an earlier marriage have grown up in part on the farm. Steve's mother lives in the old farmhouse that sits down closer to the road. That two-story century-old building is bricked now, but Wendy tells me it was originally white clapboard, as is the long canning shed that still runs off the back. The shed is dark inside, but there is a soft red-orange reflection from several dozen quart jars of tomatoes on two shelves next to a black-shaded window that lets in just enough light around the edges to keep a body from tripping on the way to get supper.

Wendy and Steve raise both beef and lamb commercially. They sell at the farmers market in nearby Princeton during the season and also have had a CSA for half a dozen years. "I did it with my dad for the first three years, and when we started we had two people. Now we have seven to ten depending on the week. But, to be honest, the problem with the local food movement is that it's a bourgeoisie movement. The majority of the folks who live around here are not, and they either raise their own gardens or don't know why they would pay $3 for a tomato when they can get three for a dollar at the grocery store. So a lot of what we do—particularly at the farm market—is education."

Education has at least two aspects for Wendy. On the one hand it is introducing her peers in the community to the pleasures of heirloom tomatoes, the delicacy of good lamb, the value of farming sustainably, and, radiating out from that, protecting the surrounding water, land, and air. Part two is creating a new generation of gardeners and farmers. She works at this second part up the road from her place, at the community garden at the Appalachian South Folklife Center, established in the 1970s by Appalachian activist Don West and his wife, Connie.

"There's a whole community of young people who come to the Folklife Center, some from the region, all to learn about Appalachia. We don't just garden. We can. We talk about the history, the troubles in the region," Wendy says, brow furrowing.

That history includes the Battle of Blair Mountain in 1921, a five-day armed civil uprising as coal miners attempted to unionize in the face of flagrant exploitative labor practices. It includes the Elk River chemical spill in early 2014, when Freedom Industries released chemicals used to clean coal into the Kanawha River system upstream from Charleston, leaving 300,000 people without potable water for at least four days. It includes mountaintop removal by coal companies that have blasted off the tops of more than five hundred mountains in West Virginia, Kentucky, Virginia, and Tennessee.

I am not sure what to say next. We sit in silence. The garden at the Folklife Center nestles on a leveling at the bottom of a steady slope. A ridge rises in the distance. There is green everywhere. It is easy to believe this might be Eden.

"Would you say your work is sustainable?" I ask, not at all sure what I mean. But Wendy takes the question in thoughtfully. She considers it for a long moment. I wonder if she is weighing it against centuries of extractive economies. Suddenly she grins. "I taught my kids to grow their own food," she says, laughing. "I'm not sure you get much more sustainable than that."

———————

And so I am on the road to Egypt, Kentucky, near the end of my journey, but with a wealth of stories in my head. Here's another one: Egypt was named when the post office was established in 1876. The story goes that the dubbers were members of the Amyx family, who had moved there after the Civil War from Hancock County, Tennessee. The place seemed so isolated that the family felt exiled, they said, as if they'd been sent to farthest Egypt. But where transplanted Tennesseans once saw isolation, 140 years later a returned eastern Kentucky native, Lora Smith, and her husband, Joe Schroeder, see potential for building community.

I first met Lora on Facebook in 2010 via the Southern Foodways Alliance. Despite our thirty-year age difference, we discovered shared passions for all things southern Appalachian, all things Dwight Yoakam, and chili buns. Lora came by the latter the same way I did, as she, too, was born in Corbin, Kentucky.

Lora grew up in Corbin, the daughter of lawyers, and was encouraged, as the best and brightest from the region have long been, both subtly and directly, to seek a life outside the mountains. For a while, this is what she did, graduating magna cum laude from New York University and continuing graduate studies in the prestigious folklore program at the University of North Carolina at Chapel Hill.

But in between her studies and labors elsewhere (she was the "goat girl" at Celebrity Dairy Inn's farm in Siler City, North Carolina, for a while), she found herself repeatedly drawn back home to work in grassroots programs in eastern Kentucky, including Kentuckians for the Commonwealth, the arts collective Appalshop in Whitesburg, and as the Oral History Director at the Laurel County African American Heritage Center.

Now Lora and Joe live on 120 acres of mixed forest and pasture land in Egypt, which lies in Jackson County, which regularly makes the list of "100 poorest counties in the country." But where the census sees poverty, Lora sees the glimmer of possibility.

Four miles from Big Switch, the name Lora and Joe have given their farm, there is a USDA-certified community kitchen, like the ones established in the early 20th century to provide home canners with equipment. This one is new, however, and available for personal use (the day we are there, shelves are filled with home-canned food waiting to be picked up by the folks who put it up earlier in the week), but primarily available to create commercial products for sale, should folks in the community desire. Lora hopes to fan that desire.

On this early Saturday in May, she has rented the kitchen so a group of friends can gather to make a feast for a party at the farm.

The county kitchen is a long metal corrugated building sitting out in a wide field off a two-lane blacktop. Unappealing on the outside, on this Saturday it's welcoming within. Lora's friends are dancing around the conventional ovens, stovetops, deep kettles, and prep areas of the kitchen to put together the feast. Emily Hilliard is elbows-deep in flour and sweet potatoes for a masterful sonker, Amelia Ruth Kirby cracks jokes and eggs as she peels a few dozen for devilment, and Anna Bogle parses tincture from eyedroppers into Chartreuse and gin to create a beverage just for the moment called Appalachian Spring. Nadia Roy sees to Wiley, Lora and Joe's two-month-old Buddha of a baby in a carrier propped on a long folding table, and Lora's mother, Marcia Smith, pops in and out bearing buttermilk, then chili buns, accompanied by impish three-year-old Alma. It seems as if Lora's dream of community is already realized, but a gathering of incredibly cool friends from near and far is not all she envisions.

The couple's five-year plan, Lora has told me, will begin with a line of eastern Kentucky foods made from produce from Big Switch Farm: "Think gourmet, but affordably priced, chowchow and heirloom tomato jams. I'm also wanting to do Joe's grandma's old-time ketchup recipe and I'm researching wild mustards so we can grow our own mustard seeds."

But the plan grows: "I want to tell the stories along with the products," Lora says, and she sees the community kitchen as a place to share not only work and recipes, but marketing strategies and ideas with others in the community. "Many regional small producers who are making really good stuff are so small they don't do a good job at marketing, and most don't understand the value of their food in other places. In a few years I'd like to launch an incubator program and curriculum for women interested in becoming food entrepreneurs on their own, out of the community kitchen. Maybe it's a nonprofit incubator, or maybe we just turn it into a women's worker-owned cooperative. Not sure yet. Gotta see how the cornbread crumbles first."

For Lora and Joe, this business built around food has a much larger dimension, one that connects to their grassroots organizing work, particularly in coal country, over the last few years.

"We are definitely in a 'moment' with sustainable food systems in the mountains," Lora notes. Coal has been the sole economic force in eastern Kentucky and West Virginia for the last century, with little attention paid to diversifying, but the reserves are running out. And with recent, more stringent emission regulations, and the nation turning away from coal-fired power plants, counties in eastern Kentucky and West Virginia have seen jobs evaporate at an alarming rate since the start of the new century.

Hydraulic fracturing, or fracking, is on the table as one potential, and controversial, economic replacement for coal; but the conversation has also included support for agricultural development of cash crops such as hemp and sorghum cane, and for development of recreation, tourism, and food businesses. For several years now, Kentucky has had an active local agriculture movement throughout its many regions, supported by the state government, and some of that attention has recently been focused on the mountains

with the state-sponsored Kentucky Proud brand expanding to include an Appalachia Proud label. The state has provided grants to assist in the establishment of The Chop Shop, the meat processing facility in Lee City that provides slaughter and butchering, including for Jay Denham's The Curehouse (see page 251). The Jackson County extension office funds the community kitchen where we talk. And at the annual Appalachian Seed Swap in Pikeville, Kentucky State University debuted its mobile canning facility in the summer of 2015, joining its mobile chicken processing facility as a means of providing affordable infrastructure for small food entrepreneurs all through the region.

"In my own experience, communities in the coalfields have been sharply divided," Lora observes, that divide breaking, often vehemently, over the economic benefits of jobs from coal versus the ecological damage. "But people still unite around food, because food taps into much deeper values. So while no one wants to talk about extractive industries, water, the uncertain economic future, people love to talk about food: a homegrown tomato, fresh corn, the seeds you saved from your mamaw's garden, where a pawpaw tree is on your uncle's homeplace. Food creates this healing space where we can come together and talk about issues of sustainability and our future in a different way.

"Everyone back home is proud of their garden or their granny's garden and that holds real value for people. The value of being able to produce our own food is something I believe Appalachians really want to hang on to. And that could provide the opportunity for local economic development and innovation as we navigate through some uncertain times ahead. I mean, did I tell you that the seal for Jackson County has a picture of Daniel Boone, a coal miner, and a farmer all fording the river together? That trips me out."

I hang on to that thought as I carry a steaming sonker to the van, nestling it between a cooler filled with pop on one side and one with deviled eggs on the other. The drive to Big Switch takes just a few minutes, but when we turn onto the dirt road that curves and dips between high brush and trees, it feels a little as if we're traveling back in time. The road was once a wagon trail. Lora and Joe bought the land from a Native American group that had used it for gatherings four times a year, and they've been told it was likely also once part of the Warrior's Path.

We come to the space where the bottom stretches out from the ridge to the creek. It's a mountain farm, so only 40 of the 120 acres is in pasture, and of that, only about 5 acres is flat enough to be tillable. By summer, that acreage will be planted with hemp and a garden bursting in an abundance of tomatoes, overflowing with peppers, Bill Best's heirloom beans, and Candy Roaster squash.

The rapid rhythmic riffs of "Sourwood Mountain" tempt us to dance out of our trucks and cars as we pull in to park near the open-air pavilion where three musicians join in lively communion. Brett Ratliff—who works at the Hindman Settlement School a few mountains over and will come back off and on all summer to help Joe clear the land, plant the hemp, clean an old logging road—mans the fiddle. Julie Shepherd-Powell—who lives in Nonesuch, Kentucky, while working on a PhD in anthropology and dreaming of homesteading with her hubby, Adrian, in Virginia (they want to start an organic pork business called Happy Hog Lard)—is woman-ing the guitar.

Mike Costello, visiting from West Virginia, is playing banjo. He's the executive director of the West Virginia Wilderness Coalition and on the board of the West Virginia Food & Farm Coalition. The Internet makes it possible for him to work remotely, as it has enabled Lora to continue working with the Mary Reynolds Babcock Foundation, now as their Network Officer for Central Appalachia, and for Joe to remain with Rural Advancement Foundation International. So Mike and his partner, Amy Dawson, are working a piece of remote West Virginia land she inherited from her grandparents, and Mike says he dreams of someday creating a farm-to-table business at Lost Creek Farm.

I speculate how the highways, both literal—many of them connecting mountain community to mountain community only in the past twenty-five years—and informational, have made it possible for these new young pioneers to diversify their personal economies in broad and once unimaginable ways. The out-migration of young people that has haunted the Appalachian South for over a century, while not stopping by any stretch, nevertheless shows sign of a shift. And of the best and brightest who have stayed or are returning, many are determined to grow community along with food.

Across the field, Joe fires up the wood oven and Lora and Emily roll out dough; a cloth is spread on a wooden picnic table under a spreading tree. The musicians grab chairs and their instruments and tote them over the grass to tableside. The rolling, tumbling spin of "Brushy Fork" is perfect for setting the table, and soon we are gathered around a bounty of fresh greens tossed in sorghum vinegar, rhubarb tart, flatbread hot from the oven with ham and pickled ramps, and more.

Anna pours the Appalachian Spring into round-bottomed glasses, sprinkles tiny violets and wildflowers in the white foam. We lift the glasses and see the field around us reflected in the tender green and violet and yellow. I look around the table and imagine I see the future in clear, young eyes.

"To Big Switch," someone says. "To the mountains," says another. We all say, "Amen." And then we dig in.

June Hill's Salt-Rising Bread

MAKES 3 LOAVES

Not long after John Matheny opened The Store at Nu-Beginnings in Staunton, he was approached by then seventy-nine-year-old June Hill.

"She said, 'What if I brought you a recipe for salt-rising bread? Would you make it?' I asked her what she wanted for it," John told me. "She said, 'You can sell it, you can give it away, you can do anything you want with it, I just want me some.' She didn't want to fool with baking it anymore, but she still wanted that bread."

June Hill passed away not long after I met John, but he still bakes her bread regularly.

Salt is not the rising agent in this bread—wild yeast in the air, attracted by the starchy sugar in the starter, is. It's a method as old as bread, but the use of potatoes with cornmeal (stone-ground, to keep the necessary germ) was a New World twist. And while its popularity has faded elsewhere (no doubt due to the starter's distinctive aroma, often likened to dirty gym socks topped with cheese), it remains a great favorite in the Appalachians. Those patient enough to endure the smell and the occasional inexplicable failure of the starter are rewarded with a bread that toasts up with a distinctly nutty sweetness.

The secret to getting the starter to work is keeping it in a place with a steady temperature between 95° and 98°F. A number of options for doing that are explained in the recipe, so I suggest that you read it through entirely before you begin.

Oh, about that "salt." The story goes that rock salt—the kind used in ice cream freezers or to defrost an icy sidewalk—was heated in a skillet, and the bowl with the starter nestled in it to keep it warm through the night, hence the name.

STARTER

2 medium russet potatoes, peeled and sliced
4 cups boiling water
¼ cup stone-ground cornmeal
2 tablespoons sugar
1 teaspoon salt

SPONGE

1½ cups whole milk
4 cups all-purpose flour
¼ teaspoon baking soda
Nonstick cooking spray, for greasing the bowl and plastic wrap

BREAD

5 to 6 cups all-purpose flour, plus more for kneading
1 tablespoon baking powder
2½ teaspoons salt
6 tablespoons vegetable oil, plus more for greasing the loaf pans

Make the starter: Place the sliced potatoes in a large bowl and pour the boiling water over them. Add the cornmeal, sugar, and salt; stir to mix completely. Cover the bowl with a cloth and set it in a warm place for 24 hours or until frothy.

The starter *must* have a frothy foam on top to succeed. If it is not frothy after 24 hours, let it set for another 3 to 6 hours. Then, if it is still not frothy, even a little, this batch will most likely fail. It's time to start over.

John Matheny told me that he uses a heating pad at its lowest temperature to keep the starter warm, which is what Charlotte Autry, my colleague and recipe tester, did, and this was the method that worked the best. However, Charlotte transferred the starter to a greased rectangular glass baking dish that was closer to the size of her heating pad, not only allowing more uniform warmth but also increasing the surface area for catching the yeast. Charlotte also noted that she started it at the highest temperature for the heating pad, but the automatic on/off function clicked it off overnight and she clicked it on again in the morning, so clearly this is not a precise art. There are other methods suggested online for coddling the starter. I have had success using cheesecloth to cover the filled containers in an old-school electric yogurt maker, but the heating pad seems to work the best. Here's what Charlotte said: "It gave me a really nice amount of foam. Kind of like halfway-done bubble bath. It was most amazing, because I almost gave up on it about two-thirds of the way through but the next time I went to check on it—BAM! Foam! It felt pretty magical. And I was most excited to have made something from nothing."

Prepare the sponge: Remove and discard the potatoes from the starter mixture. Heat the milk in a small saucepan over low heat until lukewarm (105°F), and add it to the starter. Add the flour and baking soda. Mix well with a wooden spoon until smooth.

Transfer the sponge to a large, lightly greased bowl. Cover the bowl with plastic wrap that has been sprayed with nonstick spray. Set it in a warm place until the sponge has doubled in size, 2 to 3 hours, checking the progress after 1½ hours. When it is ready, it will look creamy and light and smell slightly cheesy.

Bake the bread: Put 4 cups of the flour in a large bowl and add the baking powder, salt, and oil. Whisk until the mixture is blended and has the consistency of fine cornmeal. Add the flour mixture to the prepared sponge, and mix with a spoon to combine, adding more of the remaining 2 cups flour as needed (you probably won't need to use it all). You are aiming for a dough that is not sticky and is firm enough to be turned out and kneaded, yet is still soft. Use floured hands to keep mixing to form this soft, manageable dough.

Use floured hands to turn the dough out onto a well-floured surface and knead it for 1 to 2 minutes; then let it rest for 10 minutes. Resume kneading for 10 minutes, until the dough has taken on a slightly shiny luster and feels elastic.

Preheat the oven to 350°F and grease three 8½ × 4½-inch loaf pans.

Divide the dough into thirds and shape them into loaves. Place them in the prepared loaf pans and cover with plastic wrap that has been sprayed with nonstick spray. Set the pans in a warm place (perhaps the top of your preheating oven) and leave them there until the volume has increased by a third, 30 to 40 minutes.

Remove the plastic wrap and bake the loaves for 45 minutes, or until golden brown on top. Turn them out onto wire racks and let them cool before slicing. Store thoroughly cooled bread in tightly sealed plastic bags. The bread can be frozen for a week or two, but it does seem to lose flavor if left longer. This is a good sandwich bread, but what aficionados rave about, myself included, is salt-rising toast.

Spring Ham, Peas & New Potatoes

SERVES 4

What to do with those tasty ends of the Easter ham? This little piggy pot is both hearty and spring-fresh with new potatoes and peas. And of course you can buy a chunk of ham to start from scratch.

1 pound leftover ham with bone and some fat
Salt
12 new potatoes, no bigger than golf balls
12 pearl onions, peeled and trimmed
1 pound shelled fresh green peas
¼ cup half-and-half
Freshly ground black pepper

Separate as much meat as possible from the fat and bones. Set the meat aside for later, and put the rest in a wide soup pot or Dutch oven. Add water to cover and bring to a boil over high heat. Turn the heat down to a low and steady simmer, cover, and cook for 30 minutes.

When the broth is ready, remove the pot from the heat and spoon the solid matter into a strainer set over the pot. Press down gently to return the juices to the pot; then discard the solids. Taste the broth and add salt as needed. (Hams vary in their saltiness, so the broth will also.)

Add the potatoes and onions to the broth, return it to medium heat, and cook at a lively simmer for 20 to 25 minutes, until the potatoes are just becoming tender. Add the peas and cook for 5 minutes longer.

While the peas are cooking, break the reserved meat into bite-sized chunks. When the peas are tender, add the meat to the pot. Very slowly add the half-and-half to the pot, stir well, and then bring the heat up until the liquid boils. Boil for about 1 minute, until the broth thickens to a light sauce consistency, and then remove from the heat. Finish with salt to taste and a few grinds of black pepper.

Perfect Potato Salad

SERVES 4 TO 8

When I was a child, my mother's was the perfect potato salad, made with mayonnaise and sweet pickles. In my early teens, she switched to dill pickles and that became perfection for me. Until I added Dijon mustard. But wait. In my first cookbook, Naomi Judd's mother, Polly Rideout, shared her recipe with a ketchup-based French dressing applied while the potatoes were still warm, and that was pretty darned amazing.

So it seems that the Perfect Potato Salad is an ever-elusive dream—one to be chased at family reunions and church suppers eternally. Except, this time, I'm sure I nailed it. No. Really. See what you think.

Salt and freshly ground black pepper
2 pounds russet potatoes
1 cup diced red bell pepper
⅓ cup minced celery (tender inner stalks and leaves are best)
¼ cup minced green onions, both white and green parts
1 recipe "Clabber," Chive & Caper Tater Sauce (page 96)

Fill a large saucepan with 2 quarts of water and add ½ tablespoon salt. Cover, and bring to a boil over high heat.

While you are waiting for the water to boil, peel and cut the potatoes into ½-inch chunks. When the water boils, add the prepped potatoes to the pot, stir once, and cover the pot. Bring back to a boil and cook until the potatoes are tender, about 10 minutes. Test by removing a chunk and lightly piercing it with a fork. It should break into two pieces with a bit of "crumb." Taste to be sure it's tender, but don't let the potatoes get mushy.

Drain the potatoes, and allow them to cool until they are no longer steamy but still warm. Transfer the potatoes to a large bowl, and toss with the bell pepper, celery, and green onions. Pour the clabber sauce over the vegetables, and fold it into the salad until everything is well coated. Taste, and add salt if desired. Pass the black pepper at the table.

Redbud Caper Deviled Eggs

MAKES 2 DOZEN DEVILED EGGS

Part of the story of traditional Appalachian food involved reimagining old recipes with the abundant ingredients of the new land. That tradition continues. When Lora Smith returned to her native Kentucky in the spring, the beautiful blooming redbud trees suggested just such a possibility, and she determined to make capers with the tiniest buds.

It turned out to be both exquisite and tedious labor. "When the redbud trees first start to show signs of color, gather the unopened buds . . . " she instructs, but notes ruefully that she was late in gathering and so was able to find only a scant handful of buds among the glorious blossoms. Luckily, a scant handful is all this recipe needs.

The result is a tart and salty accent that gives great flavor but even more delightful color to deviled eggs. (They are also a gorgeous garnish for a caper-accented martini, should you decide to make one.)

Once you've gathered and stemmed the redbuds and made the capers, the rest of this recipe is deceptively simple. Deceptive because it achieves what my friend Amelia Ruth Kirby declared upon first bite is "the platonic ideal of egg devilry."

All that and they are utterly beautiful on the plate, garnished with the tiny fuchsia-hued buds. Start the capers three days before you want to make the deviled eggs.

1 dozen hardboiled eggs
½ cup mayonnaise
4 tablespoons redbud caper brine
¾ teaspoon salt
Redbud Capers (recipe follows), for garnish

Peel the eggs and slice them in half lengthwise. Gently remove the yolks, placing them in a medium bowl. Reserve the egg white "cups" on a large plate.

Use a fork to mash the yolks to a fine consistency. Add the mayonnaise and blend. Add the brine from the redbuds, 1 tablespoon at a time, stirring to incorporate well. Add the salt and stir to blend.

Use a pastry bag to pipe the yolk mixture into each egg white cup. (If you don't have a pastry bag, fill a medium plastic storage bag with the yolk mixture, cut a small hole in one corner, and press to pipe the filling out of the hole and into the egg.)

As you fill the eggs, arrange them on a serving platter, and then garnish each one with 3 to 4 redbud capers on top. (Use tweezers if you're not adept.) Keep chilled until ready to serve.

REDBUD CAPERS MAKES ⅓ CUP

2 ounces (⅓ cup) unopened buds from a redbud tree
2 tablespoons distilled white vinegar
½ teaspoon kosher salt

Gently wash the buds by lightly swishing them in a bowl of water. Set them aside in a strainer to drain well.

While the buds are draining, bring a saucepan of water to a boil and sterilize a small (4-ounce) wide-mouth jar by immersing it in the boiling water. Set the jar aside to cool on a clean cloth.

Pluck off and discard any stems, and place the redbuds in the sterilized jar.

In a small bowl, combine 2 tablespoons of water with the vinegar and salt. Stir until the salt is dissolved. Pour this brine over the redbuds. Use a smaller jar or glass as a weight to submerge the redbuds in the brine. Keep at room temperature, well away from direct sunlight, for 3 days. The capers are ready to eat on the third day. Store them, covered, in the refrigerator where they will keep for several weeks.

Sumac Oil Flatbread with Country Ham & Pickled Ramps MAKES TWO LARGE FLATBREADS (SERVES 4 TO 6)

In early mountain communities, one farmer might own a valuable tool or piece of equipment that was made available to family and neighbors as needed. There was often a trade involved, although more frequently implicit rather than directly bartered. If you were the man with the sorghum squeezer and mule, you could expect to get a couple of quarts from your neighbors' run. If you loaned a plow, you could count on borrowing the chains for hanging a freshly slaughtered hog. Or when your huge cast-iron pot was returned, it might come with several quarts of apple butter.

With a little of that same sense of sharing, Lora Smith and Joe Schroeder invested in a traveling wood-fired oven for their farm at Big Switch. In their first spring back in Kentucky, it rolled over to a couple of weddings, as well as providing the main course for the Appalachian Spring feast. Joe says plans are to take it to a couple of music festivals down the line to both share and perhaps sell enough pizzas to pay the gate.

Music makes a good metaphor for what happens in this recipe. Lora adapted a fine flatbread recipe from acclaimed chef and baker Nick Malgieri for the crust, then added some local color. In the way that European mandolins and violins were transformed by new rhythms and melodies into something purely mountain, the use of sumac-scented olive oil, tangy country ham, and pungent pickled ramps makes this a dish that tastes distinctly of its Kentucky place.

If you have access to a wood-fired oven, bake away there according to how yours works. The directions here are for a home oven.

The flatbread slices are even better when topped with a handful of arugula, mâche, or another bright, bitter green that has been drizzled with Orange Sorghum Vinegar (page 232).

2 cups all-purpose flour, plus more for rolling
⅔ cup stone-ground yellow cornmeal, plus extra for rolling the dough
½ tablespoon salt
2½ teaspoons (1 envelope) active dry yeast
1 cup warm water (110°F)
¼ cup olive oil, plus more for greasing the bowl
6 ounces country ham, sliced about ¼ inch thick and cut into bite-sized pieces
¾ cup Will Dissen's Pickled Ramps (page 223), at room temperature
¼ cup Sumac Oil (recipe follows)

Combine the flour, cornmeal, and salt in the bowl of a food processor fitted with the blade attachment. Pulse a few times to mix.

Combine the yeast with ¾ cup of the warm water in a medium bowl. Whisk in the olive oil. Add this mixture to the food processor and pulse to combine; then let the processor run continuously for about 10 seconds, or until the dough forms a ball. You may need to add up to another ¼ cup of the warm water at this point if your dough is not coming together.

Transfer the dough to a large, lightly oiled bowl. Cover the bowl with plastic wrap and allow the dough to rest for 20 minutes.

Move the rested dough to a floured work surface and flatten into a thick disk, then fold the dough over on itself. Do this several times. Return the folded dough to the oiled mixing bowl (you might have to oil it again first). Cover the bowl with plastic wrap and let the dough rise in a warm place until doubled in bulk, about 1 hour.

(recipe continues)

Line two baking sheets with parchment paper. Set oven racks in the upper and lower thirds of the oven and preheat it to 350°F.

Sprinkle a floured work surface with a little cornmeal. Transfer the risen dough to the surface and divide it in half. Working with one piece of dough at a time, gently press it into a rough rectangle. Roll the dough out as thin as possible, aiming for a roughly 10 × 15-inch rectangle. Transfer the dough to a prepared baking sheet. Repeat the process with the second half of the dough.

Pierce the dough all over at 1-inch intervals with the tines of a fork. Divide the country ham evenly between the two portions of dough.

Bake the flatbreads until golden and crisp, 20 to 30 minutes, switching the baking sheets' positions about halfway through cooking.

Remove to racks and let the flatbreads cool slightly. Divide the ramps and sumac oil evenly between the flatbreads, and serve.

SUMAC OIL MAKES ABOUT ⅓ CUP

Native people gathered the crimson berries of the sumac plant (not the noxious, poisonous white-berried variety, of course) to dry and grind them into a powder that gave a delicious lemony flavor to fish cooked over an open fire. They and the settlers who followed also used the sumac to make a drink akin to lemonade. You don't have to gather berries and make your own; you can buy good-quality ground sumac at almost any Mediterranean or Middle Eastern market and some natural foods stores.

¼ cup extra-virgin olive oil
2 tablespoons freshly squeezed lemon juice
2 teaspoons ground sumac
1 teaspoon salt
1 teaspoon sweet Hungarian paprika

Whisk all of the ingredients together in a small bowl. Use immediately.

Busy Day Cobbler SERVES 6 TO 8

Lora Smith's paternal grandparents, Alma Nadine and Ora Moss Smith of Whitley County, Kentucky, both cooked and—judging from its yellowed, splattered, dog-eared pages—often consulted the *Household Searchlight Recipe Book*, a popular cookbook of the 1930s. That doesn't mean they followed it religiously, of course, and in the front of their copy, which Lora still has, written in Alma's hand is her own rendition of Busy Day Cobbler, an easy, quickish dessert.

Alma's version, in keeping with the spirit of the mountains, is as pure and simple as it can be. Lora remembers that "She always made it with fresh peaches that she and my grandfather would prepare sitting, cutting and peeling, at the kitchen counter." Strawberries, blackberries, blueberries, huckleberries, or apricots are lovely, too. If using a large fruit such as peaches or apricots, cut it into bite-sized pieces. Strawberries can be sliced or halved, while other berries can be left whole. Of course, how you want to change this recipe is up to you—I love black walnuts with blackberries, so I added some of them. And I like to add a shot of buttermilk to my bowl before eating the cobbler.

4 cups berries or larger fresh fruit cut into
   bite-sized pieces
1¼ cups sugar
1 to 2 teaspoons grated lemon zest
½ teaspoon freshly squeezed lemon juice
½ teaspoon salt
6 tablespoons unsalted butter
1 cup all-purpose flour
2½ teaspoons baking powder
¾ cup whole buttermilk

Preheat the oven to 375°F.

In a large bowl, toss the fruit with ¼ cup of the sugar, the lemon zest, lemon juice, and salt. Set aside.

Place the butter in a 13 × 9-inch baking pan or a 10- or 12-inch cast-iron skillet, and put the pan in the preheating oven to melt the butter. Don't forget about it!

In another bowl, mix the flour with the remaining 1 cup sugar and the baking powder. Quickly add the buttermilk and stir to make a thick batter.

Remove the baking pan from the oven and carefully tip it just a bit to swirl the butter around to coat halfway up the sides of the pan. (If any butter remained unmelted, the swirling will help it to melt, as well.)

Pour most of the butter into the batter, leaving a generous coating in the pan. Stir quickly to just incorporate it (a little streaky with butter is okay), and then pour the batter right back into the pan, using the back of the mixing spoon to spread it evenly to the edges, if needed.

Turn the fruit out on top of the batter, distributing it evenly and leaving ½ inch uncovered around the sides.

Bake for 35 to 40 minutes, until golden brown on top and crisp around the edges. The cobbler can be served warm or at room temperature. Hey, it's a busy day. Whatever works best.

Appalachian Spring

MAKES I COCKTAIL

Anna Bogle is the mixologist who put Summit City in Whitesburg, Kentucky, on the map—at least my map! Of this lovely cocktail she says, "My thought was to re-create the bright, verdant color of springtime popping out in Appalachia, with an herbaceous and floral drink. Garnished with flowers, redbud blossoms, and bee pollen, it both tastes and looks like Appalachian Spring."

The redbud simple syrup and the thyme tincture are steeped for 24 hours and 4 hours respectively, so start them the day before you plan to serve the drink. If redbuds are not available, you can use fresh violets.

DRINK

1 ounce Smooth Ambler gin
1 ounce Chartreuse liqueur
2 tablespoons Cucumber and Lemon Balm Essence (recipe follows)
1 tablespoon Redbud Simple Syrup (recipe follows)
1 tablespoon freshly squeezed lemon juice
½ tablespoon Thyme Tincture (recipe follows)
1 fresh egg white

GARNISH

Small violets
Lemon balm leaf
Bee pollen
Redbuds from the syrup

Mix the gin, liqueur, essence, syrup, lemon juice, tincture, and egg white in a cocktail shaker filled with ice and shake, shake, shake. Strain into a glass and garnish as desired.

CUCUMBER AND LEMON BALM ESSENCE MAKES ½ CUP

1 large cucumber, peeled, seeded, and chopped
3 cups (loosely packed) lemon balm leaves

Puree the cucumber on a low setting in a blender until smooth. Add the lemon balm leaves and continue to blend. Strain the mixture through a fine-mesh sieve into a container, and discard the solids. Store the essence in the refrigerator. It will keep for 3 days. Any you don't use in the cocktail may be added to water for a refreshing "spa" drink.

REDBUD SIMPLE SYRUP

MAKES I ½ CUPS

1 cup water
1 cup sugar
1 cup fresh redbud (or violet) blossoms, stems removed, rinsed, and patted dry

Combine the water and sugar in a small saucepan set over medium heat, and cook until the sugar is dissolved. Continue cooking until boiling, and then reduce to a simmer. Let simmer for 3 minutes.

Transfer the sugar syrup to a heatproof bowl and allow it to cool until the mixture is warm, about 100°F. Gently fold the blossoms into the syrup. Cover the bowl with plastic wrap and allow to steep overnight. Store any extra in a lidded jar, away from the light. Do not refrigerate. It will keep 2 to 3 days.

THYME TINCTURE

MAKES ½ CUP

1 cup fresh thyme leaves
½ cup gin

Puree the thyme and gin together in a blender on a low setting. Let steep for 4 hours, and then strain the mixture through a fine-mesh sieve into a container, discarding the solids. Store the tincture in the refrigerator. It will keep for a month.

ACKNOWLEDGMENTS

I have been so richly blessed in this lifetime with family, friends, and colleagues who have supported my body, soul, and work. It is a gift beyond measure for which I am deeply grateful. It is also terrifying when I try to name everyone who has given so thoughtfully, so generously. It is inevitable that I will leave out someone deeply important and regret that for the rest of my days. So I ask all of you who know that you have been an integral part of my life and of *Victuals* to write your name here:

_____

and know it is inscribed also in my heart with deepest gratitude.

That said, there are some specific individuals without whom this very book would simply not be in your hands: Francis Lam, the extraordinary editor who could see this story and its significance, who exercised remarkable patience, and who dispensed great wisdom, humor, and commas galore to bring it to life. Lisa Ekus, friend and agent, who believed in and worked tirelessly on behalf of both me and *Victuals*. Charlotte Autry, who is not simply a patient and diligent recipe tester and inspired food stylist, but just one of the dearest people on earth. Johnny Autry, the photographer who was able to translate a fragment of a suggestion, a mood, or a pork chop into a portfolio full of breathtaking images. Designer Stephanie Huntwork, who knows the beauty of shadow as well as light. To Ash Swain, who delightfully tattooed this trip of a lifetime across my heart and endpapers. And Sheri Castle, who minded my peas and taters.

Without Meghan Lundy-Jones and Todd Kindberg I would not be here (nor would I want to be), and I thank you.

INDEX

Maybe no area of our country is more misunderstood than Appalachia, a place whose people have long been thought of as poor, backward, and unknowable.

But Ronni Lundy has been writing on the food and culture of her home region for more than thirty years with warmth, wit, and intelligence. In *Victuals*, she brings the story of Appalachian food—past and present—to life, and shows us that it's a place not just of delicious Southern cooking, but a place where tradition and modernity live side by side, a place where a new generation of people in food are fighting the stereotypes, redefining what it means to be from the mountains.

In Appalachia, contemporary ideals of seasonality and sustainability have always been the case. Young chefs, growers, and makers are stringing up shuck beans and frying apple pies just like their parents and grandparents did, but with an eye toward the rest of world. Discover the deep richness of this region through these stories and recipes as it finds itself being reborn at the dinner table.

RONNI LUNDY is a native of Corbin, Kentucky, and has written on the music, food, and culture of the Appalachian South for more than three decades. She is a founder of the Southern Foodways Alliance and the Appalachian Food Summit, has written nine previous books, and has been a finalist for an IACP Award and a two-time finalist for a James Beard Award. She lives in the mountains in Burnsville, North Carolina, a half block from the farmer's market and a half block from a McDonald's.

JOHNNY AUTRY is a photographer based in Asheville, North Carolina. He got his start in photography at age fifteen when he was given a 4x5 press camera with a broken shutter. His work has appeared in numerous publications both home and abroad. When not working on projects with his wife, Charlotte, he's riding bikes with his son, Wyatt.

CLARKSON POTTER/PUBLISHERS *New York*
crownpublishing.com | clarksonpotter.com
COVER DESIGN: STEPHANIE HUNTWORK | COVER PHOTOGRAPHS: JOHNNY AUTRY
ENDPAPER MAPS: ASH SWAIN AT GREAT SOUTHERN TATTOO CO.